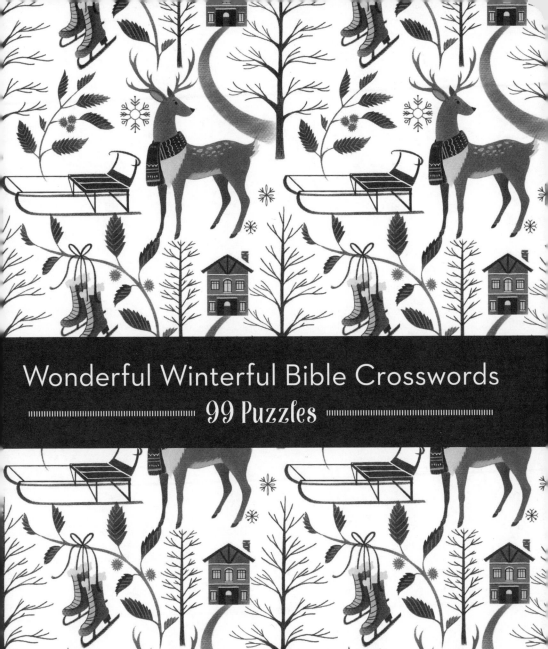

Wonderful Winterful Bible Crosswords
99 Puzzles

Wonderful Winterful Bible Crosswords
99 Puzzles

BARBOUR BOOKS
An Imprint of Barbour Publishing, Inc.

Crosswords were created using licensed Crossword Weaver software (www.crosswordweaver.com).

Puzzles were prepared by N. Teri Grottke and David K. Shortess

Cover illustration by Pimlada Phuapradit

Published by Barbour Books, an imprint of Barbour Publishing, Inc., 1810 Barbour Drive, Uhrichsville, Ohio 44683, www.barbourbooks.com

Our mission is to inspire the world with the life-changing message of the Bible.

 Member of the
Evangelical Christian
Publishers Association

Printed in China.

Need something to do on those long winter nights?

Here's something that's entertaining, educational, and even edifying.

Whether it's cold and snowy where you live, or the days are just short on sunlight, wintertime can bring the blahs—here's a book to fill that time in a positive way.

Wonderful Winterful Bible Crosswords features 99 great puzzles, perfect for beating the winter blues. Test your puzzle-solving skills with thousands of crossword clues—many of them drawn directly from the King James Version, with some taken from other fields of interest for variety's sake. You're in for hours of challenging fun.

It's a great way to learn the Bible while passing (winter)time—what could be more wonderful than that? Answers, of course, are provided, beginning after the ninety-ninth puzzle.

There's not much else to say, other than this: enjoy!

When to Trust God

For he saith, I have heard thee in a time accepted, and in the day of salvation have I succoured thee: behold, now is the accepted time; behold, now is the day of salvation.

2 CORINTHIANS 6:2

ACROSS

1 First part of a meaningless refrain
4 Ice cream component
9 "That you have come with swords and _____?" (Luke 22:52 NIV)
14 "Or with ten thousands of rivers of _____?" (Micah 6:7)
15 Persian language
16 Moreno and Hayworth
17 Coveted World Series award (abbr.)
18 Impose by trickery
19 "With _____ both the gray-headed and very aged men" (Job 15:10) (2 words)
20 Start of **CONCLUSION** to the theme verse from 2 Corinthians 6:2 (4 words)
23 Arm bones
24 "The sixth captain for the sixth month was _____" (1 Chronicles 27:9)
25 **CONCLUSION**, cont'd (2 words)
32 Where the company buck stops (abbr.)
35 "I, even I, will _____ and go away" (Hosea 5:14)
36 "That other men be _____" (2 Corinthians 8:13)
37 Heard at a school football game
39 "Put _____ on his hand" (Luke 15:22) (2 words)
42 "Shall compel thee to go a _____" (Matthew 5:41)
43 "The LORD our God _____ LORD" (Deuteronomy 6:4) (2 words)
45 "I will afflict thee no _____" (Nahum 1:12)
47 Book before Exodus (abbr.)
48 **CONCLUSION**, cont'd (4 words)
52 Native American agency (abbr.)
53 Ecological or environmental (prefix)
54 End of **CONCLUSION** (3 words)
62 "His fruit above and his roots _____" (Amos 2:9 NIV)
63 Pry
64 "For ye tithe mint and _____" (Luke 11:42)
65 "Cast alive into _____ of fire" (Revelation 19:20) (2 words)
66 "Let him seek peace, and _____ it" (1 Peter 3:11)
67 "And _____ it up" (Revelation 10:10)
68 "And they _____ fig leaves together" (Genesis 3:7)
69 Peanut butter cup originator
70 "They said unto her, Thou art _____" (Acts 12:15)

DOWN

1 "Laid it in a _____" (Mark 6:29)
2 "The _____ is mine" (Ezekiel 29:9)
3 "I am _____ and Omega" (Revelation 1:8)
4 "Taskmasters to _____ them with their burdens" (Exodus 1:11)
5 One of the seven Asian churches (Revelation 1:11)
6 "Cheese!" result
7 "One _____ near to another" (Job 41:16) (2 words)
8 Person with no sense
9 Billy Graham campaign
10 "The _____ of the men of Israel" (Nehemiah 7:7 NIV)
11 Wasatch location
12 "He _____ the sin of many" (Isaiah 53:12)
13 Opposite of NNW
21 Harem room (arch.)
22 Wrath
26 "Give ye _____, O house of the king" (Hosea 5:1)
27 Top notch
28 Scot topper
29 "They have heard that _____" (Lamentations 1:21) (2 words)
30 Donnybrook
31 "The house of _____" (Amos 1:5)
32 "Where no oxen are, the _____ is clean" (Proverbs 14:4)

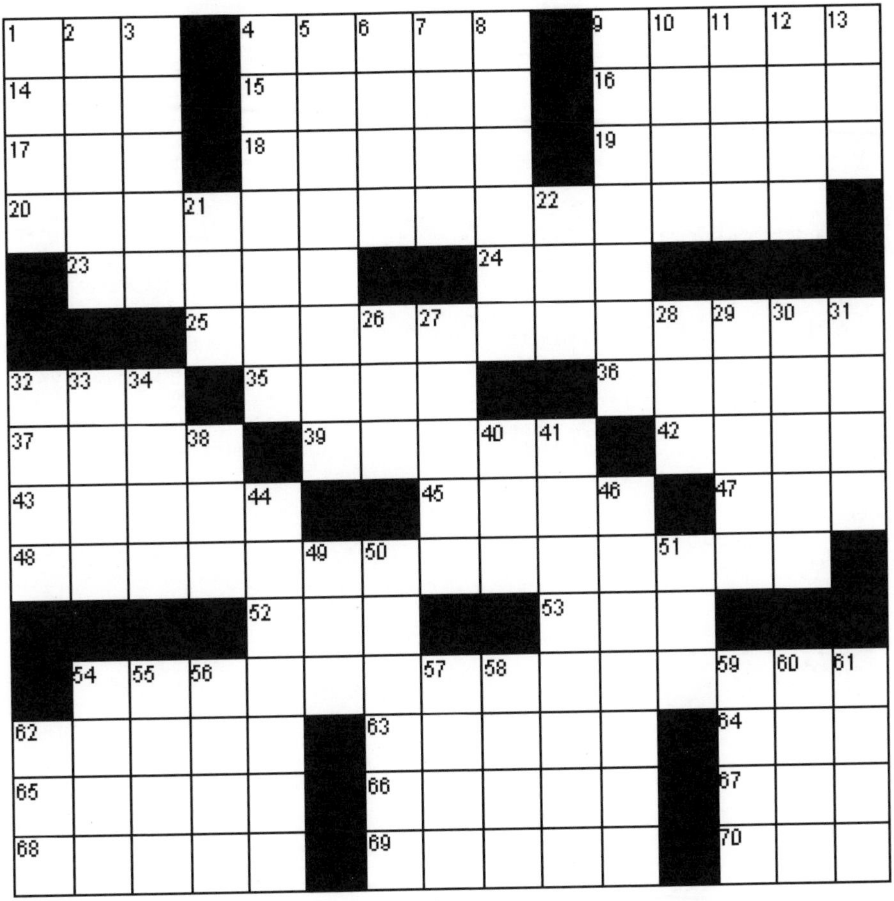

by David K. Shortess

33 "His soul shall dwell at _____" (Psalm 25:13)

34 Words at the first sign of trouble (2 words)

38 _____-Cone

40 "_____ why dost thou cry out aloud?" (Micah 4:9)

41 "_____ words stir up anger" (Proverbs 15:1)

44 Pushed ahead, as through a crowd

46 One who gets free

49 Subtraction answer (abbr.)

50 Aswan High Dam lake

51 Daycare denizen

54 Mark indicating text to be removed (var.)

55 "_____ of the God of Jacob" (Psalm 81:4) (2 words)

56 "Take my _____ upon you" (Matthew 11:29)

57 Girl from Green Gables

58 "_____ his own soul?" (Mark 8:36)

59 "Duke Magdiel, duke _____" (Genesis 36:43)

60 "There went _____ sower to sow" (Mark 4:3) (2 words)

61 "And find grace to help in time of _____" (Hebrews 4:16)

62 _____-relief

ACROSS

1 Haniel's father (1 Chronicles 7:39)

5 Rephaiah's father (1 Chronicles 4:42)

9 "_____ there yet the treasures" (Micah 6:10)

12 "God hath given thee all them that _____ with thee" (Acts 27:24)

13 Flesh food

14 "She _____ in two mites, which make a farthing" (Mark 12:42)

16 "And the stones of _____" (Isaiah 34:11)

18 Elevate

19 "The rock _____" (Judges 15:11)

20 "Fire, and _____ of fire" (2 Kings 2:11)

21 Market

23 "Then _____ destruction cometh upon them" (1 Thessalonians 5:3)

24 Epistle to a powerful empire (abbr.)

25 Bleak

29 Adam's wife

30 "Rekem, and _____, and Taralah" (Joshua 18:27)

31 "Alammelech, and _____" (Joshua 19:26)

35 Not straight

37 Consume food

38 "Helkath, and _____" (Joshua 19:25)

39 Melchi's father (Luke 3:28)

40 Baanah's brother (2 Samuel 4:2)

43 "Borders of _____ on the west" (Joshua 11:2)

44 A son of Azel (1 Chronicles 8:38)

45 "And a river went _____ of Eden" (Genesis 2:10)

46 Location of King Saul's first military victory

49 "A _____ flowing with milk and honey" (Exodus 3:8)

51 "Behold, ye fast for strife and _____" (Isaiah 58:4)

52 A place to grind flour

54 Jesus did this at the resurrection

55 "He shall bring forth the _____ thereof" (Zechariah 4:7)

60 First bird out of the ark

61 "Of _____, the family" (Numbers 26:17)

62 "Kishion, and _____" (Joshua 19:20)

63 "God created _____ heaven" (Genesis 1:1)

64 Shoham's brother (1 Chronicles 24:27)

65 Not easily found

DOWN

1 Utilize

2 Bible book of grief (abbr.)

3 "The _____ of truth shall be established for ever" (Proverbs 12:19)

4 "Nor _____ the thing" (Psalm 89:34)

5 A son of Helem (1 Chronicles 7:35)

6 "They shall _____ like torches" (Nahum 2:4)

7 Possesses

8 Possessive pronoun

9 "The day star _____ in your hearts" (2 Peter 1:19)

10 "And _____ between" (Genesis 10:12)

11 Female sheep

14 Walked (arch.); "They _____ one upon another" (Luke 12:1)

15 Difficult

17 Ribai's son (2 Samuel 23:29)

20 Throw

21 "My bowels were _____ for him" (Song of Solomon 5:4)

22 Make a correction

23 Boil (arch.)

24 A king of Midian (Numbers 31:8)

26 Abram's birthplace

27 It should "be alway with grace" (Colossians 4:6)

28 Instruct

31 "Say in their hearts, _____" (Psalm 35:25)

32 Jobab was king of this country (Joshua 11:1)

33 Audible

34 Filth

36 Titanium (sym.)

40 Thorny flower

41 Moabite border city (Numbers 21:15)

42 Male cattle

44 "Hali, and _____" (Joshua 19:25)

46 A son of Joktan (Genesis 10:26)

47 God has given Jesus a name _____ every name (Philippians 2:9)

48 Paul referred to himself as _____ among the Corinthians (2 Corinthians 10:1)

50 "Purge the _____" (Ezekiel 43:26)

51 Move quickly

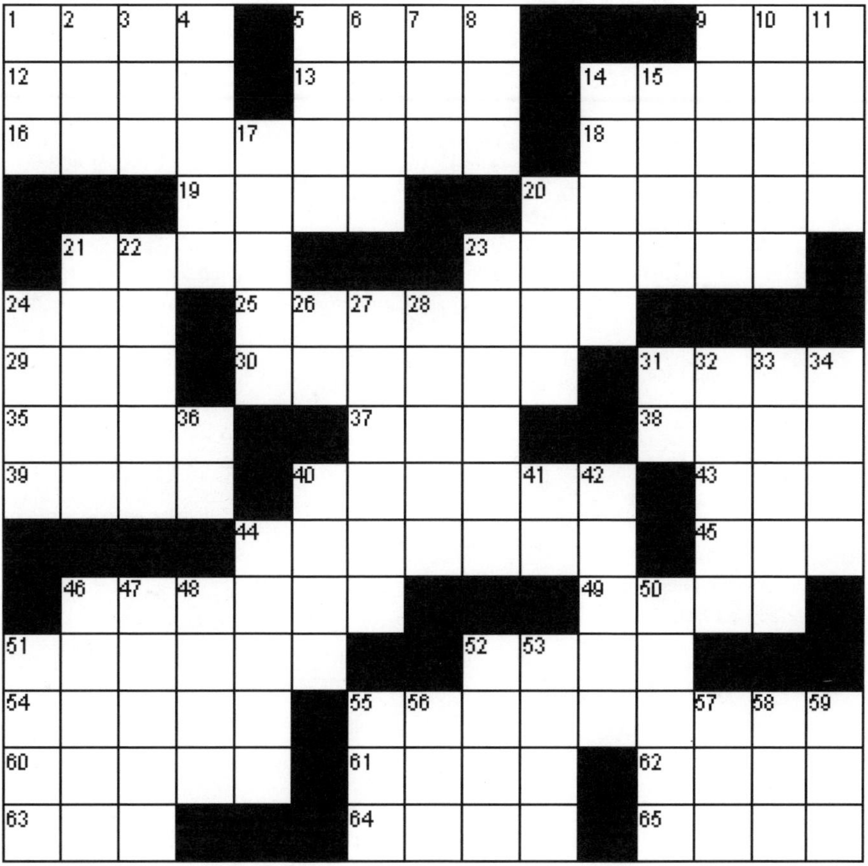

by N. Teri Grottke

52 Shammai's son (1 Chronicles 2:45)

53 Zechariah's father (Ezra 5:1)

55 Fifty-six verses make up this book (abbr.)

56 Before (arch.)

57 Shortest book of the Bible (abbr.)

58 Saul's uncle (1 Samuel 14:50)

59 Prophet to captives in Babylon (abbr.)

ACROSS

1 "The Lord is at _____"
(Philippians 4:5)

5 In this manner

9 "_____ of Judah" (2 Samuel 6:2)

14 "Tower of _____"
(Genesis 35:21)

15 "Hand by the _____ of the door"
(Song of Solomon 5:4)

16 "All the country of _____ unto
the coasts" (Deuteronomy 3:14)

17 "In _____ was there a voice"
(Matthew 2:18)

18 "The _____ that is called
Patmos" (Revelation 1:9)

19 To humble

20 "_____; which is called the
sanctuary" (Hebrews 9:2)

22 Simeon was called this (Acts 13:1)

23 Prophet who advised the kings of
Judah (abbr.)

24 "They shall be _____ and
flourishing" (Psalm 92:14)

25 "Therefore shall a _____ arise"
(Hosea 10:14)

29 "And he gave _____ his hand"
(Acts 9:41)

31 Ahira's father (Numbers 2:29)

35 Get up

36 A baptismal site of John the
Baptist (John 3:23)

38 Aka the Black River in China

39 Moza's son (1 Chronicles 8:37)

40 Unhappy

41 "The sons of Carmi; _____"
(1 Chronicles 2:7)

43 Commanded militarily

44 "Now when every _____ turn
was come" (Esther 2:12)

46 "A proverb, a _____ and a
curse" (Jeremiah 24:9)

47 Otherwise

49 "_____ up my commandments"
(Proverbs 7:1)

50 "O vine of _____, I will weep for
thee" (Jeremiah 48:32)

51 Last book of the OT (abbr.)

53 Book of *Who's* _____

54 "And the _____ which dwelt"
(Deuteronomy 2:23)

57 "Jehoiada was the leader of the
_____" (1 Chronicles 12:27)

63 Abram's wife (Genesis 11:31)

64 "Before the cock _____, thou
shalt deny" (Luke 22:61)

65 A duke of Sihon (Joshua 13:21)

66 "Why dost thou cry out _____?"
(Micah 4:9)

67 Rebuke angrily

68 "_____, and Shema"
(Joshua 15:26)

69 Hearing is one

70 "Mahli, and _____"
(1 Chronicles 23:23)

71 "The king's _____"
(Genesis 14:17)

DOWN

1 "Restore all that was _____"
(2 Kings 8:6)

2 Jabal's mother (Genesis 4:20)

3 "That at the _____"
(Philippians 2:10)

4 "Ran again unto the well to
_____ water" (Genesis 24:20)

5 "If any man _____, let him
come" (John 7:37)

6 Gomer's husband (Hosea 1:2–3)

7 Haniel's father (1 Chronicles 7:39)

8 "So shall thy _____ be"
(Romans 4:18)

9 Ahilud's son (1 Kings 4:12)

10 Paarai was one (2 Samuel 23:35)

11 Samuel killed this Amalekite king
(1 Samuel 15:33)

12 "We _____ not those things"
(2 John 1:8)

13 Salah's son (Genesis 10:24)

21 "Aner with her suburbs, and
_____" (1 Chronicles 6:70)

24 Satan went to and _____ in the
earth (Job 1:7)

25 "The _____ of the Lord"
(Malachi 1:7)

26 Michaiah's father
(2 Chronicles 13:2)

27 "Lest ye be wearied and faint in
your _____" (Hebrews 12:3)

28 Utilize

29 "Traitors, _____, highminded"
(2 Timothy 3:4)

30 Opposite of *begins*

32 "The book of the vision of _____
the Elkoshite" (Nahum 1:1)

33 "Look from the top of _____"
(Song of Solomon 4:8)

34 "For the king of the _____ shall
return" (Daniel 11:13)

36 Largest continent

37 "I will make of thee a great
_____" (Genesis 12:2)

42 Taxi

45 "Destroy _____ kings and
people" (Ezra 6:12)

48 Village about threescore
furlongs from Jerusalem
(Luke 24:13)

50 "There cometh a _____; and so
it is" (Luke 12:54)

<table>
<tr><td>1</td><td>2</td><td>3</td><td>4</td><td></td><td>5</td><td>6</td><td>7</td><td>8</td><td></td><td>9</td><td>10</td><td>11</td><td>12</td><td>13</td></tr>
</table>

52 "Turned _____ like a deceitful bow" (Psalm 78:57)

53 "I _____ unto you in an epistle" (1 Corinthians 5:9)

54 "_____ heart was perfect" (1 Kings 15:14)

55 "And in the _____" (Deuteronomy 1:7)

56 "I will make your heaven as _____" (Leviticus 26:19)

57 Land measurement

58 "_____ the Canaanite" (Numbers 21:1)

59 Mehujael's father (Genesis 4:18)

60 "The troops of _____ looked" (Job 6:19)

61 A son of Shobal (Genesis 36:23)

62 Identical

by N. Teri Grottke

ACROSS

1 "_____, and Dimonah, and Adadah" (Joshua 15:22)

6 Writing fluid

9 Adoniram's father (1 Kings 4:6)

13 Idol

14 "Shall be eaten: as a _____ tree" (Isaiah 6:13)

16 Descendants

17 "Is _____ up" (Joel 1:10)

18 "_____, and Ivah?" (Isaiah 37:13)

19 "Is anything too _____ for the LORD?" (Genesis 18:4)

20 Transgression

21 Adam's first home was in one of these

23 Anak's father (Joshua 15:13)

24 A son of Shobal (Genesis 36:23)

25 Incense was burned in this

27 "A certain island which is called _____" (Acts 27:16)

31 Always

33 "As the trees of _____ aloes" (Numbers 24:6)

34 Smelling orifice

36 Fire product

41 "_____ by his house" (Nehemiah 3:23)

43 The son of Jeroham (1 Chronicles 9:8)

45 Danger

46 Strong and _____

48 Too

49 Melchi's father (Luke 3:28)

51 "The stone was _____ away" (Mark 16:4)

53 "When _____ was the deputy of Achaia" (Acts 18:12)

57 Samson _____ 1,000 men with a jawbone (Judges 15:15)

59 Jesus cried this on the cross (Mark 15:34)

60 A city of Judah (Joshua 15:52)

62 "They reel to and _____" (Psalm 107:27)

65 Bird from the ark sent out three times

66 "All the Chaldeans, Pekod, and _____, and Koa" (Ezekiel 23:23)

67 David's eldest brother (1 Samuel 17:13)

69 "Day of _____ birth" (Ecclesiastes 7:1)

70 Opposite of *bottoms*

71 Realm

72 "Give thyself no _____" (Lamentations 2:18)

73 Jewish queen (abbr.)

74 Velocity

DOWN

1 Baby goats

2 Zaccur's father (Nehemiah 3:2)

3 Jesus raised a young man from the dead here (Luke 7:11)

4 Get older

5 "Whom God hath _____ in?" (Job 3:23)

6 Amasa's father (2 Samuel 17:25)

7 "A camel to go through a _____ eye" (Luke 18:25)

8 Cattle

9 "_____, five cities" (1 Chronicles 4:32)

10 "There came forth two she _____ out of the wood" (2 Kings 2:24)

11 A city of Lycaonia (Acts 14:6)

12 Bela's son (1 Chronicles 8:3)

15 Spear

22 A river of Damascus (2 Kings 5:12)

26 "Shuthelah: of _____" (Numbers 26:36)

27 Applaud

28 Straight distance between two points

29 Greek form of *Hagar* (Galatians 4)

30 "_____, their brethren" (Nehemiah 12:9)

32 "The _____ of the temple was rent" (Luke 23:45)

35 "Jamin, and _____" (Genesis 46:10)

37 Closure

38 "At his holy _____" (Psalm 99:9)

39 Comfort

40 "Your feet _____ with the preparation of the gospel of peace" (Ephesians 6:15)

42 "_____ the Ahohite" (1 Chronicles 11:29)

44 Paul and Silas were sent by night here (Acts 17:10)

47 "With the _____ and deacons" (Philippians 1:1)

50 "_____ thou well to be angry?" (Jonah 4:4)

52 "Of the _____ thereof" (Proverbs 1:19)

53 Penuel's son (1 Chronicles 4:4)

54 By yourself

55 "There will I give thee my _____" (Song of Solomon 7:12)

56 Go to sleep (arch.)

58 Smallest

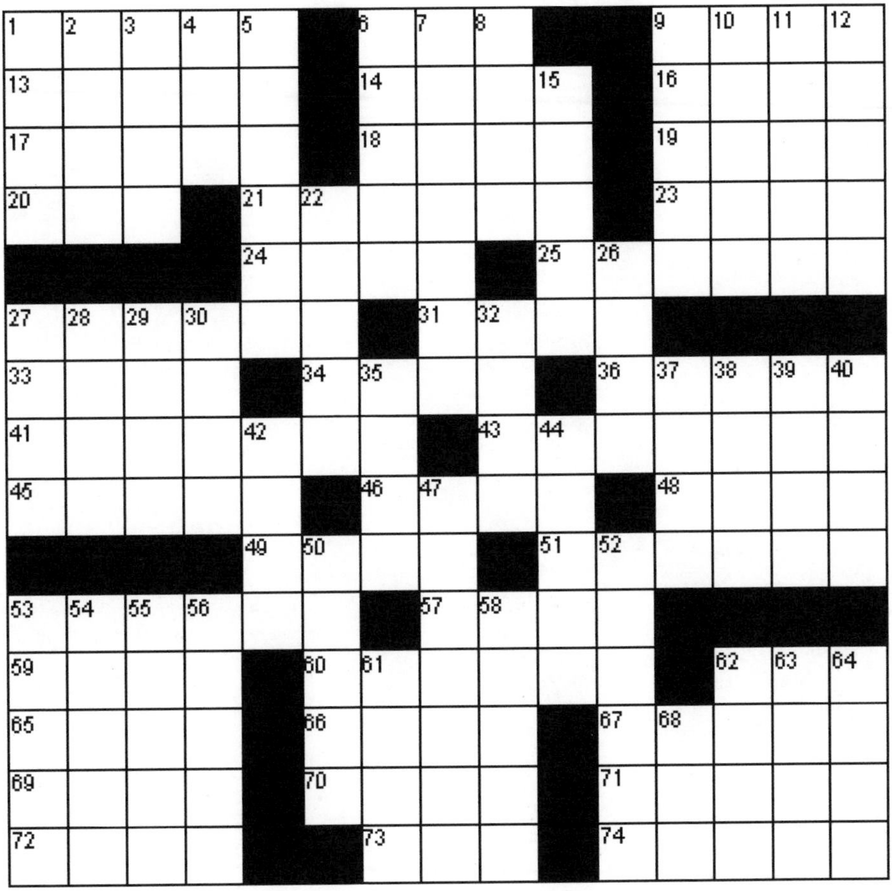

by N. Teri Grottke

61 Foot covering

62 "And he bought ______ linen" (Mark 15:46)

63 Uncontrolled anger

64 Ruth's son (Ruth 4:13–17)

68 Child's favorite seat

5

Trust in Whom?

*Trust in the Lord with all thine heart. . .
and he shall direct thy paths.*

PROVERBS 3:5–6

ACROSS

1 "Thou hast asked _____ thing" (2 Kings 2:10) (2 words)
6 "Shoo"
10 "And the _____ went forth" (Zechariah 6:7)
13 First feast of the Passover
14 "Slewest in the valley of _____" (1 Samuel 21:9)
15 "He is of _____; ask him" (John 9:21)
16 "Nor could the _____ trees" (Ezekiel 31:8 NIV)
17 Yorkshire river
18 "The name of the wicked shall _____" (Proverbs 10:7)
19 Start of **QUOTE** from Psalm 16:1 (3 words)
22 Cold War acronym
23 Modern American furniture designer

26 "The _____ day went Jesus out of the house" (Matthew 13:1)
30 Norse thunder god
33 "Because thou didst _____ on the Lord" (2 Chronicles 16:8)
34 "Is to be made _____ of rubble" (Ezra 6:11 NIV) (2 words)
36 "And Jonah _____ in the belly" (Jonah 1:17)
38 Whole lot
39 **QUOTE**, cont'd (5 words)
43 "The house of _____ in Shiloh" (1 Kings 2:27)
44 "Sinned, _____ his parents" (John 9:3)
45 "But they also have _____ through wine" (Isaiah 28:7)
46 Blind part
48 Sires' mates
51 "In the thirty-sixth year of _____ reign" (2 Chronicles 16:1 NIV)

52 Pepper-upper
54 "Arise and come to my _____" (Psalm 35:2 NIV)
56 End of **QUOTE** (4 words)
62 "To _____, the prophets of Israel" (Ezekiel 13:16)
64 "So he _____ the fare" (Jonah 1:3)
65 "That they may be _____ we are" (John 17:11) (2 words)
67 Unreturned serve
68 Sections of the small intestine
69 Start for glycerine
70 "_____, of the Gentiles also" (Romans 3:29)
71 "Yet will I not _____ thee" (Matthew 26:35)
72 Writer of Psalm 89

DOWN

1 "On the hole of the _____" (Isaiah 11:8)
2 "Come up unto me, and _____ me" (Joshua 10:4)
3 Twelfth Jewish month (Esther 3:7)
4 Descartes
5 "And _____ it first" (1 Kings 18:25)
6 "That _____ may be made in the book" (Ezra 4:15)
7 VII x XXII

8 Swiss river
9 "Are the _____ of my song" (Psalm 119:54 NIV)
10 Weather gauges
11 "Unto him that fashioned it long _____" (Isaiah 22:11)
12 "Nor _____ for your body" (Matthew 6:25)
20 "Ye shall not _____ of it" (Genesis 3:3)

21 "He that hath an _____" (Revelation 2:7)
24 Common freshwater plant
25 Church councils
26 Wisest
27 Lunar mission
28 "Because of the _____" (Judges 6:7)
29 Leprechaun's kin
31 "Into his _____ city" (Matthew 9:1)

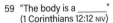
by David K. Shortess

32 "The _____, any kind of great" (Leviticus 11:29 NIV)

35 Very long time

37 "_____ obeyed not" (Zephaniah 3:2)

40 "Feed thy people with thy _____" (Micah 7:14)

41 "The sixth captain for the sixth month was _____" (1 Chronicles 27:9)

42 Pitcher's stat (abbr.)

47 "Dip the _____" (Luke 16:24)

49 Vocal SOS

50 "And made them all _____ down" (Luke 9:15)

53 Amorous archer of ancient mythology

55 He bee

57 "And the _____ of the bricks" (Exodus 5:8)

58 Demeanor

59 "The body is a _____" (1 Corinthians 12:12 NIV)

60 Father of Enos (Genesis 5:6)

61 O'Hara estate

62 "See thou tell no man; but go thy _____" (Matthew 8:4)

63 "He casteth forth his _____ like morsels" (Psalm 147:17)

66 "Whom if his _____ ask bread" (Matthew 7:9)

ACROSS

1 Became acquainted
4 Floor cover
7 King of Sodom (Genesis 14:2)
11 After the Chronicles (abbr.)
12 Puah's son (Judges 10:1)
13 Darius was of this seed (Daniel 5:31)
14 "_____ there yet the treasures" (Micah 6:10)
15 "Full ears of corn in the _____ thereof" (2 Kings 4:42)
16 "_____ the most Holy" (Daniel 9:24)
18 "_____ the Bethelite" (1 Kings 16:34)
20 Greek form of *Noah* (Matthew 24:38)
21 "_____ with her suburbs, Nahalal with her suburbs; four cities" (Joshua 21:35)
22 Consume food
24 "As a lion in his _____" (Psalm 10:9)
25 "And _____ lay at his feet until the morning" (Ruth 3:14)
26 "When saw we thee an hungered, or _____" (Matthew 25:44)
30 A son of Asher (Genesis 46:17)
32 Zorobabel's son (Luke 3:27)
33 "Even thou _____ as one of them" (Obadiah 1:11)
35 "Thou also, son of man, take thee a _____" (Ezekiel 4:1)
39 "Having _____ in the Spirit" (Galatians 3:3)
40 To the church at Ephesus (abbr.)
41 Jobab was king of this country (Joshua 11:1)
42 Eshcol's brother (Genesis 14:13)
43 "_____ the waters" (Exodus 15:25)
44 "_____ and Medad" (Numbers 11:27)
45 "For we have seen his star in the _____" (Matthew 2:2)
47 Countries
49 "Shall be astonished, and _____ his head" (Jeremiah 18:16)
52 A period of 24 hours
53 Large lake
54 Azareel's father (Nehemiah 11:13)
56 Led an army around Jericho (abbr.)
58 Smelling orifice
62 "We had been as _____" (Romans 9:29)
63 Largest continent
65 Winged mammal
66 Jehosaphat's chief captain of Judah (2 Chronicles 17:12–14)
67 "As far as the east is from the _____" (Psalm 103:12)
68 "Helez the Paltite, _____" (2 Samuel 23:26)
69 _____ priest
70 To place
71 Book of Jeremiah's tears (abbr.)

DOWN

1 "The tower of _____" (Nehemiah 3:1)
2 Chelub's son (1 Chronicles 27:26)
3 This withered before Jesus (Matthew 21:19)
4 Horses
5 Too
6 Seize
7 "Hodijah, Bani, _____" (Nehemiah 10:13)
8 "O daughter of _____" (Lamentations 4:21)
9 "Into my _____" (Lamentations 3:13)
10 "The children of _____" (Ezra 2:50)
12 Thorium (sym.)
13 "Which before these days _____ an uproar" (Acts 21:38)
17 "God created _____ heaven" (Genesis 1:1)
19 "They had no _____ so much as to eat" (Mark 6:31)
23 A son of Dishan (Genesis 36:28)
24 A son of Seir (Genesis 36:20–21)
26 The father of Anak (Joshua 15:13)
27 "See _____ that ye walk circumspectly" (Ephesians 5:15)
28 The king's chamberlain (Esther 2:3)
29 After nineteen
31 Someone from Italy
34 Capable
36 Zechariah's father (Ezra 5:1)
37 "The _____ which is lent" (1 Samuel 2:20)
38 Opposite of *begins*
41 Measure (arch.)
43 The son of Amoz (Isaiah 1:1)
46 A city in Naphtali (Joshua 19:36)
48 "That ye _____ her in whatsoever business" (Romans 16:2)
49 "God saw that it _____ good" (Genesis 1:21)
50 "Abishua, and Naaman, and _____" (1 Chronicles 8:4)
51 Susi's son (Numbers 13:11)

by N. Teri Grottke

55 Verbal music

56 "I brake the _____ of the wicked" (Job 29:17)

57 "As he saith also in _____" (Romans 9:25)

59 Ishmaelite camel driver (1 Chronicles 27:30)

60 "Through faith also _____ herself received strength to conceive seed" (Hebrews 11:11)

61 "The rock _____" (Judges 15:11)

64 Astatine (sym.)

ACROSS

1 Portion
5 A city in Benjamin (Joshua 18:25)
10 Made by worms and mulberry leaves
14 A son of Seir (1 Chronicles 1:38)
15 Ending
16 Jesus cried this on the cross (Mark 15:34)
17 A child of Gad (Numbers 26:16–18)
18 "And there came forth two she _____ out of the wood" (2 Kings 2:24)
19 Where the sun rises
20 Uncontrolled anger
21 Venture
23 "Children of _____" (Numbers 24:17)

25 "And falling into a place where two _____ met" (Acts 27:41)
26 Seasoning
29 "Which is by the coast of _____" (Ezekiel 47:16)
34 Payment
37 Zibeon's son (1 Chronicles 1:40)
39 "And he _____ upon a cherub" (Psalm 18:10)
40 "Do not _____ belong to God?" (Genesis 40:8)
45 Night sky illuminator
46 Dig
47 Obese
48 "He that gathered least gathered ten _____" (Numbers 11:32)
51 A son of Helem (1 Chronicles 7:35)

53 In this manner
56 Rain comes in this form
60 "That they turn and encamp before _____" (Exodus 14:2)
66 "Of Hena, and _____?" (2 Kings 19:13)
67 First Hebrew month (Exodus 34:18)
68 Mephibosheth's son (2 Samuel 9:12)
69 "Land from _____" (Isaiah 16:1)
70 Pears grow on this
71 Chelub's son (1 Chronicles 4:11)
72 Talmai's father (Numbers 13:22)
73 "At his holy _____" (Psalm 99:9)
74 By yourself
75 Island

DOWN

1 "Slain in the day of the plague for _____ sake" (Numbers 25:18)
2 "From Tiphsah even to _____" (1 Kings 4:24)
3 Realm
4 "The righteous God _____ the hearts and reins" (Psalm 7:9)
5 Soldiers cast lots for Jesus' _____
6 So be it
7 "To abstain from _____" (1 Timothy 4:3)
8 "_____ with thine adversary quickly" (Matthew 5:25)
9 Tikvath's father (2 Chronicles 34:22)
10 Prophet (arch.)
11 "_____ the Ahohite" (1 Chronicles 11:29)
12 A failure to win

13 "The _____ after his kind" (Leviticus 11:14)
22 Seven-plus authors contributed to this book (abbr.)
24 "_____, O Israel: The LORD our God is one LORD" (Deuteronomy 6:4)
27 Tear
28 Barrier
30 "Shallum, and Telem, and _____" (Ezra 10:24)
31 Top of a house
32 "Of Harim, _____" (Nehemiah 12:15)
33 Bird home
34 "That dippeth with me in the _____" (Mark 14:20)
35 "I have stretched out my hands _____ thee" (Psalm 88:9)
36 "The rock _____" (Judges 15:11)

38 The unknown author of this book calls Timothy "brother" (abbr.)
41 Before (arch.)
42 "When _____ king" (2 Samuel 8:9)
43 Attached to the shoulder
44 Take care of
49 Right hand (abbr.)
50 A brother of David (1 Chronicles 2:13–15)
52 A son of Haman (Esther 9:9)
54 Michaiah's father (2 Chronicles 13:2)
55 Heber's son (1 Chronicles 4:18)
57 Bread bakes in these
58 A rebuilder of the wall (Nehemiah 3:25)
59 "_____ off the dust under your feet" (Mark 6:11)
60 Way

1 2 3 4 5 6 7 8 9 10 11 12 13
14 15 16
17 18 19
20 21 22
23 24 25
26 27 28 29 30 31 32 33
34 35 36 37 38 39
40 41 42 43 44
45 46 47
48 49 50 51 52
53 54 55 56 57 58 59
60 61 62 63 64 65 66
67 68 69
70 71 72
73 74 75

by N. Teri Grottke

61 A son of Merari (1 Chronicles 24:27)

62 "______ the Bethelite" (1 Kings 16:34)

63 Cain's victim

64 "The ______ heads of grain" (Genesis 41:7)

65 Rabbit

ACROSS

1 Gained a victory
4 Applaud
8 Wrong
13 "_____ for the day!" (Joel 1:15)
15 Green citrus
16 A son of David (1 Chronicles 3:7)
17 After four
18 Greek form of *Hagar* (Galatians 4)
19 "But Ruth _____ unto her" (Ruth 1:14)
20 "_____ the death of the cross" (Philippians 2:8)
21 "_____, their brethren" (Nehemiah 12:9)
22 "Crowns shall be to _____, and to Tobijah" (Zechariah 6:14)
23 This is what the Jews did on the Sabbath
25 Too
27 Tree juice
29 "Salute _____, our helper in Christ" (Romans 16:9)
34 Mail requires this
38 "And Ahijah, Hanan, _____" (Nehemiah 10:26)
41 Isaiah's father (Isaiah 1:1)
42 "Gold, or pearls, or costly _____" (1 Timothy 2:9)
43 Commanded militarily
44 "I _____ unto you in an epistle" (1 Corinthians 5:9)
45 "Moses drew _____" (Exodus 20:21)
46 Chopped
47 Inside
48 Elisha's leprous servant (2 Kings 5:25–27)
50 Capable
52 "_____, Hizkijah, Azzur" (Nehemiah 10:17)
55 House from which fine linen was wrought (1 Chronicles 4:21)
60 "Purge the _____" (Ezekiel 43:26)
64 Boys
66 A son of Sheresh (1 Chronicles 7:16)
67 "But ye have _____" (Amos 5:26)
68 Larger than monkeys
69 Entrance
70 Pagan goddess of the Ephesians
71 You (arch.)
72 First garden
73 A son of Beriah (1 Chronicles 8:16)
74 Not easy
75 "The latter _____" (Ruth 3:10)

DOWN

1 "And one _____ out of the basket" (Exodus 29:23)
2 A shade of green
3 "And their _____, and their felloes" (1 Kings 7:33)
4 "A certain island which is called _____" (Acts 27:16)
5 "As the trees of _____ aloes" (Numbers 24:6)
6 "Look from the top of _____" (Song of Solomon 4:8)
7 Danger
8 Stabilizing weight
9 Underground rodent
10 Son of Nathan of Zobah (2 Samuel 23:36)
11 Rescue
12 "And _____ lived after" (Genesis 11:11)
14 Caused to go to a destination
24 "Sent me from Kadeshbarnea to _____ out the land" (Joshua 14:7)
26 Biggest star in our solar system
28 Little color
30 Farm building
31 Manasseh's son (2 Kings 21:18)
32 "_____ that man, and have no company with him" (2 Thessalonians 3:14)
33 Jeshua's son (Nehemiah 3:19)
34 "They _____ his praise" (Psalm 106:12)
35 Bananas grow on this
36 A son of Ulla (1 Chronicles 7:39)
37 Naomi wanted to be called this
39 Modern
40 "Of Harim, _____" (Nehemiah 12:15)
44 "Are at their _____ end" (Psalm 107:27)
46 Strike
49 "And at Enrimmon, and at _____, and at Jarmuth" (Nehemiah 11:29)
51 Went by
53 "Plain from _____" (Deuteronomy 2:8)
54 Binea's son (1 Chronicles 8:37)
56 Very large
57 "First the _____, then the ear" (Mark 4:28)
58 Consumed
59 Make a correction
60 Levite grandpa of Ethan (1 Chronicles 6:44)

61 Timothy's grandmother
(2 Timothy 1:5)

62 Snare

63 Temple prophetess in Jesus' time
(Luke 2:36–37)

65 "The fallow _____"
(Deuteronomy 14:5)

9

The Lord's Assurance

Moses said to the LORD, "...let me know whom you will send with me...."
The LORD replied, "My Presence will go with you, and I will give you rest."
Exodus 33:12, 14 NIV

ACROSS

1 "_____ from the east came" (Matthew 2:1 NIV)
5 "Drew to the _____" (Mark 6:53)
10 Taj Mahal site
14 "Become _____ of robbers in your eyes?" (Jeremiah 7:11) (2 words)
15 Ear-related
16 Thailand, once
17 Start of **QUOTE** from Matthew 11:28 (5 words)
20 "The _____ of thy strength" (Psalm 132:8)
21 Slippery swimmer
22 Very long time
23 Native-born Israeli
26 A son of Jether (1 Chronicles 7:38)
28 Transaction (abbr.)

30 **QUOTE**, cont'd (3 words)
33 "Love no false _____" (Zechariah 8:17)
34 "The pin of the beam, and with the _____" (Judges 16:14)
35 Part of 22 Across
36 Ad-less network
37 "He entered into a ship, and _____ in the sea" (Mark 4:1)
38 _____ Cruces, NM.
39 "On the hole of the _____" (Isaiah 11:8)
42 Ohs' partners
43 "They _____ him away" (Matthew 27:2)
44 Actress Hayworth
45 **QUOTE**, cont'd (3 words)
48 "Though it _____ him all the wealth" (Proverbs 6:31 NIV)

50 Blacksburg, Va., school (abbr.)
51 "To hear what your _____ are" (Acts 28:22 NIV)
52 Chinese Muslim
53 Currency of Macao
55 Apple pie maker
56 **QUOTE**, cont'd (5 words)
63 Frosts
64 "He put _____ over his face" (Exodus 34:33 NIV) (2 words)
65 "So is good _____ from a far country" (Proverbs 25:25)
66 End of **QUOTE**
67 "The upper _____ also is square" (Ezekiel 43:17 NIV)
68 "When the desire cometh, it is a _____ of life" (Proverbs 13:12)

DOWN

1 Windows rival
2 "Why make ye this _____" (Mark 5:39)
3 "The way a _____ cutter engraves" (Exodus 28:11 NIV)
4 "Thy will be done _____" (Matthew 6:10) (2 words)
5 "They _____ into the bottom as a stone" (Exodus 15:5)
6 "It sways like a _____ in the wind" (Isaiah 24:20 NIV)
7 Pizarro's gold (Sp.)
8 French composer

9 General Robert _____ (2 words)
10 Voiceless talking (abbr.)
11 "Is there no balm in _____?" (Jeremiah 8:22 NIV)
12 Synthetic fabric
13 Words at the end of Revelation 1:6, 7 (pl.)
18 _____ Mountains (European-Asian boundary)
19 "Ye shall throw down their _____" (Judges 2:2)
23 "All iniquity shall _____ her mouth" (Psalm 107:42)

24 King of Samaria (1 Kings 21:1)
25 "Moles and to the _____" (Isaiah 2:20)
26 Help a crook
27 "Will a man _____ God?" (Malachi 3:8)
29 Genetic carrier
31 Partly submerged
32 "_____ to die" (Luke 7:2)
37 "When _____ Peter" (Acts 9:40) (2 words)
38 "Of _____ he said" (Deuteronomy 33:8)

by David K. Shortess

39 "Set out with Joshua his _____"
(Exodus 24:13 NIV)

40 "The _____ was poured out"
(2 Kings 4:40 NIV)

41 "Baked it in _____"
(Numbers 11:8)

42 "I know thee who thou _____"
(Mark 1:24)

43 "The lot is cast into the _____"
(Proverbs 16:33)

44 "Thy _____ waxed not old upon
thee" (Deuteronomy 8:4)

45 Actors' words to their audiences

46 Develop slowly

47 Ukrainian city

48 "A _____ and a lamp for him"
(2 Kings 4:10 NIV)

49 437.5 grains troy

54 "Then Samuel took a _____ of
oil" (1 Samuel 10:1)

55 "Shall compel thee to go a
_____" (Matthew 5:41)

57 One who specializes in a skill
(suffix)

58 "He hath _____ me"
(Lamentations 3:2)

59 Two-wheeled cart

60 "_____ fadder's mustache!"

61 "_____ no man any thing"
(Romans 13:8)

62 "The _____ of the bow"
(2 Samuel 1:18)

ACROSS

1 Nimshi's son (2 Kings 9:20)
5 "The _____ tree" (Joel 1:12)
10 "I am a brother to dragons, and a companion to _____" (Job 30:29)
14 City in Egypt (Hosea 10:8)
15 Killed
16 "So they _____ it up" (Micah 7:3)
17 "There was a continual _____ given him of the king of Babylon" (Jeremiah 52:34)
18 "For no man ever yet _____ his own flesh" (Ephesians 5:29)
19 Smelling orifice
20 Permit (arch.)
22 Boil (arch.)
24 "And _____ destroyed of the destroyer" (1 Corinthians 10:10)

25 "Neither did we eat any man's _____ for nought" (2 Thessalonians 3:8)
26 Eliakim's son (Luke 3:30)
29 One of Jesus' brothers (Mark 6:3)
32 "Rejoice _____ her?" (Revelation 18:20)
33 A son of Naphtali (Genesis 46:24)
34 "And _____ lay at his feet until the morning" (Ruth 3:14)
37 Descendants
38 Consumed by flames
39 Show (arch.)
40 "The latter _____" (Ruth 3:10)
41 A son of Japheth (Genesis 10:2)
42 "Hand by the _____ of the door" (Song of Solomon 5:4)
43 "Plains of _____?" (Deuteronomy 11:30)

44 Troublesome plants
45 Detoxifying organ
48 Timothy's grandmother (2 Timothy 1:5)
50 Eliphaz's son (Genesis 36:12)
52 "He shall recount his _____" (Nahum 2:5)
56 Stop
57 "Hammoleketh bare _____" (1 Chronicles 7:18)
59 "Son of _____" (Nehemiah 11:12)
60 Fever
61 "The _____ of a whip" (Nahum 3:2)
62 Clothed
63 Act
64 Come in
65 Rabbit

DOWN

1 Shammai's brother (1 Chronicles 2:28)
2 Great wickedness
3 Back of foot
4 "Save yourselves from this _____ generation" (Acts 2:40)
5 One of Jacob's sons (Genesis 35:26)
6 Eating surface
7 Way
8 Untruth
9 Ceases
10 "Of the _____ thereof" (Proverbs 1:19)
11 "I _____ unto you in an epistle" (1 Corinthians 5:9)
12 "Even unto _____" (Genesis 10:19)
13 Velocity

21 "Having a _____" (Leviticus 22:22)
23 Salah's son (Genesis 10:24)
26 Eliezer's son (Luke 3:29)
27 Baking place
28 Lack
29 A son of Joktan (Genesis 10:26)
30 A child of Gad (Numbers 26:16–18)
31 To place
33 Brother of James, servant of Jesus (Jude 1:1)
34 Foot covering
35 Gripped
36 Female sheep
38 Barrier
39 "The king of _____ shall drink after them" (Jeremiah 25:26)

41 Greater
43 "The hills _____ like wax" (Psalm 97:5)
44 "To _____, that God was in Christ, reconciling the world unto himself" (2 Corinthians 5:19)
45 Jahath's son (1 Chronicles 4:2)
46 Idol
47 "Ye are of more _____ than many sparrows" (Luke 12:7)
48 "And they _____ him" (Mark 11:4)
49 "Set in _____ the things that are wanting" (Titus 1:5)
51 Cattle
52 Bit (arch.)
53 Micaiah's father (2 Chronicles 18:7)
54 A son of Seir (1 Chronicles 1:38)

55 Riverbank (Exodus 2:5)

58 "Came to Joel the _____"
(Joel 1:1)

ACROSS

1 "The linen _____ at a price" (1 Kings 10:28)

5 "Had gone six _____, he sacrificed oxen and fatlings" (2 Samuel 6:13)

10 "Valley of _____" (Psalm 84:6)

14 "As he saith also in _____" (Romans 9:25)

15 Overhead

16 "Shuthelah: of _____" (Numbers 26:36)

17 Jonathan's grandfather (2 Samuel 21:14)

18 Sixty (arch.)

20 Consume food

21 Manasseh's son (2 Kings 21:18)

22 Crown

23 Shaving tool

25 Originate

26 Employment pay

27 "The vessels of a potter shall they be broken to _____" (Revelation 2:27)

30 Sharar's son (2 Samuel 23:33)

31 Disgrace

32 Hophni's father (1 Samuel 4:4)

34 Circle

35 Meager

36 "Did _____ upon him" (Mark 15:19)

37 Partook

38 Not dead

39 "When he sowed, some _____ fell by the way side" (Matthew 13:4)

40 "His name was Doeg, an _____" (1 Samuel 21:7)

42 The sun will do this

43 Not any

44 The devil knows his time is this

45 "While I was _____ the fire burned" (Psalm 39:3)

48 Went swiftly

49 Fuss

52 Totally

54 Chew a bone

55 Precipitation

56 A circle is this shape

57 Land measurement

58 Titles of respect

59 "That of all _____" (Ecclesiastes 2:8)

60 Act

DOWN

1 Wooden collar (arch.)

2 Largest continent

3 "Scarce _____ they the people" (Acts 14:18)

4 Last historical book of the Old Testament (abbr.)

5 Isle of John's exile (Revelation 1:9)

6 Despise

7 Ear grain

8 Adam's wife

9 "_____ and harvest" (Genesis 8:22)

10 "_____ obedient unto death, even the death of the cross" (Philippians 2:8)

11 "Of _____, the family" (Numbers 26:17)

12 Feel deeply about

13 "Suburbs, and _____" (1 Chronicles 6:73)

19 Sift

21 "Baalah, and Iim, and _____" (Joshua 15:29)

24 Samuel killed this Amalekite king (1 Samuel 15:32–33)

25 Allotment

26 Free from color

27 Remove hair

28 A turning away from sin

29 "Therefore I shall not _____" (Psalm 26:1)

30 Jether's son (1 Chronicles 7:38)

31 "Thou beholdest mischief and _____" (Psalm 10:14)

33 Possessive pronoun

35 "Howbeit the _____ went about it" (2 Kings 3:25)

36 Mount where Esau lived (Genesis 36:8)

38 In the midst of

39 "Your feet _____ with the preparation of the gospel of peace" (Ephesians 6:15)

41 "The leeks, and the _____, and the garlick" (Numbers 11:5)

42 "Thou shalt break the _____ thereof" (Ezekiel 23:34)

44 "The night is far _____, the day is at hand" (Romans 13:12)

45 "Midst of _____ hill" (Acts 17:22)

46 Daniel had a vision by this river (Daniel 8:1–2)

47 Mix

48 "Wilderness of _____" (Exodus 15:22)

50 "Even _____ to die" (Romans 5:7)

51 Was indebted to

53 Also

by N. Teri Grottke

54 A son of Jacob born in
   Padanaram (Genesis 35:26)

ACROSS

1 Eliezer's son (Luke 3:29)

5 "As a roaring lion, walketh _____, seeking whom he may devour" (1 Peter 5:8)

10 Seminary (abbr.)

13 "Shelesh, and _____" (1 Chronicles 7:35)

14 A grandson of Asher (Genesis 46:17)

15 Heap

16 "Live _____, are in kings' courts" (Luke 7:25)

18 "Day of _____ birth" (Ecclesiastes 7:1)

19 Jether's son (1 Chronicles 7:38)

20 "_____ the Canaanite" (Numbers 21:1)

21 "And he sent them to _____ the kingdom of God" (Luke 9:2)

23 One of the Hebrew midwives (Exodus 1:15)

24 "_____, the children of Shobai" (Nehemiah 7:45)

25 Eshek's second son (1 Chronicles 8:39)

28 Wine is made with this

30 Bring together

31 By yourself

32 Tree juice

35 Canine

36 Absalom's captain (2 Samuel 17:25)

37 He held up Moses' hand (Exodus 17:10–12)

38 Type of tree (Isaiah 44:14)

39 "I _____ you" (Haggai 2:17)

40 "From the tower of _____ shall they fall" (Ezekiel 30:6)

42 Capture

43 After nineteen

44 Jonathan's father (2 Samuel 23:32)

47 "Mordecai for _____?" (Esther 6:3)

48 An idol of Hamath (2 Kings 17:30)

49 "Though ye have _____" (Psalm 68:13)

50 "For _____ had neither father nor mother" (Esther 2:7)

53 "And Ahijah, Hanan, _____" (Nehemiah 10:26)

54 He loved to have the preeminence (3 John 1:9)

57 Crippled

58 "The borders of _____ to Ataroth" (Joshua 16:2)

59 Recover

60 "Against Jerusalem, _____" (Ezekiel 26:2)

61 "There was a cake _____ on the coals" (1 Kings 19:6)

62 Zaccur's father (Nehemiah 3:2)

DOWN

1 Shammai's brother (1 Chronicles 2:28)

2 A seven-week liturgical period beginning with the second day of Passover

3 Heber's father (Luke 3:35)

4 Hophni's father (1 Samuel 4:4)

5 A son of Benjamin (1 Chronicles 8:1)

6 A city of Hadadezer (2 Samuel 8:8)

7 Ruth's son (Ruth 4:13–17)

8 A son of Bani (Ezra 10:34)

9 "Salute _____ and Tryphosa" (Romans 16:12)

10 Agar is this mount in Arabia

11 Selected ones

12 "Dwelling was from _____" (Genesis 10:30)

15 Rhymers

17 "For this _____ ought the woman to have power on her head" (1 Corinthians 11:10)

22 "Who said, _____ it" (Psalm 137:7)

23 "He hath _____ down the mighty" (Luke 1:52)

25 "Out of the tribe of _____" (Revelation 7:5)

26 Seth's son (Genesis 4:26)

27 Opposite of low

28 Eating surface

29 Thorny flower

31 Isaiah's father (Isaiah 1:1)

32 "Set it between Mizpeh and _____" (1 Samuel 7:12)

33 Sister of a parent

34 "Will a lion roar in the forest, when he hath no _____?" (Amos 3:4)

36 Aram's son (Matthew 1:4)

39 "They shall _____ like torches" (Nahum 2:4)

40 Pigs

41 "_____ verily, their sound" (Romans 10:18)

42 The sun will do this

43 In that respect

44 "The children of _____, the children of Darkon" (Nehemiah 7:58)

by N. Teri Grottke

45 "The children of _____"
(Ezra 2:50)

46 A son of Hothan the Aroerite
(1 Chronicles 11:44)

47 A tenth

49 Make secure

50 "And _____ lived after"
(Genesis 11:11)

51 "_____, O Israel: The Lord our
God is one Lord"
(Deuteronomy 6:4)

52 Nagge's son (Luke 3:25)

55 "Helez the Paltite, _____"
(2 Samuel 23:26)

56 Twenty-first letter of the Greek
alphabet

13

Our Now and Future Hope

"For I know the plans I have for you," declares the LORD,
"plans to prosper you and not to harm you,
plans to give you hope and a future."
JEREMIAH 29:11 NIV

ACROSS

1 Where the Mets met
5 Room at the casa
9 Urbanity
14 Alabama neighbor (abbr.)
15 "And _____ for a burnt offering" (Leviticus 9:2) (2 words)
16 "Unto him that _____ to be feared" (Psalm 76:11)
17 "It goes through _____ places" (Luke 11:24 NIV)
18 A discontinuity in geology (abbr.)
19 "And it shall rise up wholly like a _____" (Amos 9:5)
20 Start of **QUOTE** from Psalm 46:1 (4 words)
23 Redactors, briefly
24 "Then who _____ hinder him?" (Job 11:10)

25 Fury
26 **QUOTE**, cont'd (2 words)
32 "Bless all his _____, O LORD" (Deuteronomy 33:11 NIV)
36 Jazz guitarist Montgomery
37 Spanish surrealist artist Joan
38 "Which _____ him in the killing of his brethren" (Judges 9:24)
39 Nitrous for example
40 Partial to (2 words)
41 Phone or photo prefix
42 Former union of Egypt and Syria (abbr.)
43 Stewing
44 **QUOTE**, cont'd (3 words)
47 "O LORD _____ Lord" (Psalm 8:1)

48 Paradigm of simplicity
49 "_____ to teach" (1 Timothy 3:2)
52 End of **QUOTE** (3 words)
56 "The LORD caused the _____ go back" (Exodus 14:21) (2 words)
58 Fern spore producers
59 "The _____ which is lent to the LORD" (1 Samuel 2:20)
60 "And on _____ of the temple" (Daniel 9:27 NIV) (2 words)
61 Familiar DC office
62 "I went down into the garden of _____" (Song of Solomon 6:11)
63 "Thou shalt not _____ to offer the first of thy ripe fruits" (Exodus 22:29)
64 Neck part
65 "To _____" (perfectly) (2 words)

DOWN

1 "Ran at flood _____ as before" (Joshua 4:18 NIV)
2 "Days of _____ the king" (Matthew 2:1)
3 Oklahoma city and wife of Geraint (pl.)
4 "Thine eyes are upon me, _____ am not" (Job 7:8) (2 words)
5 South Pacific islanders
6 "Thy navel is like _____ goblet" (Song of Solomon 7:2) (2 words)
7 Bert, the Oz lion

8 Promised Land inhabitants (Deuteronomy 7:1)
9 Word with break or cake
10 Humdinger
11 Gung ho
12 "So he drew off his _____" (Ruth 4:8)
13 Standard (abbr.)
21 Burn with water
22 Goofs up
27 "As the LORD _____ unto them" (Deuteronomy 2:14)

28 University in Socorro, NM (abbr.)
29 Leslie Caron title role
30 1982 Disney film
31 Precedes Kong
32 "And there _____ certain man at Lystra" (Acts 14:8) (2 words)
33 Capital of Ukraine
34 "That every _____ word that men shall speak" (Matthew 12:36)
35 Eye amorously

by David K. Shortess

39 "And the men of the _____ answered Jonathan" (1 Samuel 14:12)

40 Popular dice game

42 "_____, and away!" (Superman's cry) (2 words)

43 Feverish

45 Ichth follower (it does sound fishy)

46 Each one answered to Daniel (Daniel 6:1–2 NIV)

49 An outbreak of disease (2 words)

50 "He put the golden _____" (Leviticus 8:9)

51 Edgy

52 "He gave them _____ for rain" (Psalm 105:32)

53 Sicilian volcano

54 _____ Scotia

55 It's parallel to the radius

56 "Behold, they were _____" (Genesis 40:6)

57 "Save one little _____ lamb" (2 Samuel 12:3)

ACROSS

1 Ruth's mother-in-law
6 Father (Galatians 4:6)
10 Like jelly
13 Judge after Jephthah (Judges 12:7–8)
14 Jesus' grandfather (Luke 3:23)
15 Jediael's brother (1 Chronicles 11:45)
16 "I pray you, let me _____" (Ruth 2:7)
17 Strong metal
18 Son of Judah (1 Chronicles 2:3)
19 Edges of garments
20 Above the eye
21 Place of the dead
22 Son of Zabad (1 Chronicles 7:21)
24 Son of Rimmon the Beerothite (2 Samuel 4:5)
25 Guni's son (1 Chronicles 5:15)
28 Son of Gad (Genesis 46:16)

30 "Let not thy _____ make me afraid" (Job 13:21)
31 "Even unto Ithiel and _____" (Proverbs 30:1)
32 Petroleum product
35 Border went to here from Remmonmethoar (Joshua 19:13)
36 "_____, and Idbash" (1 Chronicles 4:3)
37 Father of Menahem (2 Kings 15:14)
38 Increase
39 Priestly city of Benjamin (Joshua 21:17)
40 It's attached to your foot
41 Absalom's captain (2 Samuel 17:25)
43 Made of brass (arch.)
44 Crushed rock
47 Onion cousins

49 Forgive
50 "That at the _____ of Jesus every knee should bow" (Philippians 2:10)
51 "Unto the _____ of my kingdom" (Mark 6:23)
55 "Baalah, and Iim, and _____" (Joshua 15:29)
56 Gaddiel's father (Numbers 13:10)
57 Keeper of the women (Esther 2:3 NIV)
58 Iniquities
59 One place inherited by the children of Judah (Joshua 15:34)
60 Things
61 Unhappy
62 "Captains over _____, and officers among your tribes" (Deuteronomy 1:15)
63 Bed covering

DOWN

1 "Draw _____ to God, and he will draw nigh to you" (James 4:8)
2 Having sufficient power
3 A brother of David (1 Chronicles 2:15)
4 Zephaniah's father (Jeremiah 21:1)
5 Motel
6 Enan's son (Numbers 1:15)
7 Baladan's son (2 Kings 20:12)
8 "_____ ye the trumpet in Zion" (Joel 2:1)
9 "On the east side of _____" (Numbers 34:11)
10 Eliakim's son (Luke 3:30)
11 Ezra proclaimed a fast here (Ezra 8:21)

12 "Shall be your _____" (Ezekiel 45:12)
15 Meshullam's brother (1 Chronicles 5:13)
20 Idol of Babylon (Isaiah 46:1)
21 Girl (slang)
23 Commanded militarily
24 Another name for Zoar (Genesis 14:2)
25 "Of Harim, _____" (Nehemiah 12:15)
26 Homophone for a filling starch
27 Expired
29 "In _____ was there a voice" (Matthew 2:18)
31 Utilizes
32 Strong trees
33 Lazy

34 "Though ye have _____" (Psalm 68:13)
36 Son of Nathan of Zobah (2 Samuel 23:36)
37 "_____ upon him with his teeth" (Psalm 37:12)
40 Where the mercy seat is
41 "_____ which dwelt" (Deuteronomy 2:23)
42 Became acquainted
43 Buzzing stinger
44 "Now there was much _____ in the place" (John 6:10)
45 A son of Asher (1 Chronicles 7:39)
46 Make a correction
48 "_____ dwelt therein in times past" (Deuteronomy 2:10)
50 Not any

52 Shammah's father
   (2 Samuel 23:11)

53 Crippled

54 Closed hand

56 "The kings of the earth _____
   themselves" (Psalm 2:2)

57 "A fool's mouth is _____
   destruction" (Proverbs 18:7)

ACROSS

1 Monarch
5 Boys
9 "Letters in _____ name" (1 Kings 21:8)
14 Jesus cried this on the cross (Mark 15:34)
15 Zaccur's father (Nehemiah 3:2)
16 Paul and Silas were sent by night here (Acts 17:10)
17 Comfort
18 "_____ not unto thine own understanding" (Proverbs 3:5)
19 Judge after Jephthah (Judges 12:7–9)
20 "Speaketh like the _____ of a sword" (Proverbs 12:18)
22 Listened
23 Commanded militarily
24 "Altogether for _____ sakes?" (1 Corinthians 9:10)
25 The sorcerer Barjesus was from here (Acts 13:6)

29 Anonymous New Testament book (abbr.)
31 A son of Zophah (1 Chronicles 7:36)
35 "Ran _____ thither" (Mark 6:33)
36 Jeduthun's son (Nehemiah 11:17)
38 "_____ wings of a great eagle" (Revelation 12:14)
39 "He that _____ good is of God" (3 John 1:11)
40 "Children of _____" (Ezra 2:57)
41 "Purge the _____" (Ezekiel 43:26)
43 Are (arch.)
44 Belonging to Jacob's brother
46 Accomplishers
47 Bird home
49 Sick
50 "Let the brother of low _____ rejoice" (James 1:9)

51 She replaced Queen Vashti (abbr.)
53 "We _____ our bread" (Lamentations 5:9)
54 Goliath's brother (1 Chronicles 20:5)
57 Five sparrows are sold for two of these (Luke 12:6)
63 King David's music leader
64 A son of Ulla (1 Chronicles 7:39)
65 Pierce with horns
66 "All the house of _____" (Judges 9:6)
67 "Whosoever shall say to his brother, _____, shall be in danger" (Matthew 5:22)
68 At once (Mark 1:30)
69 One who consumes food
70 Biblical place of perfection
71 Perverse

DOWN

1 "Neither _____ they the king's laws" (Esther 3:8)
2 "_____ the Ahohite" (1 Chronicles 11:29)
3 Smelling orifice
4 Type of eagle (arch.)
5 "Consider the _____ how they grow" (Luke 12:27)
6 Make a correction
7 Pull
8 Iniquities
9 A son of Aaron (Exodus 6:23)
10 Jael was his wife (Judges 4:21)
11 Steward of the house in Tirzah (1 Kings 16:9)
12 "Should _____ rule" (Esther 1:22)

13 Beach surface
21 Put on garments
24 Prophet to the Edomites (abbr.)
25 Rachel and Leah's birthplace (Genesis 28:2; 48:7)
26 Before (arch.)
27 Rhymers
28 "My heart was _____" (Psalm 39:3)
29 A son of Pharez (Genesis 46:12)
30 Belonging to Eli
32 Complete
33 Cognizant
34 Steed
36 Ebed's son (Judges 9:26)
37 Load down (arch.)

42 Measurement for oil (Leviticus 14:10)
45 "_____ down here" (Ruth 4:1)
48 Solomon built the first
50 Abiram's brother (Numbers 16:1)
52 A river "before Egypt" (Joshua 13:3)
53 Undeserved favor
54 Crippled
55 Largest continent
56 Stop
57 "_____ ye well" (Acts 15:29)
58 "_____ the Canaanite" (Numbers 21:1)
59 Son of Nathan of Zobah (2 Samuel 23:36)
60 Not any

by N. Teri Grottke

61 "The seed should spring and ______" (Mark 4:27)

62 "I will even ______ a curse upon you" (Malachi 2:2)

ACROSS

1 Twenty-first letter of the Greek alphabet

4 First of the prophetic books (abbr.)

7 The highest point

10 "The LORD dwelleth in _____" (Joel 3:21)

11 Type of weed

13 "For as _____ was three days" (Matthew 12:40)

15 King Hoshea's father (2 Kings 15:30)

16 "The robber _____ up their substance" (Job 5:5)

18 "All the sons of _____ that dwelt" (Nehemiah 11:6)

20 Bed covering

21 "_____ that ye refuse" (Hebrews 12:25)

22 To kid or poke fun

24 "A _____ of dove's dung" (2 Kings 6:25)

25 Twisted

28 A son of Reumah (Genesis 22:24)

33 Strike

34 Untruth

36 Jehoshaphat's maternal grandfather (1 Kings 22:42)

37 In this place

38 "His _____; on the eighth" (Exodus 22:30)

40 12:00 p.m.

41 King of Damascus (2 Corinthians 11:32)

44 "But the wheat and the _____ were not smitten" (Exodus 9:32)

46 Moses' final Book of days (abbr.)

47 Magog's brother (Genesis 10:2)

49 "When thou _____, let thy companies deliver thee" (Isaiah 57:13)

51 Greek form of *Noah* (Luke 17:26)

52 Make a mistake

53 Hophni's father (1 Samuel 4:4)

56 "Ran greedily after the _____ of Balaam for reward" (Jude 1:11)

59 Absalom's captain (2 Samuel 17:25)

63 Farmer (arch.)

66 A son of Judah (1 Chronicles 2:3)

67 "All the _____ of the heathen" (Zephaniah 2:11)

68 Identical

69 "Eaten without _____?" (Job 6:6)

70 "Hundred and _____ years old" (Joshua 24:29)

71 Not cooked

72 "This is _____ blessing of Judah" (Deuteronomy 33:7)

DOWN

1 Heap

2 Gray

3 "According to his inheritance which he _____" (Numbers 35:8)

4 Possessive pronoun

5 "Put them under _____, and under harrows of iron" (2 Samuel 12:31)

6 A son of Ulla (1 Chronicles 7:39)

7 "As a thread of _____ is broken" (Judges 16:9)

8 "Day of _____ birth" (Ecclesiastes 7:1)

9 Scalp

10 Between Habakkuk and Haggai (abbr.)

12 Selected ones

13 "The daughter of Haruz of _____" (2 Kings 21:19)

14 "And _____ lay at his feet until the morning" (Ruth 3:14)

17 Belonging to Jacob's first wife

19 "Maalehacrabbim, and passed along to _____" (Joshua 15:3)

23 God of Babylon (Isaiah 46:1)

25 "_____ I hated them" (Hosea 9:15)

26 "And cut it into _____" (Exodus 39:3)

27 "God _____ tempt Abraham" (Genesis 22:1)

29 Farthest to the rear (arch.)

30 "Myrrh and _____" (Song of Solomon 4:14)

31 "The Lord. . .shall. . .descend. . . with a _____, with the voice of the archangel" (1 Thessalonians 4:16)

32 Liquid measure (Leviticus 23:13)

35 Peter cut one off

37 A son of Noah

39 He was a Morasthite (Micah 1:1) (abbr.)

42 "Man named _____" (Acts 9:33)

43 "And they laughed him to _____" (Mark 5:40)

45 Before (arch.)

48 "The _____ of cattle are perplexed" (Joel 1:18)

50 "Helez the Paltite, _____" (2 Samuel 23:26)

by N. Teri Grottke

53 A son of Benjamin (Genesis 46:21)

54 "Fulfil the ______ of the flesh" (Galatians 5:16)

55 Island

57 A son of Eliphaz (Genesis 36:11)

58 "In ______ was there a voice" (Matthew 2:18)

60 Zibeon's daughter (Genesis 36:2)

61 "______ of his patrimony" (Deuteronomy 18:8)

62 Tiny insect

64 "Zechariah, ______" (1 Chronicles 15:18)

65 "By a ______ and living way" (Hebrews 10:20)

Books of the Bible

Theme answers 20, 37, and 52 Across and 4, 7, and 10 Down are each the names of three Bible books (minus "1", "2" or "3" where it applies).

ACROSS

1 Silver salmon
6 Right now in ICU
10 "Which is the king's _____" (Genesis 14:17)
14 One of the Leeward Islands
15 *One* in Bonn (Ger.)
16 "And _____ of oil" (Leviticus 14:21) (2 words)
17 *For Me and _____* (1948 Judy Garland film) (2 words)
18 It goes into a slot (2 words)
19 "Where are the _____?" (Luke 17:17)
20 **THREE BIBLE BOOKS**
23 "The one _____ is the man; arrest him" (Matthew 26:48 NIV) (2 words)
24 "In the fig _____ her first time" (Hosea 9:10) (2 words)

25 "He would not let me _____ my breath" (Job 9:18 NIV)
28 "_____ weeping for her children" (Jeremiah 31:15)
30 Esau's first wife (Genesis 36:2)
31 R to L on a map (3 words)
33 What a fighter pilot in trouble may do
37 **THREE BIBLE BOOKS**
40 "Gold in a swine's _____" (Proverbs 11:22)
41 Rhine feeder (Swiss)
42 Butte kin
43 "Sharper than a _____ hedge" (Micah 7:4)
45 Government operation at Bikini Island

47 Irish clergyman who determined the date of creation to be 4004 BC
50 Satisfies fully
52 **THREE BIBLE BOOKS**
57 County seat of Martin County, KY
58 "Grace to thy _____" (Proverbs 3:22)
59 May be part of change in Russia
60 Twelfth Jewish month (Esther 3:7)
61 "Son of man, record this _____" (Ezekiel 24:2 NIV)
62 "Stop on _____" (very quickly) (2 words)
63 Cry from a crib
64 Relative of an organization (abbr.)
65 "Caught in a cruel _____ birds are taken in a snare" (Ecclesiastes 9:12 NIV) (2 words)

DOWN

1 "It _____ to pass" (Isaiah 37:1)
2 Gemsbok is one
3 French author Victor
4 **THREE BIBLE BOOKS**
5 Greyhound relative
6 "The Lamb opened one of the _____" (Revelation 6:1)
7 **THREE BIBLE BOOKS**
8 Father of giants in the Promised Land (Numbers 13:33)
9 Tenth Hebrew month (Esther 2:16)
10 **THREE BIBLE BOOKS**
11 "With _____ of flax in his hand" (Ezekiel 40:3) (2 words)

12 "After so _____ time" (Hebrews 4:7) (2 words)
13 The opposite of "take in" or "swallow"
21 "Thy neck is an iron _____" (Isaiah 48:4)
22 Krooked _____, where the Keystone Kops kaught katfish
25 Stadium cries
26 Location to the west of Nod (Genesis 4:16)
27 Russian-born American sculptor Naum
29 "Do not give _____ cry, do not raise" (Joshua 6:10 NIV) (2 words)
32 Romanov ruler of yesteryear

34 Jewish word for "complete truth"
35 "Counteth the _____" (Luke 14:28)
36 Relatives of IRAs
38 "Libnah, and _____, and Ashan" (Joshua 15:42)
39 Spanish lasso
44 Berkeley, California, suburb
46 Capital of Iran
47 "He said, I will go _____ as thou art" (2 Kings 3:7) (3 words)
48 "I will _____ lad" (1 Samuel 20:21) (2 words)
49 Kind of engine
51 1930 Pulitzer Prize poet Conrad

by David K. Shortess

53 "Whatsoever passeth through the paths of the _____" (Psalm 8:8)

54 Brief last "writes" (abbr.)

55 Roper of the polls

56 Ogle lecherously

ACROSS

1 "In _____ was there a voice" (Matthew 2:18)

5 Pursue

10 Revile

14 Belonging to Eli (poss.)

15 "The Amorites would dwell in mount _____" (Judges 1:35)

16 Otherwise

17 A son of Helem (1 Chronicles 7:35)

18 "Plain from _____" (Deuteronomy 2:8)

19 Haniel's father (1 Chronicles 7:39)

20 "_____ it upon the graves" (2 Chronicles 34:4)

22 Jephthah fled to there (Judges 11:3)

24 An altar (Joshua 22:34)

25 Gaal's father (Judges 9:26)

26 "And _____ destroyed of the destroyer" (1 Corinthians 10:10)

27 Shouted

30 Mourned

34 Man slain by the men of Gath (1 Chronicles 7:21)

35 Strong metal

36 "Between Bethel and _____" (Genesis 13:3)

37 Zibeon's son (1 Chronicles 1:40)

38 A city in Judah (Joshua 15:26)

40 "Shall _____ thee" (Habakkuk 2:7)

41 John's vision of the end times (abbr.)

42 Past tense of spit

43 "The streets and _____ of the city" (Luke 14:21)

44 Snooze (arch.)

46 Turn away from sin

47 Straight distance between two points

48 Not this, but _____

49 Judah's firstborn (Genesis 38:6)

51 "Garments, _____ stood" (Zechariah 3:3)

52 Dodai was one of these (1 Chronicles 27:4)

55 Perverse

57 Part of the priestly garb

59 A son of Shimei (1 Chronicles 23:10)

61 Asa's father (1 Chronicles 3:10)

62 Not those, but _____

63 "Shuthelah: of _____" (Numbers 26:36)

64 "That which _____ been" (Ecclesiastes 6:10)

65 Employs

66 Refuse to admit

DOWN

1 "Shimei, and _____, and the mighty men" (1 Kings 1:8)

2 Charity

3 "For ye tithe _____ and rue and all manner of herbs" (Luke 11:42)

4 A son of Asaph (1 Chronicles 25:2)

5 "Ere it was _____" (Numbers 11:33)

6 Baanah's son (1 Chronicles 11:30)

7 "_____ the Canaanite" (Numbers 21:1)

8 To place

9 Ishbah's son (1 Chronicles 4:17)

10 Jacob's firstborn (Genesis 35:23)

11 "Destroy _____ kings and people" (Ezra 6:12)

12 Island

13 Escort

21 Ruth's son (Ruth 4:13–17)

23 A son of Jerahmeel (1 Chronicles 2:25)

26 Opposite of cool

27 "One day is with the Lord as a thousand _____" (2 Peter 3:8)

28 "Jozabad, and _____" (2 Chronicles 31:13)

29 "Not to _____ thee" (Ruth 1:16)

30 "The whole world _____ in wickedness" (1 John 5:19)

31 Yours (arch.)

32 Consumed

33 "Where thou _____, will I die" (Ruth 1:17)

38 "He _____ as a shadow?" (Ecclesiastes 6:12)

39 Detest

40 Immersed in water

42 "Neither do they _____" (Matthew 6:28)

43 Rachel's sister (Genesis 29:16)

45 Tahath's son (1 Chronicles 7:20)

46 "Unto _____, and from thence unto Patara" (Acts 21:1)

48 Not these, but _____

49 King Hoshea's father (2 Kings 15:30)

50 A duke of Sihon (Joshua 13:21)

52 "Sons of _____" (1 Chronicles 7:12)

53 Exhaust

54 Ahira's father (Numbers 1:15)

56 "To _____, that God was in Christ, reconciling the world" (2 Corinthians 5:19)

58 Twenty-first letter of the Greek alphabet

60 No matter which

by N. Teri Grottke

ACROSS

1 Killed
5 Two of these make a farthing
10 Belonging to Eli
14 Story
15 Son of Ribai (1 Chronicles 11:31)
16 Gave a loan
17 Greek form of *Asher* (Revelation 7:6)
18 Honed
19 Measure (arch.)
20 John the Baptist's girdle was this (Matthew 3:4)
22 "Wool, and _____" (Hebrews 9:19)
24 Boy
25 Jether's son (1 Chronicles 7:38)
26 He was a herdsman (Amos 1:1) (abbr.)
27 Opposite of *wet*
28 Yelled

32 Wallet (arch.)
35 "Eaten without _____?" (Job 6:6)
36 A sibling of Lotan, Shobal, and Zibeon (1 Chronicles 1:38)
38 "Shuthelah: of _____" (Numbers 26:36)
39 "The well of _____" (2 Samuel 3:26)
40 A son of Zophah (1 Chronicles 7:36)
41 Comfort
42 Daniel had a vision by this river (Daniel 8:1–2)
43 "House, _____ Rahab" (Joshua 2:1)
44 A city of Judah's inheritance (Joshua 15:36)
46 "By his name _____" (Psalm 68:4)
47 "_____ verily, their sound" (Romans 10:18)

48 Like jelly
49 He follow Isaiah (abbr.)
52 "And will make thee as a _____" (Haggai 2:23)
56 Hodaviah's father (1 Chronicles 9:7)
58 Shammah's father (2 Samuel 23:11)
59 A son of Asher (1 Chronicles 7:30)
61 "I have stretched out my hands _____ thee" (Psalm 88:9)
62 Naomi wanted to be called this
63 Winged symbol of USA
64 Bound
65 King Hoshea's father (2 Kings 15:30)
66 "Saul leaned upon his _____" (2 Samuel 1:6)
67 "Through faith also _____ herself received strength to conceive seed" (Hebrews 11:11)

DOWN

1 Enclosure in a stable
2 A city on Crete (Acts 27:8)
3 A son of Zabad (1 Chronicles 7:21)
4 Were (arch.)
5 "Destruction and _____ are in their ways" (Romans 3:16)
6 Amasa's father (2 Samuel 17:25)
7 "Now the serpent was more subtil _____ any beast" (Genesis 3:1)
8 Used to hear
9 "In Aroer, and to them which were in _____" (1 Samuel 30:28)
10 Type of trees
11 "Punish the men that are settled on their _____" (Zephaniah 1:12)
12 "_____ the waters" (Exodus 15:25)

13 "There is but a _____ between me and death" (1 Samuel 20:3)
21 "The joy of the _____ ceaseth" (Isaiah 24:8)
23 Opposite of *me*
26 Sheshan's daughter (1 Chronicles 2:31)
27 Ate in style
28 Isaac's mother
29 A son of Reumah (Genesis 22:24)
30 "And at Bilhah, and at _____, and at Tolad" (1 Chronicles 4:29)
31 "Even _____ to die" (Romans 5:7)
32 "_____ that ye refuse" (Hebrews 12:25)
33 Rocky outcropping

34 "Who said, _____ it" (Psalm 137:7)
35 Paul's missionary partner
37 Make free
39 "That are _____ for debts" (Proverbs 22:26)
43 "That at the _____" (Philemon 2:10)
45 "But the _____" (Ezra 5:5)
46 "Is not this written in the book of _____?" (Joshua 10:13)
48 "The children of _____, the children of Darkon" (Nehemiah 7:58)
49 "Salute Andronicus and _____" (Romans 16:7)
50 One who consumes food
51 She met Peter at the door (Acts 12:13–14)

52 Identical

53 Son of Nathan of Zobah
   (2 Samuel 23:36)

54 A son of Benjamin
   (Genesis 46:21)

55 The border went to here from
   Remmonmethoar (Joshua 19:13)

56 Very large

57 Almonds, cashews, etc.

60 Tree juice

by N. Teri Grottke

ACROSS

1 "The _____ lying in a manger" (Luke 2:16)
5 King Hoshea's father (2 Kings 15:30)
9 "The _____ of the LORD" (Malachi 1:7)
14 "_____ the Canaanite" (Numbers 21:1)
15 "_____ not the world" (1 John 2:15)
16 "_____, and Bariah" (1 Chronicles 3:22)
17 "Who said, _____ it" (Psalm 137:7)
18 "The rock _____" (Judges 15:11)
19 "The streets and _____ of the city" (Luke 14:21)
20 A son of Midian (1 Chronicles 1:33)
22 "Made clay of the _____" (John 9:6)
24 Partook
25 Single
26 "_____ shall dance there" (Isaiah 13:21)
30 "When _____ the Edomite was there" (1 Samuel 22:22)
32 Not many
35 Weeps
36 Resting place
37 Another name for *Zoar* (Genesis 14:2, 8)
38 "Who shall _____ us away the stone" (Mark 16:3)
39 "Thou doest faithfully _____" (3 John 1:5)
41 Image
42 Boaz's wife
43 "Neither did we eat any man's _____ for nought" (2 Thessalonians 3:8)
44 Bowling target
45 A place to wash
46 "The rest, some on _____" (Acts 27:44)
47 Eat
48 Used to control a horse
49 "And they set the altar upon his _____" (Ezra 3:3)
52 "Get thee to _____, unto thine own fields" (1 Kings 2:26)
57 A son of Elioenai (1 Chronicles 3:24)
58 "Other _____ there" (John 6:22)
59 Beat
61 "Mint and _____" (Matthew 23:23)
62 Skeletal component
63 "Punish the men that are settled on their _____" (Zephaniah 1:12)
64 Loaded (arch.)
65 "And Ahijah, Hanan, _____" (Nehemiah 10:26)
66 "Land from _____" (Isaiah 16:1)

DOWN

1 Barrier
2 A son of Ulla (1 Chronicles 7:39)
3 "In presence am _____ among you" (2 Corinthians 10:1)
4 First garden
5 Chooses
6 "To the Israelites by _____ ordered" (Numbers 36:2 NIV) (2 words)
7 Area near Babylon (2 Kings 17:24)
8 Edges of garments
9 "Let him down through the _____ with his couch" (Luke 5:19)
10 A gem on the third row of the ephod (Exodus 28:19)
11 Not straight
12 Eliasaph's father (Numbers 3:24)
13 Otherwise
21 Hand-driven boat propellers
23 Rhymers
26 Early miners' pay
27 A son of Gad (Genesis 46:16)
28 "Benhanan, and _____" (1 Chronicles 4:20)
29 Shout
30 The end of life
31 Strong promise
32 The thing that left Peter's mother-in-law (Matthew 8:14–15)
33 Man slain by the men of Gath (1 Chronicles 7:21)
34 "Appointed the _____ of the priests and the Levites" (Nehemiah 13:30)
36 Opposite of *open*
37 King of Sodom (Genesis 14:2)
39 "So they _____ it up" (Micah 7:3)
40 Thirty-sixth encampment of the children of Israel (Numbers 21:10)
45 "Sons of Aaron were _____ in offering of burnt offerings" (2 Chronicles 35:14)
46 "Every one that is _____" (Numbers 21:8)
47 Hearing is one
48 Zadok's father (Nehemiah 3:4)
49 "Remnant of _____" (Zephaniah 1:4)
50 Temple prophetess in Jesus' time (Luke 2:36–37)

by N. Teri Grottke

51 Stated
52 Father (Galatians 4:6)
53 12:00 p.m.
54 "I am a brother to dragons, and a companion to _____" (Job 30:29)
55 You (arch.)
56 "_____ the Bethelite" (1 Kings 16:34)
60 Some of these were written by Asaph (abbr.)

21

More Biblical Mounts

*And when he had sent them away,
he departed into a mountain to pray.*

MARK 6:46

ACROSS

1 "For as in _____ all die" (1 Corinthians 15:22)

5 "And great _____ the Jews" (Esther 10:3)

10 "I _____ dream which made me afraid" (Daniel 4:5) (2 words)

14 "Not of works, _____ any man should boast" (Ephesians 2:9)

15 **MOUNT** from which Barak was victorious (Judges 4:6–16)

16 "The high places also of _____" (Hosea 10:8)

17 Laban's tender-eyed daughter (Genesis 29:16–17)

18 African pachyderm

19 "Never _____ of doing what is right" (2 Thessalonians 3:13 NIV)

20 Memory losses

22 **MOUNT** from which Jesus ascended (Acts 1:9–12)

24 "For my flesh is _____ food" (John 6:55 NIV)

25 "And to morrow is cast into the _____" (Luke 12:28)

26 **MOUNT** where Elijah called down fire from heaven (1 Kings 18:20–38)

29 "And they filled them up to the _____" (John 2:7)

30 Time in Chicago (abbr.)

33 Sometimes it's double-stuffed

34 "For he is _____, as he said" (Matthew 28:6)

35 Follows tee

36 **MOUNT** of _____, where Jesus met Moses and Elijah (Matthew 17:1–8)

40 "Give _____ to my words" (Psalm 5:1)

41 "Which is by the river _____" (Deuteronomy 3:12)

42 Flightless birds down under

43 Used to copy system files in DOS

44 "Ye _____ be born again" (John 3:7)

45 "Who go to _____ bowls of mixed wine" (Proverbs 23:30 NIV)

47 To a slight degree, in music

48 Fool

49 **MOUNT** where Noah parked (Genesis 8:4)

52 **MOUNT** where Saul was defeated (1 Samuel 31:1–8) (2 words)

56 "I will _____ Sisera" (Judges 4:7 NIV)

57 "Or loose the bands of _____?" (Job 38:31)

59 Snaky fish

60 "Everything goes _____ it has since" (2 Peter 3:4 NIV) (2 words)

61 **MOUNT** where God gave Moses the two tablets (Exodus 31:18)

62 Sobriety organization (abbr.)

63 "Their _____ shall not become garments" (Isaiah 59:6)

64 "And as soon as I had _____ it" (Revelation 10:10)

65 Threesome

DOWN

1 "_____ man's ways seem right to him" (Proverbs 21:2 NIV) (2 words)

2 Judge

3 "And _____ old lion" (Genesis 49:9) (2 words)

4 **MOUNT** on Israel's northern border (Deuteronomy 4:48) (2 words)

5 "Because it is _____" (Ezekiel 21:13) (2 words)

6 Taj _____

7 Japanese sashes

8 "_____ his son, Jehoshua his son" (1 Chronicles 7:27)

9 More "hip"

10 "And _____ ashes" (Jonah 3:6) (2 words)

11 Tel _____

12 "Though I _____ perfect" (Job 9:21)

13 "Casting _____ into the sea" (Mark 1:16) (2 words)

21 "They shall _____ God" (Matthew 5:8)

23 Duckweed genus

by David K. Shortess

25 "The scorching heat _____" (Isaiah 49:10 NASB) (2 words)

26 "_____ for flocks" (2 Chronicles 32:28)

27 "Or costly _____" (1 Timothy 2:9)

28 Raises

29 Racist

30 Simian, briefly

31 South Korean capital

32 Past or present

34 Oxydol competitor

37 Polynesian islands

38 Fruit sugar

39 **MOUNT** Moriah (2 Chronicles 3:1) (2 words)

45 Register (2 words)

46 "_____ my brother's keeper?" (Genesis 4:9) (2 words)

47 "For the _____ is full" (Joel 3:13)

48 Athenian porticos

49 "And the city shall be low in _____ place" (Isaiah 32:19) (2 words)

50 Old Germanic alphabet character

51 "And Geshem the _____ heard about it" (Nehemiah 2:19 NIV)

52 "Ye tithe _____ and rue and all manner of herbs" (Luke 11:42)

53 "I am one that _____ witness of myself" (John 8:18)

54 "In days of _____ planned it" (Isaiah 37:26 NIV) (2 words)

55 "To fear thee, _____ thy people Israel" (1 Kings 8:43) (2 words)

58 Estuary

ACROSS

1 "At Enrimmon, and at _____, and at Jarmuth" (Nehemiah 11:29)
7 Bela's father (1 Chronicles 5:8)
11 Ground moisture
14 "Mount Sinai in _____" (Galatians 4:25)
15 "We _____ not" (2 John 1:8)
16 Hophni's father (1 Samuel 4:4)
17 Bird from the ark sent out three times (Genesis 8:8–12)
18 A son of Kohath (Numbers 3:19)
20 "_____ down here" (Ruth 4:1)
21 Azariah's father (2 Chronicles 15:1)
22 Crippled
23 A son of Beriah (1 Chronicles 8:16)
25 Relatives
26 Rope web
27 Edges of garments

28 "And from _____ in the valley" (Numbers 21:20)
31 "Borders of _____" (Joshua 11:2)
32 Weeping prophet
35 One of the king's chamberlains (Esther 4:5)
38 Adam's wife
39 Type of tree (Isaiah 44:14)
40 Knight
41 "When _____ king" (2 Samuel 8:9)
42 "When thou liest down, and when thou _____ up" (Deuteronomy 6:7)
44 "Having under me _____" (Luke 7:8)
46 Songs of prayer and praise (abbr.)
47 "Will I make a _____ in the temple of my God" (Revelation 3:12)
48 Emancipate

50 Partook
51 Biggest star in our solar system
54 "Let the _____ of the hair of his head grow" (Numbers 6:5)
56 Rear end of an animal
58 "Herod was highly displeased with them of _____ and Sidon" (Acts 12:20)
59 "For _____ of the heart" (Matthew 15:19)
60 "Salute _____, our helper in Christ" (Romans 16:9)
62 The king's chamberlain (Esther 2:3)
63 Utilize
64 "Collar of my _____" (Job 30:18)
65 "_____ their mouth against thee" (Lamentations 2:16)
67 Color of blood
68 In this place
69 Cure

DOWN

1 One of David's priests (1 Kings 1:8)
2 A brother of Ezbon and Eri (Genesis 46:16)
3 First bird out of the ark (Genesis 8:7)
4 Gaal's father (Judges 9:26)
5 City conquered by Joshua (Joshua 8:26)
6 "And said, _____, King of the Jews!" (John 19:3)
7 Jehoadah's son (1 Chronicles 8:36)
8 A son of Ishi (1 Chronicles 4:20)
9 Reigned over Judah while Jeroboam ruled Israel (1 Kings 15:9)

10 "Gedaliah, and _____" (1 Chronicles 25:3)
11 "The speeches of one that is _____" (Job 6:26)
12 Bathsheba's father (2 Samuel 11:3)
13 "If they bind me with seven green _____" (Judges 16:7)
19 Jekuthiel's son (1 Chronicles 4:18)
24 "The archers _____ at king Josiah" (2 Chronicles 35:23)
28 Beryllium (sym.)
29 Absalom's captain (2 Samuel 17:25)
30 This fell on the sorcerer Elymas (Acts 13:6–11)
31 "Chalcol, and _____" (1 Kings 4:31)

32 The second prophetic book (abbr.)
33 A king of Midian (Numbers 31:8)
34 "They _____ not the persons of the priests" (Lamentations 4:16)
35 "At his holy _____" (Psalm 99:9)
36 Book with Spiritual gifts (abbr.)
37 "For Ezra had prepared _____ heart" (Ezra 7:10)
40 "Call a _____ assembly" (Joel 2:15)
43 Well of strife (Genesis 26:20)
44 "That was _____ among the rivers" (Nahum 3:8)
45 "Children of _____" (1 Chronicles 7:12)
47 "Two at _____" (1 Chronicles 26:18)

by N. Teri Grottke

48 "A measure of fine _____ be sold for a shekel" (2 Kings 7:1)

49 Wake up

51 "From the tower of _____ shall they fall" (Ezekiel 30:6)

52 "And _____ him" (Judges 16:16)

53 "Which oppress the poor, which crush the _____" (Amos 4:1)

55 "Ho, _____ a one!" (Ruth 4:1)

57 Balak brought Balaam to the top of this mountain (Numbers 23:28)

58 Those

61 Small deer

66 Physical education (abbr.)

ACROSS

1 Jezebel's husband
5 Rip
9 Son of Uriah the priest (Ezra 8:33)
14 Land next to water
15 A son of Haman (Esther 9:8)
16 A son of Benjamin (1 Chronicles 8:1)
17 "_____ that ye refuse" (Hebrews 12:25)
18 Ahian's father (Luke 3:36)
20 Type of tree (Isaiah 44:14)
21 Arphaxad's father (Luke 3:36)
22 "His _____; on the eighth" (Exodus 22:30)
23 Large lake
26 A long distance away

27 Burial place
28 Grow (arch.)
29 Get older
31 "Nor _____ the firstfruits of the land" (Ezekiel 48:14)
33 Matured
35 King Saul's father (Acts 13:21)
36 Not easily found
37 "A _____ man stirreth up strife" (Proverbs 15:18)
39 "Honour all _____" (1 Peter 2:17)
40 Zephaniah's son (Zechariah 6:14)
41 Hearing organs
42 Buzzing stinger
44 Even
45 "_____ there yet the treasures" (Micah 6:10)

46 Writing tool
47 Plant seed
50 "Thou shalt be _____, and shalt not fear" (Job 11:15)
52 "Had cast _____" (Esther 9:24)
53 "Upon this I _____" (Jeremiah 31:26)
56 "Hothan the _____" (1 Chronicles 11:44)
58 "Filled his holes with prey, and his dens with _____" (Nahum 2:12)
59 "And the king made of the algum trees _____" (2 Chronicles 9:11)
60 Snare
61 Were (arch.)

DOWN

1 Absalom's captain (2 Samuel 17:25)
2 "The Amorites would dwell in mount _____" (Judges 1:35)
3 "Argob and _____" (2 Kings 15:25)
4 Sleeping place
5 Eliel's father (1 Chronicles 6:34)
6 "Moses. . .took some of its blood and put it on. . .Aaron's right _____" (Leviticus 8:23 NIV)
7 Solomon's great-grandson (1 Kings 15:8)
8 Right hand (abbr.)
10 A son of Ishmael (1 Chronicles 1:30)
11 "Of the _____ Ruth" (Ruth 1:4)
12 People
13 A son of Noah

14 "They laid her in an upper _____" (Acts 9:37)
16 A walled city in Naphtali (Joshua 19:33)
19 "Ephraim is joined to _____" (Hosea 4:17)
23 Took an oath (arch.)
24 Consumed
25 Big hatchet
26 These are used for walking
27 These are attached to the rumps of animals
29 "_____ with thine adversary quickly" (Matthew 5:25)
30 Give
32 "Jesus" is the _____ above every name (Philippians 2:9–10)
34 "_____ flour" (Exodus 29:2)
35 "The child was _____ from that very hour" (Matthew 17:18)

37 One of five journalistic questions
38 Went
42 "They could not go over the brook _____" (1 Samuel 30:10)
43 Come in
46 Cut back
47 Seasoning
48 "Cast ye the unprofitable servant into _____ darkness" (Matthew 25:30)
49 "Every day they _____ my words" (Psalm 56:5)
50 "He maketh them also to _____ like a calf" (Psalm 29:6)
51 Obese
53 Are (arch.)
54 Fight between countries
55 Area near Babylon (2 Kings 17:24)
57 Not cooked

by N. Teri Grottke

ACROSS

1 Ishmaelite camel driver (1 Chronicles 27:30)
5 Son of Caleb (1 Chronicles 4:15)
9 Firm
13 "Shall the rich man _____ away in his ways" (James 1:11)
14 Melchi's father (Luke 3:28)
15 "Which maketh Arcturus, _____, and Pleiades" (Job 9:9)
17 Story
18 Shammai's son (1 Chronicles 2:45)
19 "Golden _____ of Ophir" (Isaiah 13:12)
20 What Dan was called before they captured it (Joshua 19:47)
22 Plow (arch.)
24 Hophni's father (1 Samuel 4:4)
25 "Shimei, and _____" (1 Kings 1:8)
26 With caution
30 Victuals

32 Jephthah fled to there (Judges 11:3)
35 "Lion's _____, and none made them afraid?" (Nahum 2:11)
36 "By faith Moses, when he was _____" (Hebrews 11:23)
37 Rodents
38 Son of Shem (Genesis 10:22)
39 "Stand up in his estate a raiser of _____" (Daniel 11:20)
40 Son of Merari (1 Chronicles 24:27)
41 "Heavens shall _____ away with a great noise" (2 Peter 3:10)
42 First garden
43 Solomon's temple was built on his threshing floor (2 Chronicles 3:1)
44 Greek convert; Paul's rep to Crete (abbr.)
45 "Day of _____ birth" (Ecclesiastes 7:1)

46 "Wherefore _____ aside all malice" (1 Peter 2:1)
47 Capable
48 High temperature
49 "Thou that _____ Joseph like a flock" (Psalm 80:1)
53 A son of Helah (1 Chronicles 4:7)
57 "_____ with her suburbs; four cities" (Joshua 21:18)
58 This priest rebuilt the temple
60 "Tappuah, and _____" (Joshua 15:34)
62 Abram lived in this plain (Genesis 13:18)
63 King of the jungle
64 Identical
65 Female red deer
66 Boys
67 "See _____ that ye walk circumspectly" (Ephesians 5:15)

DOWN

1 Often (arch.)
2 "Remnant of _____" (Zephaniah 1:4)
3 Lazy
4 "Punish the men that are settled on their _____" (Zephaniah 1:12)
5 "_____, thou shalt love thy neighbour as thyself" (Romans 13:9)
6 Walled city in Naphtali (Joshua 19:33)
7 Fuss
8 This herb can come in chocolate
9 "When they _____ upon their beds" (Hosea 7:14)
10 A son of Gad (Genesis 46:16)
11 Travel other than on foot
12 Canines

16 Rope web
21 Assist
23 Smoothes out the wrinkles (pl.)
26 Cleaned with a broom
27 Sheshan's child (1 Chronicles 2:31)
28 Celebratory meal
29 Type of trees
30 "_____ have holes" (Luke 9:58)
31 A son of Jerahmeel (1 Chronicles 2:25)
32 Ginath's son (1 Kings 16:21)
33 Pagiel's father (Numbers 1:13)
34 "For in him we live, and move, and have our _____" (Acts 17:28)
36 Sent (arch.) (Ruth 3:6)

37 "Out of the _____ clay" (Psalm 40:2)
39 "I saw the _____ of Cushan in affliction" (Habakkuk 3:7)
43 Strong promise
45 "_____ their mouth against thee" (Lamentations 2:16)
46 "_____ sister was Timna" (Genesis 36:22)
47 Decorate
48 King at the time of Jesus' birth
49 Jeremiah's book of sorrows
50 King Hoshea's father (2 Kings 15:30)
51 "Your brethren, _____" (Hosea 2:1)
52 "_____ me whether ye sold the land for so much?" (Acts 5:8)

54 Bird home

55 Zibeon's daughter (Genesis 36:2)

56 "That at the _____ of Jesus every knee should bow" (Philippians 2:10)

59 A brother of Jachan (1 Chronicles 5:13)

61 More than one man

by N. Teri Grottke

25

Improbable Encounters

These highly unlikely confrontations might elicit some strong reactions.

ACROSS

1 "What have _____ do with thee" (Mark 1:24) (2 words)

5 Cheese with red wax

9 "I _____ ease" (Job 16:12) (2 words)

14 "He built up the _____ around it" (2 Samuel 5:9 NIV)

15 19th-century popular dancer _____ Montez

16 Jung: the inner self

17 "She _____ at the door of her house" (Proverbs 9:14 NIV)

18 "_____ come unto Judah" (Micah 1:9) (2 words)

19 "This man is a _____" (Acts 22:26)

20 What Goliath (1 Samuel 17:4) did when he went to the house of Zacchaeus (Luke 19:2–3) (4 words)

23 Luster on cloth

24 "With that same _____ pottage" (Genesis 25:30)

25 Letters on some ships

28 "That _____ their tongues" (Jeremiah 23:31)

29 Swiss river

30 It helps the little entrepreneurs (abbr.)

33 He was an Elkoshite (Nahum 1:1)

35 "Saddled his _____" (Numbers 22:21)

36 "Chased you, as _____ do" (Deuteronomy 1:44)

37 What Zacchaeus (Luke 19:3–4) did when he went to the house of Rahab (Joshua 2:1–15) (3 words)

41 "Thy word is a _____ unto my feet" (Psalm 119:105)

42 "Ye shall not surely _____" (Genesis 3:4)

43 Speak pompously

44 They review manuscripts (abbr.)

45 Soviet fighter

46 "They do always _____ in their heart" (Hebrews 3:10)

48 Followed FDR

49 "The lapwing, and the _____" (Leviticus 11:19)

50 "The swallow _____ for herself" (Psalm 84:3) (2 words)

52 What Hiram, David's builder (2 Samuel 5:11), did when he went to the house where Jesus healed the palsied man (Mark 2:1–5) (4 words)

59 "He answered her not _____" (Matthew 15:23) (2 words)

60 "Jacob _____ his clothes" (Genesis 37:34 NIV)

61 Florence's river

62 Swamp plant

63 "Who is lord _____ us?" (Psalm 12:4)

64 "The fallow _____" (Deuteronomy 14:5)

65 Primp

66 "I have no _____ of thee" (1 Corinthians 12:21)

67 "Or _____ he will hold to the one" (Matthew 6:24)

DOWN

1 "_____ away thy sins" (Acts 22:16)

2 Pennsylvania port

3 Word after Psalm 119:64 NIV

4 Watering hole

5 Upper crust

6 "I will surely _____ good" (Genesis 32:12) (2 words)

7 "I am an _____ in their sight" (Job 19:15)

8 Not fem. or neut. (abbr.)

9 More cautious

10 "For he was _____ man" (1 Samuel 4:18) (2 words)

11 _____ Valley, California

12 "Every way of _____ is right in his own eyes" (Proverbs 21:2) (2 words)

13 Sharp taste

21 "Upon the _____ of his right hand" (Leviticus 8:23)

22 Expunge

25 "Saul's _____ said, Tell me" (1 Samuel 10:15)

26 Chef or Waldorf

27 Leveling devices

29 "Lifts the needy from the _____ heap" (Psalm 113:7 NIV)

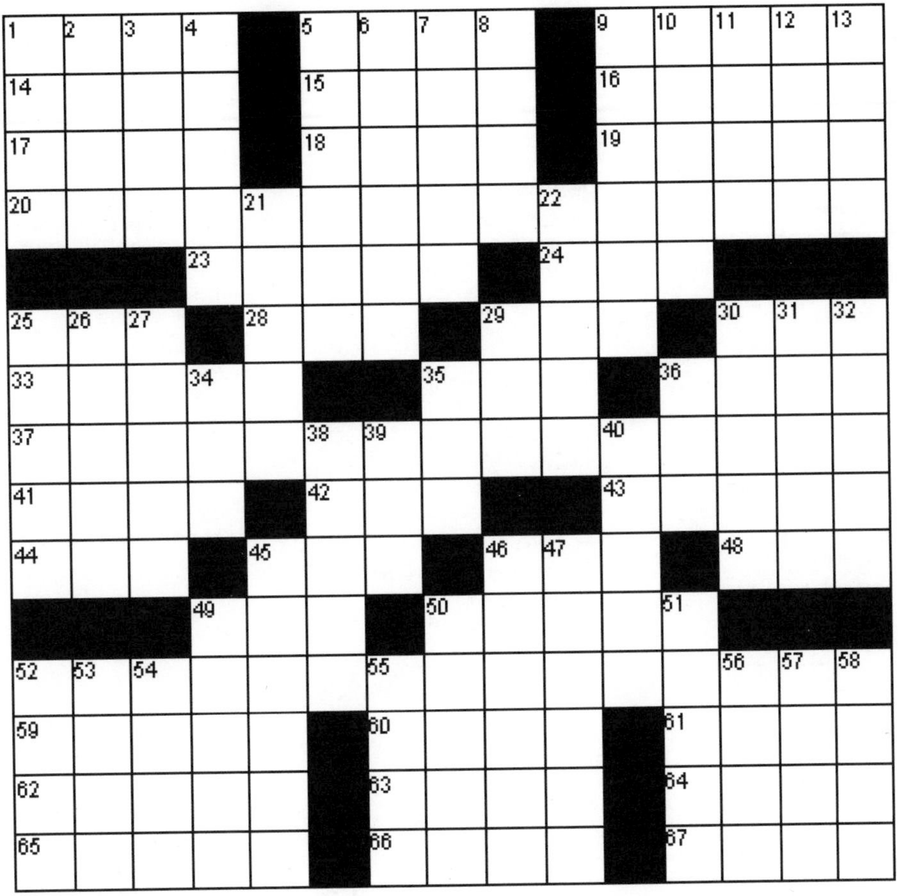

by David K. Shortess

30 Word found 71 times in the Psalms

31 "No money in your _____" (Mark 6:8 NIV)

32 "Such _____ their hearts to seek the LORD God" (2 Chronicles 11:16) (2 words)

34 Referee's kin (abbr.)

35 "_____ it up" (Revelation 10:10)

36 "Shut the doors, and _____ them" (Nehemiah 7:3)

38 Prepares for publication

39 "I cannot _____" (Luke 16:3)

40 "Is _____ than an infidel" (1 Timothy 5:8)

45 "The _____ pleased him" (Esther 2:9)

46 Main dish

47 Round up again

49 Canal craft

50 "Oh that I had wings like _____!" (Psalm 55:6) (2 words)

51 "As many as _____ by sea" (Revelation 18:17)

52 Padlock's location

53 Fancy pitcher

54 "He _____ upon a cherub" (2 Samuel 22:11)

55 School on the Thames

56 City on the Oka

57 "Every _____ bands were loosed" (Acts 16:26)

58 Precedes arm or cast (prefix)

26

ACROSS

1 Ruth's son (Ruth 4:13–17)
5 "_____ shall see God" (Matthew 5:8)
9 Male sheep
12 Bird from the ark sent out three times (Genesis 8:8–12)
13 Very large
14 "And it was about the _____ of three hours" (Acts 5:7)
16 Places to live
18 These grow from your head
19 Sister of a parent
20 "The thick _____ of his bucklers" (Job 15:26)
21 "The _____ of hell and of death" (Revelation 1:18)
23 "Shall write these _____ in a book" (Numbers 5:23)
24 Sleeping place
25 Plow (arch.)
29 Make a mistake
30 Aaron and Hur held up Moses' hands to keep them this way
31 The son of Puah (Judges 10:1)
35 Two or more deer
37 Solomon's great-grandson (1 Kings 15:8)
38 "Brought the heads of _____" (Judges 7:25)
39 Largest continent
40 "Securely as men _____ from war" (Micah 2:8)
43 A son of Jacob (Genesis 35:26)
44 Betrayal of country
45 Area near Babylon (2 Kings 17:24)
46 "For his name was _____ abroad" (Mark 6:14)
49 Eat formally
51 Johanan's father (2 Kings 25:23)
52 "And your feet _____ with the preparation of the gospel of peace" (Ephesians 6:15)
54 These cities are forsaken (Isaiah 17:2)
55 A female nonslave
60 "Even the salvation of your _____" (1 Peter 1:9)
61 "The Lord also shall _____" (Joel 3:16)
62 Crippled
63 "The latter _____" (Ruth 3:10)
64 "I am a brother to dragons, and a companion to _____" (Job 30:29)
65 Sluggish

DOWN

1 Strange
2 Arrow ejector
3 First mother
4 "Thou shalt not _____ to offer the first of thy ripe fruits" (Exodus 22:29)
5 _____ as a rail
6 "Wilt thou _____ the prey for the lion?" (Job 38:39)
7 Chicken product
8 "_____ verily, their sound" (Romans 10:18)
9 Elevate
10 43,560 square feet x 2
11 Chaos
14 The devil knows his time is this
15 "The heavens shall _____ away with a great noise" (2 Peter 3:10)
17 Selfish desires
20 Engaged in action
21 "The children of _____, the children of Siaha" (Ezra 2:44)
22 "Og the king of Bashan, which dwelt at Astaroth in _____" (Deuteronomy 1:4)
23 "His countenance is as Lebanon, excellent as the _____" (Song of Solomon 5:15)
24 King of Sodom (Genesis 14:2)
26 Boot country (abbr.)
27 "To open before him the two _____ gates" (Isaiah 45:1)
28 A city on Crete (Acts 27:8)
31 Turn over (abbr.)
32 "Sound of the _____" (Job 21:12)
33 "Not to _____ thee" (Ruth 1:16)
34 Adoniram's father (1 Kings 4:6)
36 This country's flag is made up of six colors and a Y (abbr.)
40 A son of Ulla (1 Chronicles 7:39)
41 States like Alabama, Arkansas, and the Carolinas are in this "deep" region (abbr.)
42 "He shall surely _____ her" (Exodus 22:16)
44 Product of weeping
46 "At Lydda and _____" (Acts 9:35)
47 "The Lord detests all the _____ of heart" (Proverbs 16:5 NIV)
48 "They _____ to and fro" (Psalm 107:27)
50 "Ephraim is joined to _____" (Hosea 4:17)
51 "Shall in no _____" (Matthew 5:20)
52 Closure
53 "Restore all that was _____" (2 Kings 8:6)

55 Satan went to and _____ in the earth (Job 1:7)

56 "A _____ of cedar beams" (1 Kings 6:36)

57 The last of the prophets (abbr.)

58 "What do you see, _____?" (Amos 7:8) (abbr.)

59 Opposite of *old*

by N. Teri Grottke

27

ACROSS

1 Depressed

4 "Hundred and _____ years old" (Joshua 24:29)

7 Ground moisture

10 "For he hath _____ marvellous things" (Psalm 98:1)

11 "Between Bethel and _____" (Genesis 13:3)

12 A son of Haman (Esther 9:8)

15 "Until these calamities be _____" (Psalm 57:1)

17 Dangers

18 "He shall be unto thee a _____ of thy life" (Ruth 4:15)

19 "The righteous God _____ the hearts and reins" (Psalm 7:9)

20 Loaded (arch.)

22 Eighth Hebrew month (1 Kings 6:38)

23 Satan

27 Two or more deer

29 Shackles for hands or legs

30 One of Jacob's sons (Genesis 35:25)

31 Thirty-seventh encampment (Numbers 33:45)

34 Jesus raised a young man from the dead here (Luke 7:11)

35 Capture tactic

37 Adoniram's father (1 Kings 4:6)

38 "The latter _____" (Ruth 3:10)

39 A son of Caleb (1 Chronicles 4:15)

40 "Ran greedily after the _____ of Balaam for reward" (Jude 1:11)

41 A brother of Shoham (1 Chronicles 24:27)

43 Metal pegs

44 Tear

45 A pharaoh of Egypt (2 Chronicles 35:20)

49 Hate

52 Prickly weeds

57 "And the _____ made Nibhaz" (2 Kings 17:31)

58 Uzziel's father (Nehemiah 3:8)

59 "This is a _____ place" (Mark 6:35)

60 Solomon's great-grandson (1 Kings 15:8)

61 "Who said, _____ it" (Psalm 137:7)

62 Saul's grandfather (1 Chronicles 8:33)

63 He was a governor (Nehemiah 12:26)

64 Before (arch.)

DOWN

1 "_____ not the world" (1 John 2:15)

2 "Day of _____ birth" (Ecclesiastes 7:1)

3 Were (arch.)

4 Abraham's father (Luke 3:34)

5 Comforted

6 Mineral potash (Proverbs 25:20)

7 He had to put Daniel in the lion's den

8 "Jozabad, and _____" (2 Chronicles 31:13)

9 "Knowing that thou _____ also do more than I say" (Philemon 1:21)

10 "Borders of _____" (Joshua 11:2)

12 Capable

13 A city of Lycaonia (Acts 14:6)

14 Type of tree (Isaiah 44:14)

16 "Every male by their _____" (Numbers 1:2)

21 Pull

23 Eat formally

24 "Shuthelah: of _____" (Numbers 26:36)

25 "She is empty, and _____," (Nahum 2:10)

26 Motel

28 Single

30 Last in the Pentateuch (abbr.)

31 A son of Merari (1 Chronicles 24:27)

32 Image

33 "Midst of _____ hill" (Acts 17:22)

35 Transgression

36 Strong metal

37 Jether's son (1 Chronicles 7:38)

40 "Adam, Sheth, _____" (1 Chronicles 1:1)

41 "For thou writest _____ things" (Job 13:26)

42 A son of Midian (Genesis 25:4)

44 Elevate

46 A son of Zerah (1 Chronicles 2:6)

47 Pursue

48 "A certain Adullamite, whose name was _____" (Genesis 38:1)

49 Boy

50 Baking place

51 Aka Hadassah (abbr.)

53 Type of weed

54 What the devil is

55 Comfort

56 "And _____ lay at his feet until the morning" (Ruth 3:14)

by N. Teri Grottke

28

ACROSS

1 "That at the _____" (Philippians 2:10)

5 "All the _____ of the heathen" (Zephaniah 2:11)

10 Burial place

14 Asa's father (1 Chronicles 3:10)

15 Look hard

16 Largest continent

17 Flower beginnings

18 "_____, Zeboim, Neballat, Lod, and Ono" (Nehemiah 11:34–35)

19 "_____ ye be condemned" (James 5:9)

20 "For if there come unto your _____ a man with a gold ring" (James 2:2)

22 "_____ ye have believed in vain" (1 Corinthians 15:2)

24 Allow

25 Strong wood

26 "Out of whose womb came the _____?" (Job 38:29)

27 He was swallowed by a fish (abbr.) (var.)

28 "For thou _____ bitter things against me" (Job 13:26)

32 "Gebal, and _____, and Amalek" (Psalm 83:7)

35 "Shebam, and Nebo, and _____" (Numbers 32:3)

36 "She is more precious _____ rubies" (Proverbs 3:15)

38 The border went to here from Remmonmethoar (Joshua 19:13)

39 "This was the Lord's _____" (Mark 12:11)

40 In this place

41 "The linen _____ at a price" (1 Kings 10:28)

42 Worn-out clothing

43 "To the _____ ye shall give the less inheritance" (Numbers 33:54)

44 "The mouth _____ meat" (Job 34:3)

46 Barrier

47 Possesses

48 "God saw that it _____ good" (Genesis 1:21)

49 "As for God, _____ way is perfect" (Psalm 18:30)

52 "And the woman took the child, and _____ it" (Exodus 2:9)

56 "Our soul _____ this light bread" (Numbers 21:5)

58 Jesus cried this on the cross (Mark 15:34)

59 "They traded in thy _____" (Ezekiel 27:12)

61 Shammah's father (2 Samuel 23:11)

62 "I will not _____ out his name out of the book of life" (Revelation 3:5)

63 Utilize (arch.)

64 Crippled

65 Strong promise

66 "Even unto _____" (Genesis 10:19)

67 Closed hand

DOWN

1 Abigail's foolish husband

2 Domestic violence

3 "Going through the _____ of them" (John 8:59)

4 Comfort

5 Eshtemoa's father (1 Chronicles 4:17)

6 "It hath no _____: the bud shall yield no meal" (Hosea 8:7)

7 "The elect _____" (2 John 1)

8 A son of Gad (Genesis 46:16)

9 "Giving heed to _____ spirits, and doctrines of devils" (1 Timothy 4:1)

10 Having great height

11 "As he saith also in _____" (Romans 9:25)

12 Lose

13 Winged mammal

21 This orbits the earth

23 Rope web

26 Types of golf clubs

27 "Some of _____ disciples" (John 3:25)

28 "Until ye _____ them before the chief of the priests" (Ezra 8:29)

29 "Libnah, and _____" (Joshua 15:42)

30 Show (arch.)

31 Type of weed

32 No matter which

33 Flesh food

34 Naomi wanted to be called this

35 "Howbeit there came other _____ from Tiberias" (John 6:23)

37 Saul's grandfather (1 Chronicles 8:33)

39 "O Lord, the great and _____ God" (Daniel 9:4)

43 Swift

45 "God created _____ heaven" (Genesis 1:1)

46 The son of Ahijah (2 Kings 9:9)

48 Value

by N. Teri Grottke

49 Eunuch in charge of the women
(Esther 2:3 NIV)

50 Things

51 Bed covering

52 "The other _____"
(Nehemiah 7:33)

53 Haniel's father (1 Chronicles 7:39)

54 "A _____ of Jesse" (Isaiah 11:10)

55 Since (arch.) (see Ezekiel 35:6)

56 Untruths

57 "Unto the _____ of my kingdom"
(Mark 6:23)

60 Solomon's great-grandson
(1 Kings 15:8)

29

Beginnings and Ends

Here is a quip based on John 3:3; 1 Peter 1:23; and Revelation 20:6 and 21:8. Read them to help figure out the quip.

ACROSS

1 "That which groweth of _____ own" (Leviticus 25:5)

4 "Pierce his ear with an _____" (Exodus 21:6 NIV)

7 "Come _____, and I will show you" (Revelation 4:1 NIV) (2 words)

13 Sixth-century Chinese dynasty

14 "With cords of human kindness, with _____ of love" (Hosea 11:4 NIV)

16 "To _____ the night" (Acts 16:9) (2 words)

17 Start of scripture-based **QUIP** (see above) (2 words)

19 "Also _____ past, when Saul was king over us" (2 Samuel 5:2) (2 words)

20 "And likewise a _____" (Luke 10:32)

21 "Five gold tumors and five gold _____" (1 Samuel 6:4 NIV)

23 "And for his _____" (Jeremiah 52:34)

24 "And Joseph _____" (Exodus 1:6)

26 "There he _____ Jew named Aquila" (Acts 18:2 NIV) (2 words)

30 City on the Ruhr

32 **QUIP**, cont'd (2 words)

35 "They were _____ in two" (Hebrews 11:37 NIV)

37 "Hither, _____ of the bread" (Ruth 2:14) (2 words)

38 "The _____ of the bow" (2 Samuel 1:18)

41 GE or IBM, for example (abbr.)

42 "Ye not eat of them that chew the _____" (Leviticus 11:4)

43 Sudbury Neutrino Observatory (abbr.)

44 Famous canal

46 Wooden shoe

48 **QUIP**, cont'd (2 words)

50 "He is not here: for he is _____" (Matthew 28:6)

54 "David said to Ittai, 'Go ahead, march _____.' _____ Ittai the Gittite" (2 Samuel 15:22 NIV) (2 words)

55 Sow wild _____

57 What genera are

58 "That the _____ men be sober" (Titus 2:2)

60 "As sheep in the midst of _____" (Matthew 10:16)

62 Familiar one-celled animal

66 End of **QUIP** (2 words)

68 "_____ up and go" (Acts 9:6 NIV) (2 words)

69 "And _____ through the streams" (Isaiah 47:2 NIV)

70 Opposite of *haw*

71 Hang loosely

72 "My _____ shall comfort me" (Job 7:13)

73 Sounds of hesitation

DOWN

1 Tristan's beloved

2 "Know what _____ being played" (1 Corinthians 14:7 NIV) (2 words)

3 Sifters

4 "Ye have snuffed _____" (Malachi 1:13) (2 words)

5 Hyper

6 "Ears to hear, _____ him hear" (Matthew 13:9)

7 "And shut _____ that hath the plague" (Leviticus 13:50) (2 words)

8 "And baked it in _____" (Numbers 11:8)

9 "It sways like a _____ in the wind" (Isaiah 24:20 NIV)

10 Hophni's father (1 Samuel 1:3)

11 "The _____ of a cup" (2 Chronicles 4:5 NIV)

12 Compass point (abbr.)

15 "A very _____ man" (2 Samuel 13:3 NIV)

18 "In the end it _____" (Proverbs 23:32 NIV)

22 "Why make ye this _____" (Mark 5:39)

25 Newspaper article

26 "Have I need of _____ men" (1 Samuel 21:15)

27 Parisian summers

28 "My punishment is greater _____ I can bear" (Genesis 4:13)

29 "Leisure so much _____ eat" (Mark 6:31) (2 words)

31 "And _____ said, Turn again" (Ruth 1:11)

33 "Say unto them which _____ it" (Ezekiel 13:11)

34 "Hath a familiar spirit at _____" (1 Samuel 28:7)

36 "The waters _____ the stones" (Job 14:19)

by David K. Shortess

38 "Behold, we go _____ Jerusalem" (Mark 10:33) (2 words)

39 "They were _____ asunder" (Hebrews 11:37)

40 "And Seth. . .begat ____" (Genesis 5:6)

42 "And _____ into the fire" (Luke 3:9)

45 Landsteiner blood group (abbr.)

46 "The valley of the _____ of death" (Psalm 23:4)

47 "This _____ then read many of the Jews" (John 19:20)

49 Digit

51 "_____ beasts from the land" (Leviticus 26:6 NIV)

52 Town in southeast New Hampshire

53 Kelvinator's cars of the 1940s

56 Nobel, for example

58 "From the blood of _____" (Luke 11:51)

59 "Which was before the king's _____" (Esther 4:6)

61 "Azariah the son of _____" (2 Chronicles 15:1)

62 "Is subverted, _____ sinneth" (Titus 3:11)

63 Extinct New Zealand bird

64 "His _____ hands shall bring" (Leviticus 7:30)

65 "In the white of an _____?" (Job 6:6)

67 Seize

30

ACROSS

1 Utilize

4 "Shelesh, and _____"
(1 Chronicles 7:35)

8 "And Jair died, and was buried in
_____" (Judges 10:5)

13 Heber's father (Luke 3:35)

15 Uncontrolled anger

16 Dwelling place

17 "_____, and Mikneiah, and
Obededom" (1 Chronicles 15:18)

19 Reduce the height of

20 "Hath done _____ unto the
Spirit of grace?" (Hebrews 10:29)

21 "And every _____ fled away"
(Revelation 16:20)

23 "_____ for the day!" (Joel 1:15)

24 "Let _____ glean" (Ruth 2:15)

25 Traps

28 "I have _____ and brought up"
(Lamentations 2:22)

33 Place of refuge

34 A son of Sheresh
(1 Chronicles 7:16)

35 Body part in John 18:10

36 "Neither shall _____ dwell with
thee" (Psalm 5:4)

37 "He shall deliver thee from the
_____" (Psalm 91:3)

38 "Suffered without the _____"
(Hebrews 13:12)

39 "The angels of God _____ him"
(Genesis 32:1)

40 "Children of _____, four
hundred fifty and four" (Ezra 2:15)

41 "We ought to lay down our
_____ for the brethren"
(1 John 3:16)

42 A city of the Philistines
(Judges 14:19)

45 "Backbiters, _____ of God"
(Romans 1:30)

46 "Destroy _____ kings and
people" (Ezra 6:12)

47 "They fled every man to his
_____" (2 Chronicles 25:22)

48 He had to put Daniel in the
lion's den

51 "Of Ard, the family of the _____"
(Numbers 26:40)

55 "_____ that find no pasture"
(Lamentations 1:6)

56 "All the coasts of _____?"
(Joel 3:4)

58 Another name for *Hebron*
(Genesis 35:27)

59 "Good works for necessary
_____" (Titus 3:14)

60 "Shuthelah: of _____"
(Numbers 26:36)

61 Zadok's father (Nehemiah 3:4)

62 "Knowledge is _____ unto him"
(Proverbs 14:6)

63 "The latter _____" (Ruth 3:10)

DOWN

1 "_____ the office"
(1 Timothy 3:13)

2 "_____ of his patrimony"
(Deuteronomy 18:8)

3 "The iniquity of _____ house"
(1 Samuel 3:14)

4 King of Damascus in Paul's day
(2 Corinthians 11:32)

5 "And they slew all the _____"
(Numbers 31:7)

6 Get older

7 Samson slew 1,000 Philistines
here (Judges 15:14–15)

8 "Him that hath _____ us to
glory" (2 Peter 1:3)

9 "Finding a ship. . .we went
_____" (Acts 21:2)

10 "Rain upon the _____ grass"
(Psalm 72:6)

11 Jehu's father (1 Chronicles 2:38)

12 Saul's uncle (1 Samuel 14:50)

14 "Herod, having put on his royal
_____" (Acts 12:21 NASB)

18 "And _____ with her suburbs"
(1 Chronicles 6:58)

22 Disgrace

25 A city in Judah (Joshua 15:26)

26 "And their _____, and their
felloes" (1 Kings 7:33)

27 Edom's capital
(Genesis 36:31–35)

28 "Having _____ the enmity
thereby" (Ephesians 2:16)

29 To alert

30 "Not to _____ thee" (Ruth 1:16)

31 One who consumes food

32 Clothe

34 "I will _____ all that afflict thee"
(Zephaniah 3:19)

37 Meshullam's son
(1 Chronicles 9:7)

38 Obededom was of this nationality
(2 Samuel 6:10)

41 "Possessors of _____ or houses
sold them" (Acts 4:34)

43 "And _____ with her suburbs;
three cities" (Joshua 21:32)

44 Elijah's student (1 Kings 19:19)

45 False teaching

47 Stories

48 A son of Zerah (1 Chronicles 2:6)

49 Anak's father (Joshua 15:13)

50 "_____ thee out of my mouth" (Revelation 3:16)

52 Exhaust

53 Ahira's father (Numbers 1:15)

54 "I will even _____ a curse upon you" (Malachi 2:2)

55 The prophet upon Shigionoth (Habakkuk 3:1)

57 Jehoshaphat's father (1 Chronicles 3:10)

by N. Teri Grottke

31

ACROSS

1 Make fun of
5 Eliasaph's father (Numbers 3:24)
9 Jobab was king of this country (Joshua 11:1)
14 Ahira's father (Numbers 1:15)
15 Island
16 Not dead
17 "Even _____ to die" (Romans 5:7)
18 "All the Chaldeans, Pekod, and _____, and Koa" (Ezekiel 23:23)
19 "The _____ that shrank" (Genesis 32:32)
20 "Be not forgetful to _____ strangers" (Hebrews 13:2)
22 Prophets (arch.)
23 Zephaniah's son (Zechariah 6:14)
24 Adam was the first
25 A porter (1 Chronicles 9:17)

29 Twenty-first letter of the Greek alphabet
31 Heber's father (Luke 3:35)
35 A son of Zabad (1 Chronicles 7:21)
36 Instruct
38 "Mine eye also is _____" (Job 17:7)
39 "The _____ tree" (Joel 1:12)
40 Boat paddle
41 Ezra proclaimed a fast there (Ezra 8:21)
43 "God created _____ heaven" (Genesis 1:1)
44 The devil knows his time is this
46 "Hath in due _____ manifested his word" (Titus 1:3)
47 "Through faith also _____ herself received strength to conceive seed" (Hebrews 11:11)
49 Sick
50 A son of Becher (1 Chronicles 7:8)

51 A whit, an iota, a tittle
53 Barrier
54 Sharar's son (2 Samuel 23:33)
57 "_____ then as Christ hath suffered for us" (1 Peter 4:1)
63 "The _____ of the Lord" (Malachi 1:7)
64 454 of his descendants returned from exile (Ezra 2:15)
65 "_____ the Ahohite" (1 Chronicles 11:29)
66 "Ran greedily after the _____ of Balaam for reward" (Jude 1:11)
67 A king of Midian (Numbers 31:8)
68 Israel's first king
69 "Into my _____" (Lamentations 3:13)
70 The perfect place
71 Plow

DOWN

1 Darius was one (Daniel 11:1)
2 A son of Judah (1 Chronicles 2:3)
3 Small wagon
4 "Every _____ should bow" (Philippians 2:10)
5 "_____, O isles, unto me" (Isaiah 49:1)
6 "_____, five cities" (1 Chronicles 4:32)
7 "_____, lana Sabachthani?" (Mark 15:34)
8 "_____ not unto thine own understanding" (Proverbs 3:5)
9 A son of Ishmael (1 Chronicles 1:30–31)
10 Foreigners
11 Eat formally

12 "Be thou also _____ five cities" (Luke 19:19)
13 Current events
21 "Unto _____, and from thence unto Patara" (Acts 21:1)
24 He had a house of gods (Judges 17:5) (abbr.)
25 "Lament for the _____" (Isaiah 32:12)
26 First letter of the Greek alphabet
27 One afflicted with a skin disease
28 Final Old Testament book (abbr.)
29 Found in an oyster
30 Male red deer
32 Walled city in Naphtali (Joshua 19:32–33)
33 Detoxifying organ

34 Absalom's captain (2 Samuel 17:25)
36 "Nor any _____ of iron heard in the house" (1 Kings 6:7)
37 "Backbiters, _____ of God" (Romans 1:30)
42 Opposite of *her*
45 Town in modern-day Iraq
48 "_____, and Jethlah" (Joshua 19:42)
50 "The inhabitant of _____ came not forth" (Micah 1:11)
52 Manna was measured in these units
53 "Have I received any _____ to blind mine eyes" (1 Samuel 12:3)
54 "_____, Hizkijah, Azzur" (Nehemiah 10:17)

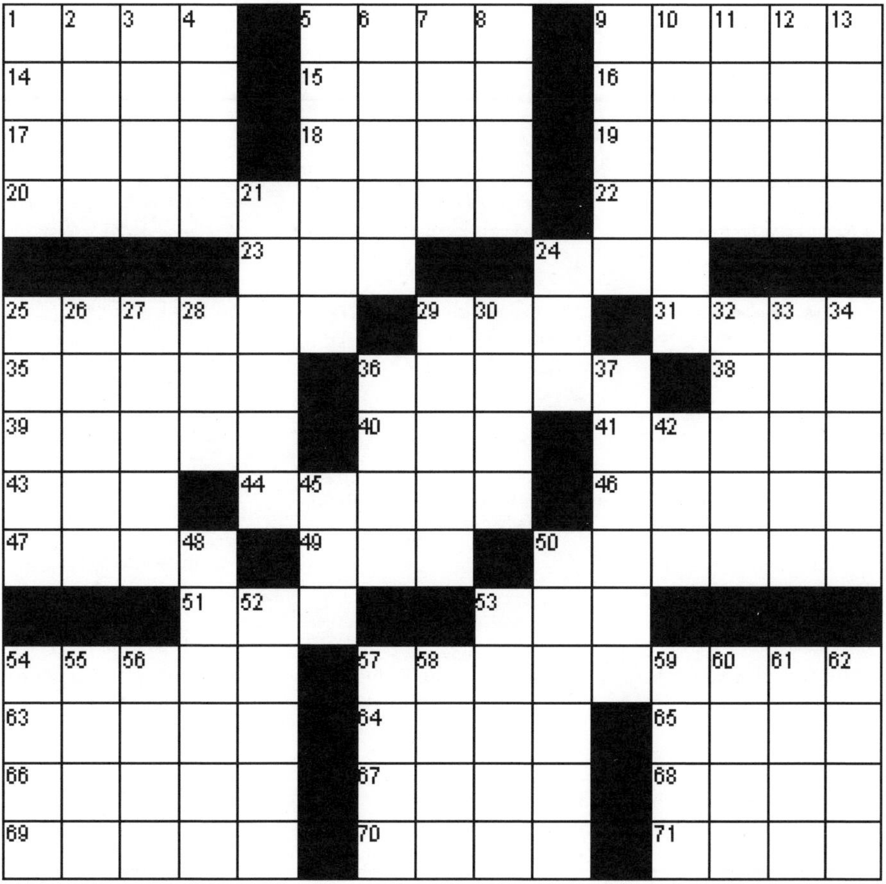

by N. Teri Grottke

55 Rabbit

56 A son of Merari (1 Chronicles 24:27)

57 "______ ye well" (Acts 15:29)

58 Azariah's father (2 Chronicles 15:1)

59 This watered the earth before the flood

60 Daniel had a vision by this river (Daniel 8:1–2)

61 "Rend the ______ of their heart" (Hosea 13:8)

62 "At his holy ______" (Psalm 99:9)

32

ACROSS

1 Tree juice

4 "Came to Joel the _____" (Joel 1:1)

7 A son of Bela (1 Chronicles 7:7)

10 "Every _____ should bow" (Philippians 2:10)

12 Agar is this mount in Arabia (Galatians 4:25)

14 "Shuthelah: of _____" (Numbers 26:36)

15 "The linen _____ at a price" (1 Kings 10:28)

16 Things

17 "He _____ down with sleep" (Acts 20:9)

18 "The tents of _____" (Psalm 120:5)

20 A pause or musical note used in the Psalms

22 A king of Midian (Numbers 31:8)

23 Jewish queen of Persia (abbr.)

24 His Excellency (abbr.)

26 "For ye lade men with _____ grievous to be borne" (Luke 11:46)

30 A son of Esau (Genesis 36:5)

32 The fourth prophetic book (abbr.)

33 "_____, and goeth out" (Joshua 19:27)

36 Salathiel's father (Luke 3:27)

37 "There was a man in the land of _____" (Job 1:1)

38 "Chalcol, and _____" (1 Kings 4:31)

39 Physical education (abbr.)

40 Banner

42 This Hararite was father to Jonathan in David's army (1 Chronicles 11:34)

43 Eat

44 Jorkoam's father (1 Chronicles 2:44)

46 "And their border was _____, and Hali" (Joshua 19:25)

48 River border of WV and KY (abbr.)

49 "Sin is the transgression of the _____" (1 John 3:4)

51 "Helez the Paltite, _____" (2 Samuel 23:26)

52 "Wherefore putting away _____" (Ephesians 4:25)

55 Shamgar's father (Judges 3:31)

57 Shoe bottom

60 These were in the tops of the curtains of the tabernacle

62 "_____ the Bethelite" (1 Kings 16:34)

64 Carry out directions

65 A son of Micah (1 Chronicles 8:35)

66 Very (arch.)

67 "Shall be astonished, and _____ his head" (Jeremiah 18:16)

68 Zephaniah's son (Zechariah 6:14)

69 Rope web

DOWN

1 "So many as the stars of the _____ in multitude" (Hebrews 11:12)

2 Talmai's father (Numbers 13:22)

3 "The name of the place _____ to this day" (2 Samuel 6:8)

4 "_____ down here" (Ruth 4:1)

5 "Day of _____ birth" (Ecclesiastes 7:1)

6 "That at the _____" (Philippians 2:10)

7 A son of Caleb (1 Chronicles 4:15)

8 "And _____ greedily after the error of Balaam" (Jude 1:11)

9 Writing fluid

11 "Weeping may _____ for a night" (Psalm 30:5)

12 Knight

13 Island

14 Paseah's father (1 Chronicles 4:12)

19 Naaman's brother (Numbers 26:40)

21 Question

24 Bethgader's father (1 Chronicles 2:51)

25 A son of Benjamin (Genesis 46:21)

26 "Thou shalt be called Hephzibah, and thy land _____" (Isaiah 62:4)

27 "The _____ of the earth were afraid" (Isaiah 41:5)

28 The border went to here from Remmonmethoar (Joshua 19:13)

29 "The well of _____" (2 Samuel 3:26)

31 "But made himself of no _____" (Philippians 2:7)

34 Farthest part

35 Eliasaph's father (Numbers 3:24)

40 Satan went to and _____ in the earth (Job 1:7)

41 "Wherein shall go no _____ with oars" (Isaiah 33:21)

43 Belonging to Abraham's wife

45 Month before June

47 Relatives

50 "Knowing that thou _____ also do more than I say" (Philemon 1:21)

53 The eighth person (2 Peter 2:5)

54 Pierce with horns
55 Succeeded Abijam (1 Kings 15:8)
56 In this place
57 Plant small seeds
58 He feared the Lord greatly
   (1 Kings 18:3) (abbr.)
59 Appendage
61 Writing tool
63 Allow

by N. Teri Grottke

33

Donkey Business

You are now with child and you will have a son. You shall name him Ishmael. . . . He will be a wild donkey of a man.

GENESIS 16:11–12 NIV

ACROSS

1 "Without an inhabitant, _____ this day" (Jeremiah 44:22) (2 words)

5 "As it _____ we had not delayed" (Genesis 43:10 NIV) (2 words)

9 "He shall gather the _____ with his arm" (Isaiah 40:11)

14 "The Jews of _____ sought to stone thee" (John 11:8)

15 "How _____ dispossess them?" (Deuteronomy 7:17) (2 words)

16 "There shall be _____ of Jesse" (Romans 15:12) (2 words)

17 What Samson used to kill a thousand men (Judges 15:16 NIV) (3 words)

20 Presbyterian parsonage

21 "They _____ not, they spin not" (Luke 12:27)

22 "Sing unto him _____ song" (Psalm 33:3) (2 words)

23 Followes *printemp* (Fr.)

24 Caesar's "I"

26 "He planteth an _____" (Isaiah 44:14)

28 _____-cone

29 "I cannot find one _____ man among you" (Job 17:10)

31 "Why make ye this _____, and weep?" (Mark 5:39)

34 Formerly Siamese

37 "But as my beloved sons I _____ you" (1 Corinthians 4:14)

39 "The law is not _____ on faith" (Galatians 3:12 NIV)

41 What happened when Balaam saw the angel? (Numbers 22:27–28) (3 words)

44 "Watch ye and pray, lest ye _____ into temptation" (Mark 14:38)

45 "There was one Anna. . .of the tribe of _____" (Luke 2:36)

46 "Because I am a man of unclean _____" (Isaiah 6:5)

47 European theater of operations (abbr.)

48 "He _____ save himself!" (Mark 15:31 NIV)

50 "Give _____ king" (1 Samuel 8:6) (2 words)

52 "Under your arms to _____ the ropes" (Jeremiah 38:12 NIV)

53 Metro maker

54 "Thou sayest that I _____ king" (John 18:37) (2 words)

57 "Do not give _____ cry" (Joshua 6:10 NIV) (2 words)

60 "By this time there is a bad _____" (John 11:39 NIV)

63 Where Moses saw the burning bush (Exodus 3:1–2)

65 Jesus entered Jerusalem this way (Matthew 21:4–5 NIV) (4 words)

68 "Beast had _____ as a man" (Revelation 4:7) (2 words)

69 Hoodwink

70 Giant Mel's family

71 "When _____ with us" (Acts 20:14) (2 words)

72 "Their throat is an _____ sepulchre" (Romans 3:13)

73 Flag-maker Betsy

DOWN

1 "A blind man, or _____" (Leviticus 21:18) (2 words)

2 "He was _____ that saying" (Mark 10:22) (2 words)

3 "Slain by him _____ time" (1 Chronicles 11:11) (2 words)

4 "Captains over _____" (Deuteronomy 1:15)

5 "He casteth forth his _____ like morsels" (Psalm 147:17)

6 "Thus shall ye _____ David" (1 Samuel 18:25) (2 words)

7 "Give him drink: for _____ doing" (Romans 12:20) (2 words)

8 South Pacific country of 320 islands

9 "The _____ of the LORD is perfect" (Psalm 19:7)

10 Another name for *Hebron* (Genesis 35:27)

11 "Nor the _____ by night" (Psalm 121:6)

12 "A _____ of him shall not be broken" (John 19:36)

13 "Some bread and some lentil _____" (Genesis 25:34 NIV)

18 "This man Daniel. . .was found to have a _____ mind" (Daniel 5:12 NIV)

19 "_____ for the day!" (Joel 1:15)

25 "Her _____ is interwoven with gold" (Psalm 45:13 NIV)

27 First son of Cush (Genesis 10:7)

28 "A thousand shall fall at thy _____" (Psalm 91:7)

29 "Every day they _____ my words" (Psalm 56:5)

30 "Them that were entering _____ hindered" (Luke 11:52) (2 words)

by David K. Shortess

31 "Whatever you _____ will give you" (Mark 6:23 NIV) (2 words)

32 "I sink in _____ mire" (Psalm 69:2)

33 Chances

34 "Make _____ an ark of gopher wood" (Genesis 6:14)

35 "Not be even a _____ of sexual immorality" (Ephesians 5:3 NIV)

36 "I speak _____ wise men" (1 Corinthians 10:15) (2 words)

38 A son of Ezer (Genesis 36:27)

40 "_____ man's ways seem right to him" (Proverbs 21:2 NIV) (2 words)

42 Free Willy, for example

43 "That was the _____ Light" (John 1:9)

49 "As _____ lappeth" (Judges 7:5) (2 words)

51 Fashionable London district

52 "Her _____ is far above rubies" (Proverbs 31:10)

53 "The vines with the tender _____" (Song of Solomon 2:13)

54 "Prepared an _____ the saving of his house" (Hebrews 11:7) (2 words)

55 "The church that _____ at their house" (1 Corinthians 16:19 NIV)

56 "Darkened by the smoke from the _____" (Revelation 9:2 NIV)

57 First son of Ulla (1 Chronicles 7:39)

58 "But his _____ looked back" (Genesis 19:26)

59 "As in _____ all die" (1 Corinthians 15:22)

61 "And whatsoever ye _____ it heartily" (Colossians 3:23) (2 words)

62 "He went _____ the mountain" (Exodus 24:18 NIV) (2 words)

64 _____ about (approximately) (2 words)

66 "He hath spread a _____ for my feet" (Lamentations 1:13)

67 "Ye have made it a _____ of thieves" (Luke 19:46)

34

ACROSS

1 "Our Lord sprang out of _____" (Hebrews 7:14)

5 Asa's father (1 Chronicles 3:10)

9 Not cooked

12 A faithful spy

13 Swamps

14 Jesus' grandfather (Luke 3:23)

15 Shaphat's father (1 Chronicles 27:29)

16 Strong promise

17 Manasseh's son (2 Kings 21:18)

18 "From mount _____ unto the entering in of Hamath" (Judges 3:3)

20 "A fool uttereth all his _____" (Proverbs 29:11)

21 Makes use of

22 Type of quartz

24 "Children of _____" (Ezra 2:55)

28 A son of Ham (Genesis 10:6)

29 Jerahmeel's son (1 Chronicles 2:25)

30 "Even unto Ithiel and _____" (Proverb 30:1)

33 Tunnel core

37 Spear

39 Be indebted

40 "A certain Adullamite, whose name was _____" (Genesis 38:1)

41 "He shall surely _____ her" (Exodus 22:16)

42 Support

44 Story

45 Blood vessel

47 "He made a shew of them _____" (Colossians 2:15)

49 "Which was a _____, and believed" (Acts 16:1)

52 "Shelesh, and _____" (1 Chronicles 7:35)

54 "Tower of _____" (Genesis 35:21)

55 "And shall go on to _____, and pass on to Azmon" (Numbers 34:4)

61 "_____ him vehemently" (Luke 11:53)

62 Thummim's partner

63 "For this _____ ought the woman to have power on her head" (1 Corinthians 11:10)

64 Descendants

65 "_____, Hizkijah, Azzur" (Nehemiah 10:17)

66 Made a mistake

67 "So _____ strength was not known" (Judges 16:9)

68 Island

69 Night sky illuminator

DOWN

1 Shammai's brother (1 Chronicles 2:28)

2 Haniel's father (1 Chronicles 7:39)

3 "Lookest thou upon them that _____ treacherously" (Habakkuk 1:13)

4 Bela's son (1 Chronicles 8:3)

5 Before (arch.)

6 "Who layeth the _____ of his chambers" (Psalm 104:3)

7 "_____ the waters" (Exodus 15:25)

8 "And Jiphtah, and _____, and Nezib" (Joshua 15:43)

9 Forgive

10 By yourself

11 "Carried about of _____" (Jude 1:12)

12 "A _____ of dove's dung" (2 Kings 6:25)

14 "The _____: and afterward were the families of the Canaanites spread abroad" (Genesis 10:18)

19 Jacob's brother

23 Flow

24 "Upon a _____" (Numbers 21:8)

25 "Shuthelah: of _____" (Numbers 26:36)

26 Tear apart

27 "They _____ the roof where he was" (Mark 2:4)

28 Guilty or not guilty

31 Ear grain

32 Reverent fear

34 A son of Dishan (Genesis 36:28)

35 Topple

36 "_____ shall see God" (Matthew 5:8)

38 Several female sheep

43 "The LORD also shall _____" (Joel 3:16)

46 A son of Asher (1 Chronicles 7:30)

48 "Against spiritual wickedness in high _____" (Ephesians 6:12)

49 Aholibamah's son (Genesis 36:5)

50 "Og the king of Bashan, which dwelt at Astaroth in _____" (Deuteronomy 1:4)

51 Employment pay

52 "And Zechariah, and _____" (1 Chronicles 15:20)

53 Abram lived in this plain (Genesis 13:18)

56 "Used curious _____" (Acts 19:19)

57 Move quickly

58 "The plain of _____" (Daniel 3:1)

59 Greek form of *Asher* (Revelation 7:6)

60 Color of blood

by N. Teri Grottke

35

ACROSS

1 Cry loudly
5 "_____ him vehemently"
   (Luke 11:53)
9 A city on Crete (Acts 27:8)
14 "Believed the master and the
   _____ of the ship" (Acts 27:11)
16 A duke of Edom (Genesis 36:43)
18 "A _____ giveth ear to a
   naughty tongue" (Proverbs 17:4)
19 Realm
20 Smelling orifice
21 After the proper time
22 "In heaven forgive your _____"
   (Mark 11:26)
24 A son of Zerubbabel
   (1 Chronicles 3:19–20)
25 "_____ mouth is smoother than
   oil" (Proverbs 5:3)
26 Makes use of
27 A son of Immer (Ezra 10:20)

29 Joseph mourned for Jacob at his
   threshing floor (Genesis 50:10)
30 Uterus
31 Traps
34 Hodesh's son (1 Chronicles 8:9)
35 Physical education (abbr.)
37 "_____, Zeboim, Neballat, Lod,
   and Ono" (Nehemiah 11:34–35)
38 King of Sodom (Genesis 14:2)
39 A city of Hadarezer
   (1 Chronicles 18:8)
41 "_____, and Shema"
   (Joshua 15:26)
42 A son of Baanah
   (2 Samuel 23:29)
43 Injured
44 A son of Benjamin
   (Genesis 46:21)
45 "_____ for the day!" (Joel 1:15)
46 "Under the _____"
   (Galatians 3:10)

47 An altar (Joshua 22:34)
48 Ephraim's son
   (1 Chronicles 7:22–25)
50 Joseph was in jail with Pharaoh's
51 "That which _____ been"
   (Ecclesiastes 6:10)
52 Goliath was from here
53 Beerothite who was one of
   David's "mighty men"
   (2 Samuel 23:37)
56 A son of Ulla (1 Chronicles 7:39)
57 "A _____ of dove's dung"
   (2 Kings 6:25)
60 Shammah's father
   (2 Samuel 23:11)
61 "Shemaiah the _____"
   (Jeremiah 29:31)
64 "_____, and Ivah?" (Isaiah 37:13)
65 "Bring down my _____ hairs
   with sorrow" (Genesis 42:38)
66 "The son of _____" (1 Kings 4:10)

DOWN

1 Value
2 Cognizant
3 Inside
4 Walking appendages
6 Washed with water
7 "For the heart of this people is
   waxed _____" (Acts 28:27)
8 Comfort
10 "The name of it was called
   _____" (Genesis 35:8)
11 "Children of _____" (Ezra 2:44)
12 Consumed
13 A son of Gad (Genesis 46:16)
15 "And _____ vile in your sight?"
   (Job 18:3)
17 "And _____, and Jamlech, and
   Joshah" (1 Chronicles 4:34)

23 "Nevertheless _____ heart"
   (1 Kings 15:14)
28 A family of returned exiles
   (Ezra 2:57)
29 "Joseph of _____, an honourable
   counsellor" (Mark 15:43)
30 "And cut it into _____"
   (Exodus 39:3)
31 This Hararite was father to
   Jonathan in David's army
   (1 Chronicles 11:34)
32 "House, _____ Rahab"
   (Joshua 2:1)
33 Twelfth Hebrew month
   (Esther 9:1)
34 Burial site of Saul and Jonathan
   (2 Samuel 21:14)
35 "No scrip, no bread, no money in
   their _____" (Mark 6:8)

36 Come in
38 A son of Benjamin
   (Genesis 46:21)
40 Throw
42 "All my familiars watched for my
   _____" (Jeremiah 20:10)
46 "Men from Babylon, and from
   _____" (2 Kings 17:24)
49 Peter cut one off
50 "Remnant of _____"
   (Zephaniah 1:4)
52 "The beauty of old men is
   the _____ head"
   (Proverbs 20:29)
53 Prophet of the destruction of
   Nineveh (abbr.)
54 Get older
55 Zephaniah's son (Zechariah 6:14)

by N. Teri Grottke

56 "Against Jerusalem, _____"
   (Ezekiel 26:2)
57 King Saul's father (Acts 13:21)
58 Partook
59 Sleeping place
62 Judah's firstborn (Numbers 26:19)
63 Maine (abbr.)

36

ACROSS

1 Gentle
5 Aharhel's father (1 Chronicles 4:8)
10 Puah's son (Judges 10:1)
14 A son of Joktan (Genesis 10:26–29)
15 Jesus did this at the resurrection
16 City in Egypt (Hosea 10:8)
17 "The Hittites, the _____, the Jebusites" (Ezra 9:1)
19 "_____, and Ivah?" (Isaiah 37:13)
20 Chief captain (Acts 24:22)
21 Fireplace
23 Buzzing stinger
24 "Let us go into the next _____" (Mark 1:38)
25 "The children of Shephatiah, the children of _____" (Nehemiah 7:59)
29 Soldiers cast lots for Jesus' _____

30 Praise and worship poetry (abbr.)
33 "Down in _____" (Acts 27:27)
34 "Land from _____ to the wilderness" (Isaiah 16:1)
35 "Used curious _____" (Acts 19:19)
36 Eliasaph's father (Numbers 53:24)
37 David's eldest brother (1 Samuel 17:13)
38 "The tower of _____" (Nehemiah 3:1)
39 "Shelesh, and _____" (1 Chronicles 7:35)
40 Give for temporary use
41 One of Shaharaim's wives (1 Chronicles 8:8)
42 "Abraham lifted up _____ eyes" (Genesis 22:4)
43 Parts of the mouth

44 "The priest shall take the _____ shoulder" (Numbers 6:19)
45 "As thou _____ to do unto those" (Psalm 119:132)
47 Large lake
48 "But _____ for a while" (Matthew 13:21)
50 Paul's hometown
54 David hid by this stone (1 Samuel 20:18–19)
55 "The conscience of him which is weak be _____" (1 Corinthians 8:10)
59 Book after 2 Chronicles
60 "_____ of Judah" (2 Samuel 6:2)
61 A brother of Eshcol (Genesis 14:13)
62 Hasty
63 Increased
64 "Out of the _____ clay" (Psalm 40:2)

DOWN

1 Spinning toy
2 Cain's victim
3 Jesus' mother
4 Belonging to Eli
5 "I will send a fire into the house of _____" (Amos 1:4)
6 Get up
7 Decay
8 Utilize
9 "And _____, and Jamlech" (1 Chronicles 4:34)
10 A son of Ephraim (Numbers 26:35)
11 "Of them was the whole earth _____" (Genesis 9:19)
12 Gave a loan
13 Zibeon's daughter (Genesis 36:2)

18 A son of Hodesh (1 Chronicles 8:9)
22 Female sheep
24 "And at _____" (1 Chronicles 4:29)
25 The king of Assyria placed Israel here (2 Kings 17:6)
26 "And their coast was from Heleph. . .and _____, Nekeb" (Joshua 19:33)
27 "To all the _____ which are beyond the river" (Ezra 7:21)
28 Plow
29 "Into my _____" (Lamentations 3:13)
31 Look hard
32 "_____, five cities" (1 Chronicles 4:32)

34 "Many bodies of the saints which _____ arose" (Matthew 27:52)
35 "Alammelech, and _____" (Joshua 19:26)
37 Aaron's wife (Exodus 6:23)
41 "Under every _____ two sockets" (Exodus 36:30)
43 Allow
44 "_____ with the king's ring" (Esther 3:12)
46 A pause or musical note used in the Psalms
47 "Let him that _____" (Ephesians 4:28)
48 "The roebuck, and the fallow _____" (Deuteronomy 14:5)
49 Manasseh was buried in this garden (2 Kings 21:18)

51 "Now the coat was without _____" (John 19:23)

52 "_____, their brethren" (Nehemiah 12:9)

53 Prophet (arch.)

56 Insane

57 Spoiled

58 Arid

by N. Teri Grottke

37

God's Requirement

He hath shewed thee, O man, what is good;
and what doth the Lord require of thee. . . ?

Micah 6:8

ACROSS

1 "And with the one _____ tenth deal of flour" (Exodus 29:40) (2 words)
6 "Shew I unto you _____ excellent way" (1 Corinthians 12:31) (2 words)
11 "There _____ man in the land of Uz" (Job 1:1) (2 words)
15 "Even upon _____ by the wall" (1 Samuel 20:25) (2 words)
16 Third son of Micah (1 Chronicles 8:35)
17 "And the _____ arose" (Job 29:8)
18 Start of **ANSWER** to the question in the quote from Micah 6:8 (above) (5 words)
21 _____-cone
22 "Lead _____ Benjamin" (Hosea 5:8 NIV) (2 words)
23 Chinese general of chicken fame
24 Baton Rouge school (abbr.)

25 Copiers' needs
28 "They are as a _____" (Psalm 90:5)
30 **ANSWER**, cont'd (2 words)
33 "From wing _____ wing tip" (1 Kings 6:24 NIV) (2 words)
36 "So long" in Lyon
37 "Great is _____ of the Ephesians" (Acts 19:28)
39 "A _____ of horses" (Isaiah 21:9 NIV)
43 "Attack them and _____ them open" (Hosea 13:8 NIV)
44 **ANSWER**, cont'd (2 words)
47 Organization of attorneys (abbr.)
48 "Though you _____ me" (Psalm 17:3 NIV)
50 What Jefferson was
51 Playful swimmer
53 Uncle Tom's creator

55 **ANSWER**, cont'd (2 words)
56 Extent
59 "That they which _____ race run all" (1 Corinthians 9:24) (3 words)
62 Clumsy fellow
63 Morning hours (abbr.)
66 "_____ his son" (1 Chronicles 7:27)
67 "Why make ye this _____" (Mark 5:39)
70 End of **ANSWER** (4 words)
75 "And when _____ the blood" (Exodus 12:13) (2 words)
76 Spokes
77 He played Superman
78 "Even so _____ I you" (John 20:21)
79 "_____ from the blue" (2 words)
80 Exceptional mount

DOWN

1 Retrieving dogs, for example
2 "God is _____ and shield" (Psalm 84:11) (2 words)
3 "And shaken _____ pieces" (Job 16:12) (2 words)
4 "The lapwing, and the _____" (Leviticus 11:19)
5 From _____ Z (2 words)
6 "Is taken _____ end" (Jeremiah 51:31) (2 words)
7 "Every _____ town" (2 Kings 3:19 NIV)
8 Tulsa school (abbr.)
9 "I will give you _____"

(Matthew 11:28)
10 "He who _____ meat" (Romans 14:6 NIV)
11 "I am the _____" (John 14:6)
12 "Like chaff swept away by _____?" (Job 21:18 NIV) (2 words)
13 "Where would the _____ of smell be? (1 Corinthians 12:17 NIV)
14 Make sense (2 words)
19 "If I have _____ this" (Psalm 7:3)
20 "That remain, that nothing be _____" (John 6:12)

25 "The great _____ of his right foot" (Leviticus 14:14)

26 Egg
27 "And two lions standing by the _____" (2 Chronicles 9:18)
29 Abram's nephew (Genesis 12:5)
30 Acidy
31 Garfield's friend
32 "My _____ shall praise thee" (Psalm 63:3)
34 "Enter ye _____ the strait gate" (Matthew 7:13) (2 words)
35 "And she took a _____" (2 Samuel 13:9)
37 "He _____ out his sword" (Acts 16:27)
38 More wintry

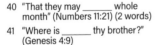

The crossword grid with numbered cells.

40 "That they may _____ whole month" (Numbers 11:21) (2 words)

41 "Where is _____ thy brother?" (Genesis 4:9)

42 "They _____ my steps" (Psalm 56:6)

45 Former name of Tokyo

46 "Not lawful to _____ the sabbath days?" (Luke 6:2) (2 words)

49 Recipe measurement (abbr.)

52 Hughes' airline

54 Small duck

55 Slight hair alteration

56 "_____ strength was not known" (Judges 16:9) (2 words)

57 "Whether we be sober, it is for your _____" (2 Corinthians 5:13)

58 "Was it from heaven, or _____?" (Luke 20:4) (2 words)

60 "_____ I make thy foes thy footstool" (Acts 2:35)

61 Kind of ball game pitchers dream of (2 words)

64 British pianist Dame _____ Hess

65 Q-tip, for example

67 Shammah's father, one of David's mighty men (2 Samuel 23:11)

68 "I did mourn as a _____" (Isaiah 38:14)

69 Azariah's father (2 Chronicles 15:1)

71 "A man sick of the palsy, lying on a _____" (Matthew 9:2)

72 "_____ set my bow in the cloud" (Genesis 9:13) (2 words)

73 Points of days (abbr.)

74 "It is _____ high day" (Genesis 29:7)

by David K. Shortess

ACROSS

1 "_____ that man, and have no company with him" (2 Thessalonians 3:14)
5 The eighth person (2 Peter 2:5)
9 "Holy and without _____" (Ephesians 1:4)
14 Gaal's father (Judges 9:26)
15 Zaccur's father (Nehemiah 3:2)
16 "Neither _____ nor sown" (Deuteronomy 21:4)
17 Gentle
18 Lack
19 "In whatsoever _____" (Philippians 4:11)
20 False personal report
22 Aram's son (Genesis 10:23)
23 Possessive pronoun
24 "_____ after his kind" (Leviticus 11:14)
25 "_____ beloved, I beseech you" (1 Peter 2:11)
29 Saul's grandfather (1 Chronicles 8:33)
30 A son of Benjamin (Genesis 46:21)
34 "Seek peace, and _____ it" (1 Peter 3:11)
35 Young females
37 Bind
38 "_____ the son" (1 Chronicles 11:42)
39 Time past
40 One of Jacob's sons (Genesis 35:26)
42 "_____, Hadid, and Ono" (Ezra 2:33)
43 Identifications
45 Realm
46 Cherries grow on this
48 A king of Midian (Numbers 31:8)
49 Women
50 Cain's victim
52 He was an Elkoshite (Nahum 1:1) (abbr.)
53 "The _____, and the mouse" (Leviticus 11:29)
56 "In the _____ of the multitude" (Luke 22:6)
61 "Down in _____" (Acts 27:27)
62 "Out of the tribe of _____" (Revelation 7:5)
64 "Yea, what _____, yea, what revenge!" (2 Corinthians 7:11)
65 "Desire to walk in long _____" (Luke 20:46)
66 "Shuthelah: of _____" (Numbers 26:36)
67 Weapons
68 Hurt
69 Eve was made from one of these
70 "The harvest is _____" (Joel 3:13)

DOWN

1 Peter and Andrew left these and followed Jesus (Matthew 4:18–20)
2 A son of Joktan (Genesis 10:26–29)
3 Arabian city (Isaiah 21:13–14)
4 First garden
5 After eighty-nine
6 Ancient Hebrew units of dry capacity
7 "_____ there yet the treasures" (Micah 6:10)
8 Kept from detection
9 "The sin which doth so easily _____ us" (Hebrews 12:1)
10 "The former rain, and the _____ rain" (Joel 2:23)
11 A son of Ulla (1 Chronicles 7:39)
12 Measure (arch.)
13 "Mahli, and _____" (1 Chronicles 23:23)
21 "And _____, and Mizpeh" (Joshua 15:38)
22 Young female
24 "The children of _____, the children of Siaha" (Ezra 2:44)
25 Reached a state of acceptance or reconcilement
26 Jabin and Sisera perished there (Psalm 83:9–10)
27 Away
28 Sprint
29 Simeon was called this (Acts 13:1)
31 Shemaiah's son (1 Chronicles 26:7)
32 Capture tactic
33 "The Amorites would dwell in mount _____" (Judges 1:35)
35 "The two and twentieth to _____" (1 Chronicles 24:17)
36 Belonging to Abraham's wife
41 Unhappy
44 "_____ had six sons" (1 Chronicles 9:44)
47 "Whether is it _____ to say to the sick" (Mark 2:9)
49 "And he heard the words of _____ sons" (Genesis 31:1)
51 Partner of the false prophet in the book of Revelation
52 A son of Elisheba (Exodus 6:23)
53 "_____ and fightings" (James 4:1)

54 "O daughter of _____"
(Lamentations 4:21)

55 Anak's father (Joshua 15:13)

57 A son of Seir (1 Chronicles 1:38)

58 Salathiel's father (Luke 3:27)

59 "And compassed the _____ of
the saints about"
(Revelation 20:9)

60 Otherwise

62 Author of Lamentations (abbr.)

63 "Shallum, and Telem, and
_____" (Ezra 10:24)

by N. Teri Grottke

39

ACROSS

1 Turn quickly
5 Crucifixion instrument
9 Realm
14 Arabian city (Job 6:19)
15 Levite grandfather of Ethan (1 Chronicles 6:44)
16 "_____, and Bariah," (1 Chronicles 3:22)
17 A son of Shem (Genesis 10:22)
18 At once (arch.)
19 "Waiting at the _____ of my doors" (Proverbs 8:34)
20 "Sherezer and _____" (Zechariah 7:2)
23 "God created _____ heaven" (Genesis 1:1)
24 A son of Buzi (Ezekiel 1:1) (abbr.)
25 Boat paddle
26 Strong wood

28 "Let this be your _____" (Job 21:2)
34 Father of Rachel and Leah (Genesis 29:16)
37 Make clean
38 Greek form of *Noah* (Luke 17:26)
39 "_____, and Dumah" (Joshua 15:52)
40 Cleaned with a broom
42 Detest
43 One of Jacob's sons
44 "Archers _____ at king Josiah" (2 Chronicles 35:23)
45 "_____ of barley" (Hosea 3:2)
46 "_____, and Suchathites" (1 Chronicles 2:55)
50 "Latter _____ than at the beginning" (Ruth 3:10)
51 "Cheeks, and the _____" (Deuteronomy 18:3)

52 Book after Job (abbr.)
55 Type of snake
58 "At _____ also the day shall be darkened" (Ezekiel 30:18)
62 "Therefore I shall not _____" (Psalm 26:1)
64 Sadoc's father (Matthew 1:14)
65 "Gedaliah, and _____" (1 Chronicles 25:3)
66 "Golden _____ empty the golden oil out of themselves?" (Zechariah 4:12)
67 "Who said, _____ it" (Psalm 137:7)
68 Gaal's father (Judges 9:26)
69 "The night is far _____, the day is at hand" (Romans 13:12)
70 Guilty or not guilty
71 Darius was one (Daniel 11:1)

DOWN

1 Look hard
2 "All the sons of _____ that dwelt" (Nehemiah 11:6)
3 Idol
4 "That at the _____" (Philippians 2:10)
5 Syrian leper (Luke 4:27)
6 "Of _____ men" (2 Samuel 2:31)
7 Image
8 Straight distance between two points
9 A son of Gomer (1 Chronicles 1:6)
10 Time past
11 Bird home
12 Goliath was from here
13 Otherwise
21 This orbits the earth
22 Land next to water

27 Kings (abbr.)
28 "A _____ of dove's dung" (2 Kings 6:25)
29 Be in debt to (arch.)
30 Child's favorite seat
31 A son of Shobal (Genesis 36:23)
32 "_____ that man, and have no company with him" (2 Thessalonians 3:14)
33 Prophet (arch.)
34 Boys
35 A son of Ulla (1 Chronicles 7:39)
36 Mighty man of David (2 Samuel 23:36)
40 Jonah appreciated this
41 "_____ ye not what the scripture saith" (Romans 11:2)
42 Gomer's husband (Hosea 1:3) (abbr.)

44 Did send (arch.)
45 Chopped
47 State of lobsters (abbr.)
48 "It shall not be lawful to _____ toll, tribute, or custom, upon them" (Ezra 7:24)
49 "Sons of Micah were, Pithon, and Melech, and _____" (1 Chronicles 9:41)
52 Servant of the church at Cenchrea (Romans 16:1)
53 A son of Zebulun (Genesis 46:14)
54 Out of the way
55 Poisonous snakes
56 "Lest at any time we should let them _____" (Hebrews 2:1)
57 "Whether _____ or harp" (1 Corinthians 14:7)

59 "Joy of the _____ ceaseth"
(Isaiah 24:8)

60 "Mountains shall reach unto
_____" (Zechariah 14:5)

61 "At Bilhah, and at _____, and at
Tolad" (1 Chronicles 4:29)

63 "As a lion in his _____"
(Psalm 10:9)

by N. Teri Grottke

40

ACROSS

1 "Two nations are in thy _____"
(Genesis 25:23)

5 Money used by miners

10 Son of Asaph the recorder
(Isaiah 36:22)

14 "Spread his tent beyond the
tower of _____" (Genesis 35:21)

15 "For her _____ is far above
rubies" (Proverbs 31:10)

16 "Of Harim, _____"
(Nehemiah 12:15)

17 Another name for *Zoar*
(Genesis 14:2)

18 "They _____ against me"
(Hosea 7:14)

19 Twelfth Hebrew month
(Esther 3:7)

20 "Imagine _____ all the day long"
(Psalm 38:12)

22 Pose a question

24 Beryllium (sym.)

25 Farthest part

26 Dog parasite

27 "Neither let me give flattering
_____ unto man" (Job 32:21)

30 "Man that hath friends must shew
himself _____" (Proverbs 18:24)

34 "Name of the _____ Ruth"
(Ruth 1:4)

35 Raise

36 "Wheat and the _____ were not
smitten" (Exodus 9:32)

37 Bit (arch.)

38 "For he shall be like the _____
in the desert" (Jeremiah 17:6)

40 Simon Peter's father (John 1:42)

41 "Thrust it through his _____
unto the door"
(Deuteronomy 15:17)

42 A son of Caleb (1 Chronicles 4:15)

43 "But a _____ of hospitality"
(Titus 1:8)

44 "Speedy _____ of all them that
dwell in the land"
(Zephaniah 1:18)

46 "Do ye not know their _____"
(Job 21:29)

47 Zibeon's son (1 Chronicles 1:40)

48 "Priest of the _____ high God"
(Hebrews 7:1)

49 South Africa (abbr.)

51 Motel

52 Shemaiah's father
(1 Chronicles 9:14)

55 First garden

57 Things

59 This priest rebuilt the temple

61 Small wagon

62 Cognizant

63 Jeshua's son (Nehemiah 3:19)

64 "_____ shall see God"
(Matthew 5:8)

65 "Now faith is the substance of
things _____ for" (Hebrews 11:1)

66 Load (arch.)

DOWN

1 Spider's art

2 Azariah's father
(2 Chronicles 15:1)

3 Not female

4 "_____ that was on his arm"
(2 Samuel 1:10)

5 Shoots

6 "For this cause left I thee in
_____" (Titus 1:5)

7 Eve was made from one of these

8 "Out of whose womb came the
_____?" (Job 38:29)

9 Amzi's son (Nehemiah 11:12)

10 "Children of _____ to Mosera"
(Deuteronomy 10:6)

11 Strange

12 A Canaanite city (Joshua 11:21)

13 Rabbit

21 "Mahli, and _____"
(1 Chronicles 23:23)

23 Prophet (arch.)

26 Worry

27 "Thy neck is like the _____ of
David" (Song of Solomon 4:4)

28 Ribai's son (1 Chronicles 11:31)

29 After second

30 "They will not _____ their
doings" (Hosea 5:4)

31 "He _____ them all out of the
temple" (John 2:15)

32 Flax cloth

33 "One day is with the Lord as a
thousand _____" (2 Peter 3:8)

38 Shadrach's former name
(Daniel 1:6)

39 Individually

40 "Called the name of it _____
unto this day" (2 Kings 14:7)

42 Jesus raised a young man from
the dead here (Luke 7:11)

43 A decrease in amount

45 "His soul _____ meat"
(Job 33:20)

46 "Driven with the wind and
_____" (James 1:6)

48 The Lord appeared to Abraham
in the plain of _____

49 Adherents of a creed

by N. Teri Grottke

50 Jabal's mother (Genesis 4:20)

52 "For in so doing thou shalt
_____ coals of fire on his head"
(Romans 12:20)

53 Shimei's son (1 Chronicles 6:29)

54 Impregnated

56 Before (arch.)

58 "_____ wings of a great eagle"
(Revelation 12:14)

60 "_____ there yet the treasures"
(Micah 6:10)

41

"Simon, Simon..."

Jesus had a brother named Simon: "Is not this the carpenter, the son of Mary, the brother of James, and Joses, and of Juda, and Simon?" (Mark 6:3). However, he is not found in this puzzle.

ACROSS

1 An early city of the tribe of Judah (Joshua 15:26)

5 "Behold the ____ of God!" (John 1:36)

9 A **SIMON** who had an infamous son named _____ (John 13:26)

14 *Nothing* in Nogales

15 A grandson of Esau (Genesis 36:10–11)

16 "We spend our years as _____ that is told" (Psalm 90:9) (2 words)

17 "_____ with joy receiveth it" (Matthew 13:20)

18 "Change my _____, because I am perplexed" (Galatians 4:20 NIV)

19 Faux silk

20 A **SIMON** from Samaria who practiced _____ (Acts 8:9, 11 NIV)

22 Ukrainian capital

24 "_____ God blessed them" (Genesis 1:22)

25 Short literary pieces

27 A **SIMON,** one of the twelve, called _____ (Luke 6:15)

30 Canadian First Nation member

32 City in Harar province, Ethiopia

33 "Stand in _____, and sin not" (Psalm 4:4)

36 "They may _____ whole month" (Numbers 11:21) (2 words)

38 "O God, do not _____ my plea" (Psalm 55:1 NIV)

42 A **SIMON** as Jesus addressed him (John 21:15) (4 words)

45 Artist's workplace

46 Lute, harp, and piano ensemble

47 "Neither hath the _____ seen" (Isaiah 64:4)

48 "_____ my Father are one" (John 10:30) (2 words)

50 "Keep a tight _____ on his tongue" (James 1:26 NIV)

52 A **SIMON** who lived by the sea and was _____ (Acts 10:6) (2 words)

55 Epitomes of slowness

59 "_____ his son" (1 Chronicles 7:27)

60 "Some would even _____ to die" (Romans 5:7)

63 One of the seven first deacons (Acts 6:5)

64 Dizzy with joy

67 "God _____ the increase" (1 Corinthians 3:6)

69 Bathe

70 "Death will _____ them" (Revelation 9:6 NIV)

71 "An _____ for every man" (Exodus 16:16)

72 "Had no _____ who it was" (John 5:13 NIV)

73 A **SIMON** living in Bethany who was a _____ (Matthew 26:6)

74 "Where are the _____?" (Luke 17:17)

75 Social misfit

DOWN

1 "He had _____ written" (Revelation 19:12) (2 words)

2 "I said, Should such a _____ I flee?" (Nehemiah 6:11) (2 words)

3 "Am I _____ head" (2 Samuel 3:8) (2 words)

4 "The inspired man a _____" (Hosea 9:7 NIV)

5 "From the _____ of our inheritance" (Numbers 36:3)

6 "Sallu, _____, Hilkiah" (Nehemiah 12:7)

7 "What a wretched _____ am!" (Romans 7:24 NIV) (2 words)

8 "A passing _____ that does not return" (Psalm 78:39 NIV)

9 "With her _____ on her shoulder" (Genesis 24:45 NIV)

10 Actress Hagen

11 "Then the same _____ evening" (John 20:19) (2 words)

12 "He _____ on the land" (Mark 6:47)

13 "He _____ you abundant showers" (Joel 2:23 NIV)

21 A **SIMON** who bore the cross for Jesus and was a _____ (Mark 15:21)

23 Substantiates

26 "Wherewith shall it be _____?" (Luke 14:34)

28 Knee (2 words)

29 "Whether he be a sinner _____, I know not" (John 9:25) (2 words)

by David K. Shortess

31 Arena where 65 Down commanded (abbr.)

33 "The foal of an _____" (Matthew 21:5)

34 "To _____, Israel" (Nehemiah 11:3)

35 Australian big bird

37 "Go to the _____, thou sluggard" (Proverbs 6:6)

39 "Love _____ another" (1 John 3:23)

40 "Without a _____ of brightness?" (Amos 5:20 NIV)

41 NNE + 90 degrees

43 Viking's Zeus

44 Hockey's Bobby

49 "Wounded the _____?" (Isaiah 51:9)

51 "To give us a _____ his holy place" (Ezra 9:8) (2 words)

52 "It is his _____" (Acts 12:15)

53 Sheer fabric

54 "On to Daberath _____ to Japhia" (Joshua 19:12 NIV) (2 words)

56 "Which _____ before Titus" (2 Corinthians 7:14) (2 words)

57 "A _____ of good men" (Titus 1:8)

58 Golfer Sammy

61 "The two-horned _____ had seen" (Daniel 8:6 NIV) (2 words)

62 "And, behold, I, _____ I" (Genesis 6:17)

65 WWII general (initials)

66 "Your" to a hillbilly

68 "_____ the lamp of God went out" (1 Samuel 3:3)

42

ACROSS

1 "Before _____ by the way"
(2 Samuel 2:24)

5 "I will send a fire on the wall of
_____" (Amos 1:7)

9 "Ran again unto the well to
_____ water" (Genesis 24:20)

13 "_____ him vehemently"
(Luke 11:53)

14 Eshcol's brother (Genesis 14:13)

15 This turns into a raisin

16 Amos's father (Luke 3:25)

17 "Where there is no _____, the
strife ceaseth" (Proverbs 26:20)

19 A son of Zophah
(1 Chronicles 7:36)

21 Shows ownership (arch.)

22 Rope web

24 The people of Syria go into
captivity here (Amos 1:5)

25 Girl (slang)

28 Great sorrow

30 A descendant of Manasseh
(Numbers 32:39–42)

35 Old

37 Amoz was his father (Isaiah 2:1)
(abbr.)

39 Tahath's son (1 Chronicles 7:20)

41 "_____ up a child"
(Proverbs 22:6)

43 "Dip the _____ of his finger
in water" (Luke 16:24)

45 "Chalcol, and _____"
(1 Kings 4:31)

46 "And the fame _____ went
abroad into all that land"
(Matthew 9:26)

48 Novel

50 "I shall be a _____ like unto you"
(John 8:55)

51 Come in

52 City of the priests
(1 Samuel 22:19)

54 Naaman's brother
(Numbers 26:40)

55 A son of Bani (Ezra 10:34)

58 "Hundred and _____ years old"
(Joshua 24:29)

60 "And they made war with the
_____" (1 Chronicles 5:19)

66 Penuel's son (1 Chronicles 4:4)

70 "Joseph of _____, an honourable
counsellor" (Mark 15:43)

72 Center

73 First bird out of the ark

74 Always

75 "Every _____ should bow"
(Philippians 2:10)

76 "See _____ that ye walk
circumspectly" (Ephesians 5:15)

77 Lease

78 "I will even _____ a curse upon
you" (Malachi 2:2)

DOWN

1 Jahzeel's brother (Genesis 46:24)

2 A duke of Edom (Genesis 36:43)

3 Jakeh's son (Proverbs 30)

4 "_____, and Chalcol"
(1 Kings 4:31)

5 "We _____ our bread"
(Lamentations 5:9)

6 A Canaanite city (Joshua 11:21)

7 "_____ the Ammonite"
(2 Samuel 23:37)

8 A son of Gad (Genesis 46:16)

9 Pull

10 Not easily found

11 Larger than monkeys

12 Were (arch.)

15 Creation's book (abbr.)

18 "But ye have _____"
(Amos 5:26)

20 Chop (arch.)

23 "When _____ king"
(2 Samuel 8:9)

25 Goliath was from here

26 "_____ with thine adversary
quickly" (Matthew 5:25)

27 "This only would I _____ of you"
(Galatians 3:2)

29 Jewish queen (abbr.)

31 Elderly

32 "Remnant of _____"
(Zephaniah 1:4)

33 "Down in _____" (Acts 27:27)

34 A son of Ishmael
(Genesis 25:13–15)

36 "There was a continual _____
given him of the king of Babylon"
(Jeremiah 52:34)

38 "On the east side of _____"
(Numbers 34:11)

40 Opposite of easy

42 Greek form of Noah (Luke 17:26)

44 Writing tool

47 An orange, for example

49 "_____ ye not what"
(Romans 11:2)

53 Panhandle

56 "Libnah, and _____"
(Joshua 15:42)

57 "Not to _____ thee" (Ruth 1:16)

59 They connect our heads with our
shoulders

60 Male red deer

by N. Teri Grottke

61 Had 775 descendants in captivity (Ezra 2:1, 5)

62 Opposite of *take*

63 So be it

64 "And _____ greedily after the error of Balaam" (Jude 1:11)

65 Viewed

67 "For he hath _____ marvellous things" (Psalm 98:1)

68 Jerahmeel's son (1 Chronicles 2:25)

69 "A _____ shaken with the wind?" (Luke 7:24)

71 Are (arch.)

43

ACROSS

1 "He _____ horns" (Habakkuk 3:4)

4 "Neither had they...more than one _____" (Mark 8:14)

8 Zibeon's son (Genesis 36:24)

12 Hosea's wife

14 "I have stretched out my hands _____ thee" (Psalm 88:9)

15 "Lest he _____ thee to the judge" (Luke 12:58)

16 To humble

17 "The fallow _____" (Deuteronomy 14:5)

18 "Of _____, the family" (Numbers 26:17)

19 "The children of Uzza, the children of _____" (Ezra 2:49)

21 "Why stand ye _____ up into heaven?" (Acts 1:11)

23 "To _____ the goads" (1 Samuel 13:21)

25 "_____, and Magog, to gather them together to battle" (Revelation 20:8)

26 Buzzing stinger

27 "Husham of the land of the _____ reigned in his stead" (1 Chronicles 1:15)

30 A herds man of Tekoa (Amos 1:1) (abbr.)

33 "_____ weeping for her children" (Jeremiah 31:15)

34 Comforted

38 "They _____ his praise" (Psalm 106:12)

40 "And their _____, and their felloes" (1 Kings 7:33)

42 Heap

43 "The LORD will destroy the house of the _____" (Proverbs 15:25)

45 Belonging to Jacob's first wife

47 Word preceding Psalm 119:121

48 "_____ not thee, O king" (Daniel 6:13)

51 Take action

54 A god of Babylon (Isaiah 46:1)

55 Tanhumeth's son (2 Kings 25:23)

59 "To the _____ which are at Ephesus" (Ephesians 1:1)

61 "Wheat with a _____" (Proverbs 27:22)

62 Certain

63 "_____, O Israel: The LORD our God is one LORD" (Deuteronomy 6:4)

67 In the edge of the wilderness (Exodus 13:20)

68 Largest continent

69 "_____ him vehemently" (Luke 11:53)

70 Product of weeping

71 365 days

72 "A _____ shaken with the wind?" (Luke 7:24)

73 Dull

DOWN

1 This place is on the left hand of Damascus (Genesis 14:15)

2 Absalom's captain (2 Samuel 17:25)

3 "This is a _____ place" (Mark 6:35)

4 A son of Shem (1 Chronicles 1:17)

5 Single

6 Partook

7 Failed to remember

8 "Jotham, _____" (Hosea 1:1)

9 "For Elnathan, and for _____" (Ezra 8:16)

10 By yourself

11 "Hast not thou made an _____ about him" (Job 1:10)

12 Breaches

13 "The plowman shall overtake the _____" (Amos 9:13)

20 "_____, and Chalcol" (1 Kings 4:31)

22 Shammah's father (2 Samuel 23:11)

24 "Dimnah with her suburbs, _____ with her suburbs; four cities" (Joshua 21:35)

25 "And _____ wife bare him sons" (Judges 11:2)

28 "For if ye do these things, ye shall _____ fall" (2 Peter 1:10)

29 Tree juice

30 "And the sucking child shall play on the hole of the _____" (Isaiah 11:8)

31 Disfigure

32 Japanese musician Yoko _____

35 "Of Keros, the children of _____" (Nehemiah 7:47)

36 Hophni's father (1 Samuel 4:4)

37 "As a lion in his _____" (Psalm 10:9)

39 "Going up to _____" (2 Kings 9:27)

41 Fleecy ruminant

44 Amount owed

46 Lane

49 Talmai was king of this place (2 Samuel 3:3)

50 "_____ to deceit" (Job 31:5)

51 Analysis of an ore

52 "For this _____ ought the woman to have power on her head" (1 Corinthians 11:10)

53 A son of Jehaleleel
   (1 Chronicles 4:16)

56 Ribai's son (1 Chronicles 11:31)

57 "Against the fenced cities"
   (Zephaniah 1:16)

58 Edges of garments

60 "Moses drew _____"
   (Exodus 20:21)

64 Before (arch.)

65 Get older

66 Scarlet

by N. Teri Grottke

44

ACROSS

1 One of Shaharaim's wives (1 Chronicles 8:8)
6 "_____, and Dumah" (Joshua 15:52)
10 King Hoshea's father (2 Kings 15:30)
14 Sychem's father (Acts 7:16)
15 "A _____ language" (Zephaniah 3:9)
16 "Shall compel thee to go a _____" (Matthew 5:41)
17 Zophar was one (Job 2:11)
19 Destitute
20 Elderly
21 "Into my _____" (Lamentations 3:13)
22 "A feast of _____ on the lees" (Isaiah 25:6)
23 "Flowed over all his _____" (Joshua 4:18)
24 Part of the handwriting on the wall (Daniel 5:28)
25 Island (abbr.)

27 Possessive pronoun
28 "Golden _____ empty the golden oil" (Zechariah 4:12)
29 Not straight
31 Very little
33 "And Jacob _____ pottage" (Genesis 25:29)
36 "_____, and the mighty men which belonged to David" (1 Kings 1:8)
37 Product of weeping
38 The Ten Commandments' book (abbr.) (var.)
39 "There was no room for them in the _____" (Luke 2:7)
40 "That _____ to the sound of the viol" (Amos 6:5)
41 "_____ the office" (1 Timothy 3:13)
42 Belonging to Jacob's brother
44 Barrier
46 Nobelium (sym.)

47 Bread bakes in these
48 "Their coast was from Heleph. . . and _____" (Joshua 19:33)
50 "Dead indeed unto sin, but _____ unto God" (Romans 6:11)
51 "As many as _____ by sea" (Revelation 18:17)
52 A son of Jether (1 Chronicles 7:38)
55 "Shall _____ thee" (Habakkuk 2:7)
56 "Declaring the _____ of the Gentiles" (Acts 15:3)
58 "_____ the death of the cross" (Philippians 2:8)
59 "_____ the Ahohite" (1 Chronicles 11:29)
60 Stop
61 Opposite of *more*
62 Beach surface
63 "Libnah, and _____" (Joshua 15:42)

DOWN

1 A brother of Shoham (1 Chronicles 24:27)
2 "Shelesh, and _____" (1 Chronicles 7:35)
3 "Alammelech, and _____" (Joshua 19:26)
4 Paul's letter to a great empire (abbr.)
5 Resting place of Noah's ark (Genesis 8:4)
6 "Nor of Helbah, nor of _____, nor of Rehob" (Judges 1:31)
7 "I will raise up his _____" (Amos 9:11)
8 "Used curious _____" (Acts 19:19)
9 Buzzing stinger

10 Kingdom
11 Female lions
12 "Myrrh and _____" (Song of Solomon 4:14)
13 "Restore all that was _____" (2 Kings 8:6)
18 "Captains over _____, and officers" (Deuteronomy 1:15)
22 "Jesus _____" (John 11:35)
23 "A serpent _____ him" (Amos 5:19)
24 "All the _____. . .shall be of brass" (Exodus 27:19)
25 A son of Merari (1 Chronicles 24:27)
26 Viewed

28 "Abundant honour to that _____ which lacked" (1 Corinthians 12:24)
30 "For as Jonas was a sign unto the _____" (Luke 11:30)
31 "And falling into a place where two _____ met" (Acts 27:41)
32 Is able
34 "Doth God take care for _____?" (1 Corinthians 9:9)
35 Puah's father (Judges 10:1)
37 In this manner
40 Sugar plant
41 "Shallum, and Telem, and _____" (Ezra 10:24)
43 The numbers of the clean animals on the ark (Genesis 7:2)

44 Sent (arch.) (Ruth 3:6)

45 "Shall _____ him" (Deuteronomy 22:19)

47 Shade of green

48 "The sons of Rephaiah, the sons of _____" (1 Chronicles 3:21)

49 A son of Jesse (Ruth 4:17)

50 Cain's victim (Genesis 4:8)

51 Puah's son (Judges 10:11)

52 Zibeon's son (1 Chronicles 1:40)

53 Thorny flower

54 Eshcol's brother (Genesis 14:13)

56 King Saul's father (Acts 13:21)

57 To place

by N. Teri Grottke

45

Biblical Beasts of Burden

And God made the beast of the earth after his kind.
GENESIS 1:25

ACROSS

1 "To whom I shall give _____" (John 13:26) (2 words)

5 "They made a calf in _____" (Psalm 106:19)

10 "For thou art my _____" (Psalm 71:5)

14 "With the _____ grain offering" (Numbers 28:12 NIV) (2 words)

15 "But I am afraid that just _____ was deceived" (2 Corinthians 11:3 NIV) (2 words)

16 "_____ when we were dead in sins" (Ephesians 2:5)

17 "Throughout all _____, world without end" (Ephesians 3:21)

18 Doomed one

19 "And they were _____ before the king" (Esther 6:1)

20 **BEAST** and burden referred to in Jeremiah 51:21 NIV (3 words)

23 Office of Natural Resources (abbr.)

24 Classical Portuguese writer _____ Miranda (2 words)

25 "_____ na na"

28 "And what _____ this day unto these" (Genesis 31:43) (3 words)

31 "Give everyone what you _____" (Romans 13:7 NIV) (2 words)

33 Prince Valiant's son

34 **BEAST** of burden prophesied in Zechariah 9:9 (4 words)

37 Nugget source

39 "I wouldn't do that for all the _____ in China!"

40 "In the _____ of the land of Edom" (Numbers 33:37)

41 **BEAST** carrying "Faithful and True" found in Revelation 19:11 (3 words)

46 "Went Jesus _____ of the house" (Matthew 13:1)

47 "Into the _____ one of them survived" (Exodus 14:28 NIV) (2 words)

48 "Their dead were _____ along the Shaaraim road" (1 Samuel 17:52 NIV)

50 "Wherewith the _____ number of them is" (Numbers 3:48)

51 Expression of resignation (2 words)

54 "Four days _____ I was fasting until this hour" (Acts 10:30)

55 **BEAST** with a question (Numbers 22:28 NIV) (2 words)

61 Former boxer Max

63 "Sat like a _____ in the desert" (Jeremiah 3:2 NIV)

64 "Seeing _____ stranger?" (Ruth 2:10) (3 words)

65 Part of a list

66 "All her vows, _____ her bonds" (Numbers 30:14) (2 words)

67 "And Anab, and Eshtemoh, and _____" (Joshua 15:50)

68 "Lest ye _____ your God" (Joshua 24:27)

69 Column of items in Paris

70 "Mending their _____" (Matthew 4:21)

DOWN

1 "The children of _____, six hundred fifty and two" (Nehemiah 7:10)

2 Asian palm tree

3 "An _____ for every man" (Exodus 16:16)

4 "After that ye shall _____" (Genesis 18:5) (2 words)

5 "What is the matter, _____ not be afraid" (Genesis 21:17 NIV) (2 words)

6 "But thou, _____ of man" (Ezekiel 3:25) (2 words)

7 Tears

8 "For Hiram was _____ lover of David" (1 Kings 5:1) (2 words)

9 "Your houses may _____ the frogs" (Exodus 8:9 NIV) (3 words)

10 "_____ am I; send me" (Isaiah 6:8)

11 "The power of the Highest shall _____ thee" (Luke 1:35)

12 It's split in soup

13 "An _____ is come" (Ezekiel 7:6)

21 Star in Pegasus

22 "Out the _____ bowlful of water" (Judges 6:38 NIV) (2 words)

26 A policeman's defense (2 words)

27 "And I _____ in my ward whole nights" (Isaiah 21:8) (2 words)

28 "Immediately a rooster _____" (Matthew 26:74 NIV)

by David K. Shortess

29 "Alive, _____ seen of her" (Mark 16:11) (3 words)

30 "And his _____ unto Isaac" (Psalm 105:9)

32 Halfway between due east and northeast (abbr.)

33 "And Joshua said, _____ Lord GOD" (Joshua 7:7) (2 words)

35 Baseball's Durocher

36 "Wherein shall go no galley with _____" (Isaiah 33:21)

38 *One* in Essen (Ger.)

42 "For if thou lift up thy _____ upon it" (Exodus 20:25)

43 Gasoline additive

44 Hay platform

45 Consequently

49 Pertaining to a very long time

52 New Zealand native

53 Namesakes of Ms. Lazarus

56 "An exceeding great _____" (Ezekiel 37:10)

57 "Ye are the _____ of the earth" (Matthew 5:13)

58 Welles's citizen

59 Give off

60 Sweet potatoes down South

61 "For me, except I _____ thee" (2 Kings 4:24)

62 "And _____ it up" (Revelation 10:10)

46

ACROSS

1 "_____ of asps within him" (Job 20:14)

5 Bed covering

10 A type of eagle (arch.) (Deuteronomy 14:17)

14 "_____ the Ahohite" (1 Chronicles 11:29)

15 Ishmael's mother

16 Nagge's son (Luke 3:25)

17 "_____ not the world" (1 John 2:15)

18 "Not selfwilled, not soon _____" (Titus 1:7)

19 Rear end of an animal

20 Philemon's runaway servant

22 "_____ ye the LORD" (Judges 5:2)

24 "_____ mouth is smoother than oil" (Proverbs 5:3)

25 "I will make you fishers of _____" (Matthew 4:19)

26 Feminine pronoun

27 Elderly

28 "Say ye to the _____ of the house" (Mark 14:14)

32 A son of Cush (1 Chronicles 1:9)

35 "With three _____ of great stones" (Ezra 6:4)

36 Shammah's father (2 Samuel 23:11)

38 King Hoshea's father (2 Kings 15:30)

39 A son of Micah (1 Chronicles 8:35)

40 Head covers

41 Tell about danger

42 "Sons of _____" (1 Chronicles 7:12)

43 Most horrible

44 "The mountains _____ like rams" (Psalm 114:4)

46 Letter to the church at Colosse (abbr.)

47 A son of Bani (Ezra 10:34)

48 "To Joel the _____ of Pethuel" (Joel 1:1)

49 Not cooked

52 "Against the band of the _____" (1 Chronicles 12:21)

56 Close (arch.)

58 "_____ the death of the cross" (Philippians 2:8)

59 "_____ whose fruit" (Jude 1:12)

61 Detest

62 A brother of Shoham (1 Chronicles 24:27)

63 Ithai's father (1 Chronicles 11:31)

64 "Even unto Ithiel and _____" (Proverbs 30:1)

65 "Used curious _____" (Acts 19:19)

66 Long for

67 Deep-water vehicle

DOWN

1 "Even from _____, while he offered sacrifices" (2 Samuel 15:12)

2 By yourself

3 Priests had to wash here

4 Untruths

5 Humiliated

6 Sixth son of Zalaph (Nehemiah 3:30)

7 Chicken products

8 "Give _____ to me, O son of Zippor!" (Numbers 23:18 NASB)

9 "Salute Tryphena and _____" (Romans 16:12)

10 A son of Benjamin (Genesis 46:21)

11 A son of Asher (Genesis 46:17)

12 Type of trees

13 "Harvest is _____" (Joel 3:13)

21 Micaiah's father (2 Chronicles 18:7)

23 Scarlet

26 "A _____ went out to sow his seed" (Luke 8:5)

27 A son of Shemaiah (1 Chronicles 26:7)

28 "Whether he have _____" (Exodus 21:31)

29 Chalcol's father (1 Kings 4:31)

30 Greek form of *Hagar* (Galatians 4:24–25)

31 Peter fished with these

32 Stitch

33 "_____ for the day!" (Joel 1:15)

34 "They are all dumb dogs, they cannot _____" (Isaiah 56:10)

35 "_____ weeping for her children" (Jeremiah 31:15)

37 Mordecai's beautiful cousin (abbr.)

39 "She maketh herself coverings of _____" (Proverbs 31:22)

43 "Seven times more than it was _____ to be heated" (Daniel 3:19)

45 "Haman. . .had devised against the Jews. . .and had cast _____" (Esther 9:24)

46 Mary had this relationship with Elisabeth

48 "Laban went to _____ his sheep" (Genesis 31:19)

49 Stretch

50 Abijah's brother
(2 Chronicles 11:20)

51 "The lion's _____, and none
made them afraid?" (Nahum 2:11)

52 A prince of Midian (Joshua 13:21)

53 Above

54 "My belly is as wine which hath
no _____" (Job 32:19)

55 Seth's son (Genesis 4:26)

56 "_____ shall offer gifts"
(Psalm 72:10)

57 In this manner

60 "The wheat and the _____ were
not smitten" (Exodus 9:32)

47

ACROSS

1 "Died Abner as a _____ dieth?" (2 Samuel 3:33)

5 "Habor, and _____" (1 Chronicles 5:26)

9 Boy

12 "According to this _____" (Galatians 6:16)

13 Seth's son (Genesis 4:26)

14 "No more _____" (Hosea 2:16)

16 "He _____ his arrows against the persecutors" (Psalm 7:13)

18 "Seek peace, and _____ it" (1 Peter 3:11)

19 Night sky illuminator

20 Best

21 Detest

23 "The children of _____" (Ezra 2:35)

24 "_____ mouth is smoother than oil" (Proverbs 5:3)

25 "_____ himself to go afoot" (Acts 20:13)

29 Hophni's father (1 Samuel 4:4)

30 A set of steps

31 "Shuthelah: of _____" (Numbers 26:36)

35 "Who said, _____ it" (Psalm 137:7)

37 King Hezekiah's mother (2 Kings 18:1–2)

38 Not easily found

39 Slough off

40 "Now gather thyself in _____" (Micah 5:1)

43 Place where Goliath's brother was slain (2 Samuel 21:19)

44 "The LORD shall beat off from the _____" (Isaiah 27:12)

45 Fuss

46 "Nineveh is laid waste: who will _____ her?" (Nahum 3:7)

49 A son of Asher (Genesis 46:17)

51 Rebel

52 "Shall the rich man _____ away in his ways" (James 1:11)

54 Utilizes (arch.)

55 Abiathar's father (1 Samuel 22:20)

60 "That of all _____" (Ecclesiastes 2:8)

61 Heber's father (Luke 3:35)

62 A son of Jehiel (1 Chronicles 9:35–37)

63 Test

64 Slay

65 Snake sound

DOWN

1 Satan went to and _____ in the earth (Job 1:7)

2 "Altogether for _____ sakes?" (1 Corinthians 9:10)

3 Elderly

4 Smallest

5 "_____, and Ivah?" (Isaiah 37:13)

6 Eshcol's brother (Genesis 14:13)

7 Decay

8 Type of tree (Isaiah 44:14)

9 A city on Crete near the Fair Havens (Acts 27:8)

10 Encampment in the wilderness (Numbers 33:13)

11 "There was a continual _____ given him of the king of Babylon" (Jeremiah 52:34)

14 "For in him we live, and move, and have our _____" (Acts 17:28)

15 Temple prophetess in Jesus' time (Luke 2:36)

17 Things

20 Old English word for marshes or swampy areas

21 One of the wives of Ashur, the father of Tekoa (1 Chronicles 4:5)

22 Get up

23 "_____ like a young unicorn" (Psalm 29:6)

24 "Restore all that was _____" (2 Kings 8:6)

26 Italy (abbr.)

27 "And eastward _____" (1 Chronicles 7:28)

28 "And upon _____" (Jeremiah 48:22)

31 Judah's firstborn (Numbers 26:19)

32 Saruch's father (Luke 3:35)

33 A son of Gad (Genesis 46:16)

34 "The other _____" (Nehemiah 7:33)

36 An altar (Joshua 22:34)

40 Specific one

41 Physical education (abbr.)

42 "Therefore I shall not _____" (Psalm 26:1)

44 Foals

46 "They could not go over the brook _____" (1 Samuel 30:10)

47 "Prepared unto _____ good work" (2 Timothy 2:21)

48 "Priest of the _____ high God" (Hebrews 7:1)

50 A pause or musical note used in the Psalms

51 Decomposing metal

52 Opposite of empty

53 "Shelesh, and _____"
(1 Chronicles 7:35)

55 Present a question

56 "Between Bethel and _____"
(Genesis 13:3)

57 A son of Benjamin
(Genesis 46:21)

58 King Saul's father (Acts 13:21)

59 Loruhamah's father (Hosea 1:6)
(abbr.)

by N. Teri Grottke

ACROSS

1 "He _____ horns"
(Habakkuk 3:4)

4 Abdiel's son (1 Chronicles 5:15)

7 Barrier

10 Simple

11 Floor cover

12 "Or will he _____ the valleys
after thee?" (Job 39:10)

15 "Eubulus _____ thee"
(2 Timothy 4:21)

17 Jedidah's father (2 Kings 22:1)

18 Mary Magdelene thought Jesus
was this at the tomb

19 "Destruction and _____ are in
their ways" (Romans 3:16)

20 Bela's son (1 Chronicles 8:3)

22 Last historical book of the OT
(abbr.)

23 Land of Joseph's captivity

27 "_____ your lusts" (James 4:3)

29 Belonging to Jacob's first wife

30 Book before Proverbs (abbr.)

31 "Maalehacrabbim, and passed
along to _____" (Joshua 15:3)

34 A son of Merari
(1 Chronicles 24:27)

35 Elkanah's grandfather
(1 Samuel 1:1)

37 Exhaust

38 Adam was the first

39 Mary was told by the angel to
regard fear this way

40 A river "before Egypt"
(Joshua 13:3)

41 Idols

43 A son of Elioneai
(1 Chronicles 3:24)

44 Modern

45 Er's wife (Genesis 38:6)

49 Arachnid

52 Consecrate

57 Consume (arch.)

58 A son of Haman (Esther 9:7-10)

59 Built by the children of Gad
(Numbers 32:34-36)

60 "For they loved the praise of"
(John 12:43)

61 Prophet (arch.)

62 Zephaniah's son (Zechariah 6:14)

63 First prophetic book of the Old
Testament (abbr.)

64 Test

DOWN

1 "Habor, and _____"
(1 Chronicles 5:26)

2 Greek form of *Asher*
(Revelation 7:6)

3 Colored

4 Make a correction

5 "For no man ever yet _____ his
own flesh" (Ephesians 5:29)

6 Amasa's father (2 Samuel 17:25)

7 Made of brass (arch.)

8 "Argob and _____"
(2 Kings 15:25)

9 "The LORD also shall _____"
(Joel 3:16)

10 Chicken product

12 A son of Noah

13 Chief among the captains
of David's mighty men
(2 Samuel 23:8)

14 One of five journalistic questions

16 "Lament for the _____"
(Isaiah 32:12)

21 "_____, in one day" (Isaiah 9:14)

23 The fifth encampment
(Numbers 33:9)

24 A priestly city of Benjamin
(Joshua 21:17)

25 "The linen _____ at a price"
(1 Kings 10:28)

26 Twenty-first letter of the Greek
alphabet

28 "His city was _____"
(Genesis 36:39)

30 Deep hole

31 "_____ and Gispa were over the
Nethinims" (Nehemiah 11:21)

32 Strong metal

33 Salathiel's father (Luke 3:27)

35 "The latter _____" (Ruth 3:10)

36 "My people hath been _____
sheep" (Jeremiah 50:6)

37 Another name for stannum

40 Zebulun's border turned
eastward from this city
(Joshua 19:12)

41 Greek form of *Gideon*
(Hebrews 11)

42 Be indebted to (arch.)

44 Mineral potash (Proverbs 25:20)

46 Zaanannim, and _____,
(Joshua 19:33)

47 "Tarshish, _____, Marsena"
(Esther 1:14)

48 "_____ the son"
(1 Chronicles 11:42)

49 Large lake

50 Way

51 Right hand (abbr.)

53 Throw out

54 "_____, Hizkijah, Azzur"
(Nehemiah 10:17)

55 "_____ shall see God"
(Matthew 5:8)

56 "If thou wilt. . . give _____ to his
commandments" (Exodus 15:26)

by N. Teri Grottke

A Pinwheel of Prophets

*And beginning at Moses and all the prophets,
he expounded unto them in all the scriptures
the things concerning himself.*

LUKE 24:27

ACROSS

1 Alcohol abuse program
5 Mentalist's claim
8 Word found 71 times in the Psalms
13 Away from the weather
14 "And pass _____ Zin" (Numbers 34:4) (2 words)
15 Muse of lyric poetry
16 **BIBLICAL PROPHET**
17 "They shall _____ their swords into" (Isaiah 2:4)
18 **BIBLICAL PROPHET**
19 "Let come _____ what will" (Job 13:13) (2 words)
20 Meg and Beth's sis
21 "I have covered my bed with colored _____ from Egypt" (Proverbs 7:16 NIV)
22 Scrutinize again

24 "_____ we find such a one as this is" (Genesis 41:38)
25 Samuel's mentor (1 Samuel 3:1)
26 **BIBLICAL PROPHET**
31 "Precious stones, wood, _____, stubble" (1 Corinthians 3:12)
34 City in Georgia
36 He played Superman
37 Baseball family
39 "He delighteth not in the strength of the _____" (Psalm 147:10)
41 "For with _____ and with malice" (Ezekiel 36:5 NIV)
42 Wet thoroughly
44 Kosher unleavened bread
46 "In a _____ it shall be made with oil" (Leviticus 6:21)
47 **BIBLICAL PROPHET**
49 Baseball statistic (abbr.)

51 Question response (abbr.)
52 Comedian Red
56 "Some fell among _____" (Matthew 13:7)
60 He said, "Float like a butterfly, sting like a bee"
61 "Never _____ of doing what is right" (2 Thessalonians 3:13 NIV)
62 **BIBLICAL PROPHET**
63 General Robert (2 words)
64 **BIBLICAL PROPHET**
65 "Rise _____ us go" (Mark 14:42) (2 words)
66 Two-person contest
67 "The _____ is made worse" (Mark 2:21)
68 Two-element electron tube
69 Baseball official (abbr.)
70 Lyric poems

DOWN

1 "Every fortified city and every _____ town" (2 Kings 3:19 NIV)
2 "Neither pray I for these _____" (John 17:20)
3 Has an opinion
4 Frequently used computer key
5 "Still the _____ and the avenger" (Psalm 8:2)
6 "None can _____ his hand" (Daniel 4:35)

7 "The fining _____ is for silver" (Proverbs 17:3)
8 Conference
9 The Emerald Isle
10 "With a _____ of blue" (Exodus 28:28)
11 "_____ hour when he is not aware" (Luke 12:46) (2 words)
12 Coastal Washington tribal members

14 **BIBLICAL PROPHET**
21 Test site, for short
23 City on the Danube
24 "Jesus said unto him, If thou _____ believe" (Mark 9:23)
26 Israeli folk dance (var.)
27 A hundred pounds of nails
28 Large brown alga
29 Eye layer

30 "Was found to have a _____ mind" (Daniel 5:12 NIV)

31 Islamic pilgrimage

32 Medicinal plant

33 "Love ye _____ enemies" (Luke 6:35)

35 Traumatic periods of unconsciousness

38 "That _____ their tongues, and say" (Jeremiah 23:31)

40 **BIBLICAL PROPHET**

43 Give off

45 Metal-bearing mineral mass that can be profitably mined

48 _____ and outs

50 "So will I compass thine _____ LORD" (Psalm 26:6) (2 words)

52 "I _____, but my heart waketh" (Song of Solomon 5:2)

53 Clocked

54 "Jeremias, _____ of the prophets" (Matthew 16:14) (2 words)

55 "Where the birds make their _____" (Psalm 104:17)

56 Dull sound

57 Arizona tribe

58 European capital

59 "A _____ shaken with the wind?" (Matthew 11:7)

60 Grad

63 Prof's email suffix, perhaps

50

ACROSS

1 Weeps
6 Take action
9 "Unto the _____ of my kingdom" (Mark 6:23)
13 "Even unto _____" (Genesis 10:19)
14 Cleaning agent
16 Jakeh's son (Proverbs 30:1)
17 Eliud's father (Matthew 1:14)
18 Certain
19 "We _____ not" (2 John 1:8)
20 "Name of his city was _____" (1 Chronicles 1:50)
21 One who charges interest
23 Picnic pests
24 Hearing organs
25 Ira's father (2 Samuel 23:26)
27 A son of Merari (Exodus 6:19)
31 Nagge's son (Luke 3:25)

33 First Hebrew month (Exodus 34:18)
34 Smelling orifice
36 "The true worshippers _____ worship the Father in spirit and in truth" (John 4:23)
41 "But he that _____ me before men shall be denied before the angels of God" (Luke 12:9)
43 Joab's armour bearer (1 Chronicles 11:39)
45 "_____ and Medad" (Numbers 11:27)
46 "Used curious _____" (Acts 19:19)
48 Endurance test
49 Menahem's father (2 Kings 15:14)
51 "But have renounced the _____ things" (2 Corinthians 4:2)

53 "The _____ with the mice of gold" (1 Samuel 6:11)
57 A son of Ham (Genesis 10:6)
59 Ahab's father (1 Kings 16:28)
60 Belonging to Abraham's brother
62 Zephaniah (abbr.)
65 Support
66 Greek form of *Hagar* (Galatians 4:24–25)
67 A Harodite guard of David's (2 Samuel 23:25)
69 Fever
70 Peter fished with these
71 Battles are drawn on these
72 Boys
73 "And _____ lay at his feet until the morning" (Ruth 3:14)
74 "Delivered me from all my _____" (Psalm 34:4)

DOWN

1 Applaud
2 "Whosoever shall say to his brother, _____, shall be in danger of the council" (Matthew 5:22)
3 Rephaiah's father (1 Chronicles 4:42)
4 A son of Benjamin (Genesis 46:21)
5 Hannah's firstborn
6 Esarhaddon was king here (Ezra 4:2)
7 "The Levites in their _____" (Ezra 6:18)
8 Type of weed
9 "Even from the mount _____" (Joshua 11:17)
10 "Three days _____ I fell sick" (1 Samuel 30:13)
11 Selfish desires

12 "So can no fountain both yield salt water and _____" (James 3:12)
15 Danger
22 Child of God
26 Saul's father
27 "He _____ havock of the church" (Acts 8:3)
28 Cain's victim
29 Female red deer
30 Asa's father (1 Chronicles 3:10)
32 Caused to go to a destination
35 "Jamin, and _____" (Genesis 46:10)
37 Firm
38 "_____ the Canaanite" (Numbers 21:1)
39 "_____ of blue" (Exodus 39:31)

40 "Though ye have _____" (Psalm 68:13)
42 Farthest part
44 Abiah's son (1 Chronicles 2:24)
47 A son of Gomer (1 Chronicles 1:6)
50 "The sons of Rephaiah, the sons of _____" (1 Chronicles 3:21)
52 Alone
53 "No mention shall be made of _____" (Job 28:18)
54 The ending
55 "His mouth is full of cursing and deceit and _____" (Psalm 10:7)
56 "Glorify ye the LORD in the _____" (Isaiah 24:15)
58 Steed
61 Generations
62 A son of Shimei (1 Chronicles 23:10)

63 A son of Ram (1 Chronicles 2:27)

64 "The heavens shall _____ away
with a great noise" (2 Peter 3:10)

68 Untruth

by N. Teri Grottke

51

ACROSS

1 Not straight
5 Daughter of Caleb (1 Chronicles 2:49)
10 A mighty man of David (2 Samuel 23:36)
14 Jesus cried this on the cross (Mark 15:34)
15 "Plucked up by the _____" (Jude 1:12)
16 Jeshua's son (Nehemiah 3:19)
17 "The LORD also shall _____" (Joel 3:16)
18 "And they set the altar upon his _____" (Ezra 3:3)
19 Son of Zerah (1 Chronicles 2:6)
20 "He that overcometh shall _____ all things" (Revelation 21:7)
22 "For the LORD shall rise up as in mount _____" (Isaiah 28:21)
24 Possessive pronoun
25 Insane
26 Next to
30 Tasks
32 King Hezekiah's mother (2 Kings 18:1–2)
35 Sibling of Dishon and Dishan (1 Chronicles 1:38)
36 "_____ of Judah" (2 Samuel 6:2)
37 Rope web
38 Asa's father (1 Chronicles 3:10)
39 Abram lived in this plain (Genesis 13:18)
40 Rabbit
41 "And _____ greedily after the error of Balaam" (Jude 1:11)
42 "Into my _____" (Habakkuk 3:16)
43 "And _____ with her suburbs" (1 Chronicles 6:73)
44 "_____ down here" (Ruth 4:1)
45 Stops
46 Chief captain (Acts 24:7)
48 Son of Nun (Numbers 11:28) (abbr.)
49 Small deer
50 Places of very little rain
54 Elimelech was Naomi's (Ruth 1:3)
59 Jacob's brother
60 Finished
62 Sadoc's father (Matthew 1:14)
63 Primary color
64 Wake up
65 Entrance
66 Plow
67 "_____ not, neither by heaven, neither by the earth" (James 5:12)
68 Killed

DOWN

1 A son of Zophah (1 Chronicles 7:36)
2 Esau's father-in-law (Genesis 26:34)
3 The eighth person (2 Peter 2:5)
4 Exhaust
5 Paarai was one (2 Samuel 23:35)
6 "Unto Adam also and to his wife did the LORD God make _____ of skins" (Genesis 3:21)
7 Hosea (abbr.)
8 "There is but a _____ between me and death" (1 Samuel 20:3)
9 "_____ yourselves, and come" (Joel 3:11)
10 Hadad's father (Genesis 36:35)
11 Bela's father (1 Chronicles 5:8)
12 Salathiel's father (Luke 3:27)
13 A duke of Edom (Genesis 36:43)
21 To free
23 "Who said, _____ it" (Psalm 137:7)
26 "And there came forth two she _____ out of the wood" (2 Kings 2:24)
27 Naarai's father (1 Chronicles 11:37)
28 Child of God
29 "Helez the Paltite, _____" (2 Samuel 23:26)
30 One of the sons of thunder
31 Hand-driven boat propellers
32 A son of Elioneai (1 Chronicles 3:24)
33 Paul and Silas were sent by night here (Acts 17:10)
34 Things
36 Group of people
39 "Even the sea _____ draw out the breast" (Lamentations 4:3)
40 Possesses
42 Balaam's father (Micah 6:5)
46 Noisier
47 "_____ verily, their sound" (Romans 10:18)
48 A son of Zerah (1 Chronicles 9:6)
49 Son of Zorobabel (Luke 3:27)
50 Amount owed
51 Nagge's son (Luke 3:25)
52 Israel's first king
53 White precipitation
55 "Bound two talents of silver in two _____" (2 Kings 5:23)
56 "The mountains shall reach unto _____" (Zechariah 14:5)

by N. Teri Grottke

57 "_____ that man, and have no company with him" (2 Thessalonians 3:14)

58 "And _____ away much people after him" (Acts 5:37)

61 Payment

ACROSS

1 Portion
5 "Look from the top of _____" (Song of Solomon 4:8)
10 Lengthwise threads
14 Greek form of *Hagar* (Galatians 4:24–25)
15 "No man _____ for my soul" (Psalm 142:4)
16 "_____, Hizkijah, Azzur" (Nehemiah 10:17)
17 "From the villages of _____" (Nehemiah 12:28)
19 Thorny flower
20 "Thou _____ up mine iniquity" (Job 14:17)
21 After nineteen
23 No (slang)
24 Particular ones
25 A son of Japhlet (1 Chronicles 7:33)

29 "Shuthelah: of _____" (Numbers 26:36)
30 Became acquainted
33 "Nor _____ my love, until he please" (Song of Solomon 8:4)
34 Jesus cried this on the cross (Mark 15:34)
35 Jesus' grandfather (Luke 3:23)
36 "In _____ was there a voice" (Matthew 2:18)
37 Bathsheba's father (2 Samuel 11:3)
38 "Eshtemoh, and _____" (Joshua 15:50)
39 Son of Dishan (Genesis 36:28)
40 Untruths
41 A tenth
42 Saul's grandfather (1 Chronicles 8:33)
43 "Yea, what _____, yea, what revenge!" (2 Corinthians 7:11)
44 Paul's hometown

45 Things
47 Boat paddle
48 "My son, if sinners _____ thee, consent thou not" (Proverbs 1:10)
50 Go to different places
54 Male pig
55 "In the borders of Zabulon and _____" (Matthew 4:13)
59 Temple prophetess in Jesus' time (Luke 2:36–37)
60 A son of Micah (1 Chronicles 8:35)
61 Gentle
62 "How much _____ shall I answer him" (Job 9:14)
63 "Yea, the _____ in the heaven knoweth her appointed times" (Jeremiah 8:7)
64 "Set it between Mizpeh and _____" (1 Samuel 7:12)

DOWN

1 Cooking vessel
2 Generations
3 Charge
4 "I _____ not" (Luke 17:9)
5 Caleb's daughter (Judges 1:12)
6 Mattathias's son (Luke 3:26)
7 Are (arch.)
8 Precedes Esther (abbr.)
9 "Sharaim, and _____, and Gederah" (Joshua 15:36)
10 Goods
11 "The sin offering of _____" (Exodus 30:10)
12 "Give thyself no _____" (Lamentations 2:18)
13 "Will a lion roar in the forest, when he hath no _____?" (Amos 3:4)

18 "Three hundred _____" (John 12:5)
22 Opposite of *lost*
24 "They passing by Mysia came down to _____" (Acts 16:8)
25 Ishmael and Hagar lived in this wilderness (Genesis 21:17–21)
26 Cognizant
27 "The Jews have no dealings with the _____" (John 4:9)
28 A son of Ezer (Genesis 36:27)
29 "Jozabad, and _____" (2 Chronicles 31:13)
31 Elkanah's grandfather (1 Samuel 1:1)
32 "But hath in due _____ manifested his word" (Titus 1:3)
34 Elijah (Romans 11:2)

35 Delilah cut Samson's
37 "In bondage under the _____ of the world" (Galatians 4:3)
41 "Pitched at _____" (Numbers 33:27)
43 Book before Malachi (abbr.)
44 "Made Nibhaz and _____" (2 Kings 17:31)
46 A son of Japheth (Genesis 10:2)
47 "One was Adah, and the name of the _____ Zillah" (Genesis 4:19)
48 A son of Shobal (Genesis 36:23)
49 Not any
51 Tubs
52 King Hoshea's father (2 Kings 15:30)
53 Green citrus
56 Consume food

57 Professional (abbr.)

58 "Wise _____ lay up knowledge" (Proverbs 10:14)

by N. Teri Grottke

Salvation Instructions

When his disciples heard it, they were exceedingly amazed,
saying, Who then can be saved?

MATTHEW 19:25

ACROSS

1 "Look from the top of _____" (Song of Solomon 4:8)

6 He sold his soul

11 "The head of the _____" (Leviticus 8:22)

14 French painter

15 "_____ also is joined with them" (Psalm 83:8)

16 "His mother's name also was _____" (2 Kings 18:2)

17 Start of **QUOTE** from Acts 2:21 NIV (2 words)

19 "_____ of renown" (Genesis 6:4)

20 Cowardly lion

21 It may be humble

22 One kind of value

24 Ike's command (abbr.)

25 "Of oil olive an _____" (Exodus 30:24)

26 They may be put on

27 **QUOTE**, cont'd (4 words)

33 "This _____ your health" (Acts 27:34) (2 words)

35 "_____ the nations be glad" (Psalm 67:4) (2 words)

36 "The _____ appeareth" (Proverbs 27:25)

37 "Casting all your _____ upon him" (1 Peter 5:7)

38 Low, heavy carts

40 "Never _____ of doing what is right" (2 Thessalonians 3:13 NIV)

41 "They had a great while _____ repented" (Luke 10:13)

42 "As a _____ offering" (Leviticus 5:13)

43 "Then appeared the _____ also" (Matthew 13:26)

44 **QUOTE**, cont'd (4 words)

48 Sandusky's lake

49 "The grove of _____ trees" (Song of Songs 6:11 NIV)

50 "Eat not of it _____" (Exodus 12:9)

53 "I will _____ the dawn" (Psalm 57:8 NIV)

56 "Unto me men gave _____" (Job 29:21)

57 Actress Hayworth

58 "He said, _____ is a lion's whelp" (Deuteronomy 33:22)

59 End of **QUOTE** (3 words)

62 "I said in my haste, All men _____ liars" (Psalm 116:11)

63 It may surround a lagoon

64 "Jesus saw that a crowd was running to the _____" (Mark 9:25 NIV)

65 "Against her; and she _____ them" (1 Samuel 25:20)

66 Utilize again

67 Edible Asian root vegetables

DOWN

1 "If it be _____" (Leviticus 27:7) (2 words)

2 "Stood every _____ his tent door" (Exodus 33:8) (2 words)

3 "_____ infancy you have known the holy Scriptures" (2 Timothy 3:15 NIV) (3 words)

4 At no time, poetically

5 Four-wheeler (abbr.)

6 Finely milled grain for cooked cereal

7 "As long _____ do well" (1 Peter 3:6) (2 words)

8 "Not unto _____ Lord" (Psalm 115:1) (2 words)

9 "As surely as the _____" (Hosea 6:3 NIV) (2 words)

10 Silvan fungal infestation (2 words)

11 "In _____ was there a voice" (Matthew 2:18)

12 Cain's brother

13 "I will lift up _____ eyes" (Psalm 121:1)

18 Big heroic tale

23 Familiar US ID (abbr.)

25 "Came unto mount _____" (Numbers 20:22)

26 "The Lord's chosen _____" (Isaiah 48:14 NIV)

28 "Once cultivated by the _____" (Isaiah 7:25 NIV)

29 Reluctant

30 "The name of the _____ is Hiddekel" (Genesis 2:14) (2 words)

31 "The _____, because he cheweth" (Leviticus 11:6)

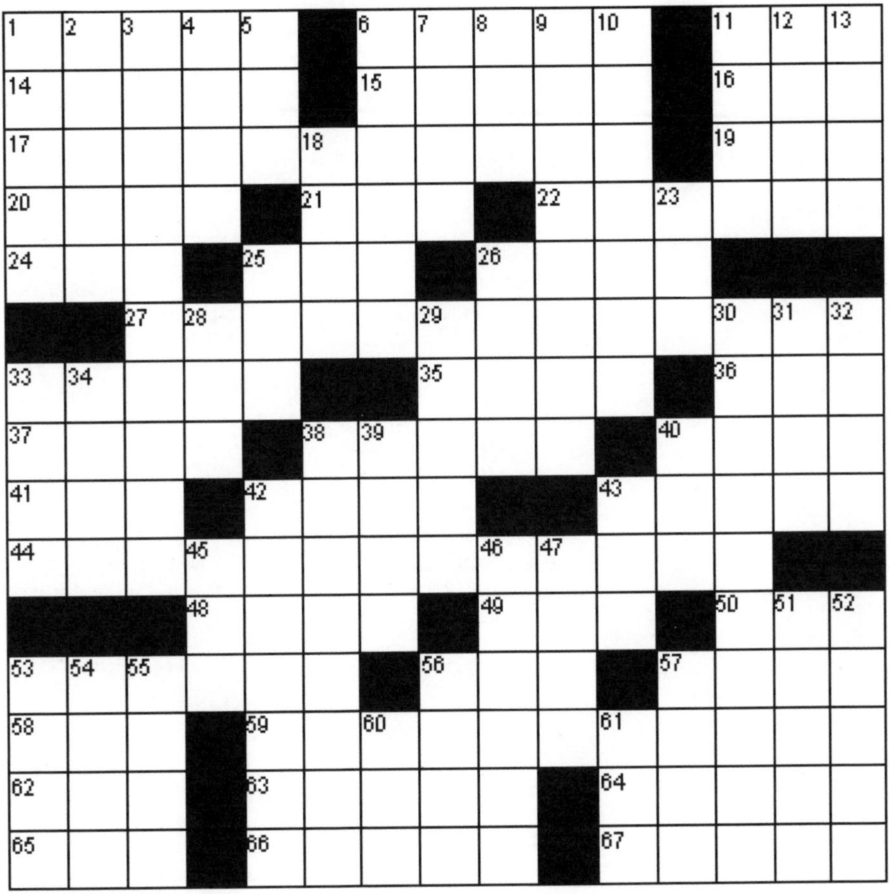

by David K. Shortess

32 "Lift up now thine _____"
(Genesis 13:14)

33 "_____ do all things through
Christ" (Philippians 4:13)
(2 words)

34 A long story about past events or
people

38 "I have nothing _____ to write
to His Majesty" (Acts 25:26 NIV)

39 "A daily _____ for every day"
(2 Kings 25:30)

40 "Coated it with _____ and pitch"
(Exodus 2:3 NIV)

42 "There was no _____"
(2 Chronicles 15:19) (2 words)

43 Toddler

45 Response to a mouse?

46 "To _____ us to serve him"
(Luke 1:74 NIV)

47 "I will _____ Sisera"
(Judges 4:7 NIV)

51 "I _____ pleasant bread"
(Daniel 10:3) (2 words)

52 Walks in water

53 "For as in _____ all die"
(1 Corinthians 15:22)

54 "_____ no clothes" (Luke 8:27)

55 "As a wild bull in _____"
(Isaiah 51:20) (2 words)

56 Right-angle pipes

57 "Whosoever shall say to his
brother, _____" (Matthew 5:22)

60 Bud's comic pal in early films

61 Mach 2 flier (abbr.)

54

ACROSS

1 A son of Zerah (1 Chronicles 2:6)
6 Salah's son (Genesis 10:24)
10 Child's favorite seat
13 Ezra proclaimed a fast there (Ezra 8:21)
14 "Even _____ to die" (Romans 5:7)
15 A son of Dishan (Genesis 36:28)
17 A pause or musical note used in the Psalms
18 Not easily found
19 Repulsive
20 Even
21 Cain's victim
23 "_____ up all the rivers" (Nahum 1:4)
25 A servant of King Josiah (2 Chronicles 34:20)
27 Rephaiah's father (1 Chronicles 4:42)

28 "The first man is of the earth, _____" (1 Corinthians 15:47)
31 Grinders
33 "In the middle of the garden were the _____ of life" (Genesis 2:9 NIV)
34 Possess
35 "God created man in _____ own image" (Genesis 1:27)
38 Amashai's father (Nehemiah 11:13)
42 Hate intensely
44 Insane
45 A son of Ham (Genesis 10:6)
47 We will give account for these kinds of words (Matthew 12:36)
48 A son of Gershon (Exodus 6:17)
49 Hold in high regard
51 A son of Jehiel (1 Chronicles 9:37)
53 "Ye shall eat in _____" (Joel 2:26)
55 Recompense

57 Load (arch.)
58 "Sin is the transgression of the _____" (1 John 3:4)
61 Sunrise
62 ".The sons of Mushi; Mahli, and _____, and Jeremoth, three" (1 Chronicles 23:23)
64 Eznite who slew 800 people at one time (2 Samuel 23:8)
66 "As he saith also in _____" (Romans 9:25)
67 "Fulfil the _____ of the flesh" (Galatians 5:16)
68 "The waters of _____" (Isaiah 15:9)
69 Naaman's brother (Numbers 26:40)
70 With "bat," a crescent-shaped, two-ended sword
71 "The night is far _____, the day is at hand" (Romans 13:12)

DOWN

1 "For my yoke is _____" (Matthew 11:30)
2 You (arch.)
3 Stop
4 Area near Babylon (2 Kings 17:24)
5 He gouged out the right eyes of eight people (1 Samuel 11:1–2)
6 "Og the king of Bashan, which dwelt at Astaroth in _____" (Deuteronomy 1:4)
7 "_____, and Tadmor in the wilderness" (1 Kings 9:18)
8 Make a mistake
9 "A _____ shaken with the wind?" (Luke 7:24)
10 "They _____ gold out of the bag" (Isaiah 46:6)

11 "Argob and _____" (2 Kings 15:25)
12 Raphu's son (Numbers 13:9)
16 After Ezra (abbr.)
22 Color of a horse
24 "The _____ of it" (Numbers 9:3)
25 "_____, Hizkijah, Azzur" (Nehemiah 10:17)
26 "The same is made the _____ of the corner" (1 Peter 2:7)
28 "The rock _____" (Judges 15:11)
29 Steward of the house in Tirzah (1 Kings 16:9)
30 "_____ before the king" (Esther 6:1)
32 "For Adam was first formed, then _____" (1 Timothy 2:13)
35 Pelt

36 Island
37 "They shall _____ like torches" (Nahum 2:4)
39 David wore one made of linen (1 Chronicles 15:27)
40 A son of Benjamin (Genesis 46:21)
41 "A little leaven leaveneth the whole _____" (Galatians 5:9)
43 "Be jealous for his land, and _____ his people" (Joel 2:18)
46 "When thou _____ the ground" (Genesis 4:12)
48 Transgressed
49 "The latter _____" (Ruth 3:10)
50 "They dwelt in their _____" (1 Chronicles 5:22)

by N. Teri Grottke

51 Absalom's captain (2 Samuel 17:25)

52 Woodsman

54 "The elements shall melt with fervent heat, the _____ also" (2 Peter 3:10)

55 Fuss

56 "Buy and _____, and get gain" (James 4:13)

58 Green citrus

59 At once (arch.) (Mark 1:30)

60 "Seven times more than it was _____ to be heated" (Daniel 3:19)

63 Payment

65 "He may _____ the tip of his finger" (Luke 16:24)

55

ACROSS

1 "Ye shall point out for you mount _____" (Numbers 34:7)

4 "_____ mouth is smoother than oil" (Proverbs 5:3)

7 "Of Keros, the children of _____" (Nehemiah 7:47)

10 Son of Pharez (Genesis 46:12)

12 "_____, and Shema" (Joshua 15:26)

14 "What do thy eyes _____ at" (Job 15:12)

15 Son of Gad (Genesis 46:16)

16 Eat formally

17 "_____, and Ivah?" (Isaiah 37:13)

18 "Can any understand the _____ of the clouds" (Job 36:29)

20 Baking place

21 Travel other than on foot

22 "_____ of barley" (Hosea 3:2)

24 Division

28 The border went to here from Remmonmethoar (Joshua 19:13)

30 "King _____ the Canaanite" (Numbers 21:1)

31 Strong promise

33 In the edge of the wilderness (Exodus 13:20)

38 Virgins

40 "I am not worthy to stoop down and _____" (Mark 1:7)

42 Fat king of Moab (Judges 3:17)

43 Adoniram's father (1 Kings 4:6)

45 So be it

46 Too

48 "Diverse from all the _____" (Daniel 7:19)

50 Bread from heaven

53 Arrived

55 "Habor, and _____" (1 Chronicles 5:26)

56 Of the sons of the giant (2 Samuel 21:16)

62 Thummim's partner (Exodus 28:30)

63 Viewed

64 By yourself

65 "Who said, _____ it" (Psalm 137:7)

66 Rabbit

67 Son of Igdaliah (Jeremiah 35:4)

68 "God created _____ heaven" (Genesis 1:1)

69 Temple gate (2 Kings 11:6)

70 "Lowborn _____ are but a breath" (Psalm 62:9)

DOWN

1 "Joy of the _____ ceaseth" (Isaiah 24:8)

2 Manna was measured in this unit (Exodus 16:15–16)

3 "According to this _____" (Galatians 6:16)

4 "_____, Zeboim, Neballat" (Nehemiah 11:34)

5 Famous

6 Resounded

7 Strain

8 Inside

9 Son of Ezer (Genesis 36:27)

10 Possesses

11 "Cretians are alway _____" (Titus 1:12)

13 "Dwelling was from _____" (Genesis 10:30)

14 "To _____ is reserved the blackness of darkness for ever" (Jude 1:13)

19 "Waters of _____" (Isaiah 15:9)

23 Son of Zerubbabel (1 Chronicles 3:19–20)

24 Identical

25 Rocky outcropping

26 "Said, _____, King of the Jews!" (John 19:3)

27 Zechariah's father (Ezra 5:1)

29 Judge of Israel (Judges 3:15)

32 "Nevertheless _____ heart" (1 Kings 15:14)

34 Zuph's father (1 Chronicles 6:34–35)

35 Dwelling

36 Greek form of *Asher* (Revelation 7:6)

37 "Having _____ persons in admiration" (Jude 1:16)

39 Ahira's father (Numbers 1:15)

41 Ruth's mother-in-law

44 A son of Azel (1 Chronicles 8:38)

47 Phaltiel's father (2 Samuel 3:15)

49 Son of Reumah (Genesis 22:24)

50 Naomi's chosen name

51 Get up

52 "That at the _____ of Jesus every knee should bow" (Philippians 2:10)

54 Saul's first cousin (1 Samuel 14:50)

55 Injured

57 "Falling into a place where two _____ met" (Acts 27:41)

58 Son of Shem (Genesis 10:22)

59 Not any

60 Son of Judah (1 Chronicles 2:3)

61 "Zechariah, _____, and Jaaziel" (1 Chronicles 15:18)

by N. Teri Grottke

56

ACROSS

1 "But who is able to build _____ an house" (2 Chronicles 2:6)

4 Detest

8 "Son of _____, in Makaz" (1 Kings 4:9)

13 "Tower of _____" (Genesis 35:21)

15 Esau's father-in-law (Genesis 26:34)

16 A Harodite guard of David's (2 Samuel 23:25)

17 Ostracized

19 Melea's father (Luke 3:31)

20 "Learn to do well; seek judgment, _____ the oppressed" (Isaiah 1:17)

21 "Even all one as if she were _____" (1 Corinthians 11:5)

23 A type of eagle (arch.)

24 Single

25 "Suddenly there _____ round about him a light" (Acts 9:3)

28 Daring courage

33 Humpbacked animal

34 "No _____ in the stalls" (Habakkuk 3:17)

35 "The _____ of truth shall be established for ever" (Proverbs 12:19)

36 "Alammelech, and _____" (Joshua 19:26)

37 Employment pay

38 Common tree

39 Measurement for oil (Leviticus 14:10)

40 "_____, and Dumah" (Joshua 15:52)

41 Undeserved favor

42 "When one came to the _____ for to draw" (Haggai 2:16)

45 Shut

46 Female sheep

47 "And _____ lived after" (Genesis 11:11)

48 Written account

51 "And _____, and Uzal, and Diklah" (Genesis 10:27)

55 Shaving tool

56 "Him that _____ was blind" (John 9:13)

58 Make a correction

59 Resounded

60 First garden

61 "Appointed the _____ of the priests and the Levites" (Nehemiah 13:30)

62 "The LORD shewed him a _____" (Exodus 15:25)

63 "The latter _____" (Ruth 3:10)

DOWN

1 "_____, O Israel: The LORD our God is one LORD" (Deuteronomy 6:4)

2 Lazy

3 Body armor (arch.)

4 "When ye have _____ the best" (Numbers 18:30)

5 "Nor _____ the thing" (Psalm 89:34)

6 Connected to the foot

7 Ceases

8 "I will speak: I will _____ of thee" (Job 42:4)

9 Disciples left after death of Judas

10 Cattle

11 A child of Ezer (Genesis 36:27)

12 "And _____ greedily after the error of Balaam" (Jude 1:11)

14 "Ye have _____ as kings without us" (1 Corinthians 4:8)

18 "_____, and goeth out" (Joshua 19:27)

22 "All thy strong _____ shall be like fig trees" (Nahum 3:12)

25 Head

26 Shechem's father (Genesis 33:19)

27 Idol

28 "Of his own will _____ he us with the word of truth" (James 1:18)

29 "Brought the heads of _____" (Judges 7:25)

30 Elijah (Romans 11:2)

31 "For _____ the fathers fell asleep" (2 Peter 3:4)

32 Velocity

34 "Habor, and _____" (1 Chronicles 5:26)

37 "And one _____ out of the basket" (Exodus 29:23)

38 "Exalt her, and she shall _____ thee" (Proverbs 4:8)

41 "And the _____, and the kite" (Deuteronomy 14:13)

43 Gihon was this river coming out of Eden (Genesis 2:13)

44 "Beat your plowshares into _____" (Joel 3:10)

45 "Who shall lay any thing to the _____ of God's elect?" (Romans 8:33)

47 "Suddenly there _____ from heaven a great light" (Acts 22:6)

48 "In _____ was there a voice" (Matthew 2:18)

49 Jeshua's son (Nehemiah 3:19)

50 Move quickly

52 Travel other than on foot

by N. Teri Grottke

53 So be it

54 Repair

55 Not cooked

57 Kidman and Cruise movie:
_____ *and Away*

Snake in the Grass

The theme answer is a long, familiar Bible quote that snakes up and down and back and forth across the grid, even jumping across black spaces. Follow the arrows and stay within the shaded squares.

ACROSS

1 Start of **QUOTE** from Genesis 3 (see note above)
5 Part of **QUOTE**
9 Part of **QUOTE**
14 "And _____ bare Jabal" (Genesis 4:20)
15 "_____ abhor me" (Job 30:10)
16 Wealthy or powerful person
17 "Or clothe his neck with a flowing _____?" (Job 39:19 NIV)
18 Negative replies
19 Recover metal by heating ore
20 "The LORD shall judge the _____ of the earth" (1 Samuel 2:10)
21 Charlotte Brontë's Jane and family
23 Asian inland sea
24 Part of **QUOTE**
25 Oklahoma town
27 Avenue crossers (abbr.)
30 "_____ to your faith virtue" (2 Peter 1:5)

32 Part of **QUOTE**
36 "Round about the _____ thereof" (Exodus 28:33)
37 "I know it _____ of a truth" (Job 9:2) (2 words)
39 "For whether is _____" (Matthew 9:5)
40 Ecology watchdog group (abbr.)
41 Part of **QUOTE**
43 "They _____ the ship aground" (Acts 27:41)
44 "Now learn this _____ from the fig tree" (Matthew 24:32 NIV)
46 "Ye shall find a colt _____" (Mark 11:2)
47 "We _____ many" (Mark 5:9)
48 Part of **QUOTE**
49 "Jerusalem, _____, she is broken" (Ezekiel 26:2)
50 Manuscripts (abbr.)
51 "As it had been the face _____ angel" (Acts 6:15) (2 words)

53 Part of **QUOTE**
55 "_____ do all things through Christ" (Philippians 4:13) (2 words)
58 "Who will _____ us?" (Isaiah 6:8) (2 words)
61 Expression of annoyance
65 Natives of northern Ohio, once
67 Friskies rival
68 "Why should _____ with thee?" (2 Samuel 13:26) (2 words)
69 "Get a new _____ on life" (start over)
70 Afrikaans, language of South Africa
71 Swiss river
72 Part of **QUOTE**
73 Part of **QUOTE**
74 Part of **QUOTE**

DOWN

1 "He shall have no _____ in the street" (Job 18:17)
2 "Thy god, _____, liveth" (Amos 8:14) (2 words)
3 Baton
4 Part of **QUOTE**
5 Part of **QUOTE**
6 Nautical greeting
7 "O thou _____, go, flee thee away" (Amos 7:12)

8 "That thou wilt not cut off _____ after me" (1 Samuel 24:21) (2 words)
9 _____ and offs
10 Southwestern covered porches
11 Salah's son (Genesis 10:24)
12 *Alone* (Sp.)
13 Part of **QUOTE**
22 Tin in Chemistry 101

26 "Shall go _____ out" (John 10:9) (2 words)
27 Off-the-_____ (not custom-made)
28 Conical abode
29 "_____ her jugs" (Jeremiah 48:12 NIV)
30 Abijam's son (1 Kings 15:8)
31 "This man _____ many miracles" (John 11:47)

by David K. Shortess

33 "Solomon sent to _____, saying" (1 Kings 5:2)

34 "They that sow in _____ shall reap in joy" (Psalm 126:5)

35 Sea eagles

37 "Let them break _____" (Exodus 32:24) (2 words)

38 Nine-digit ID (abbr.)

39 "Mine _____ is consumed because of grief" (Psalm 6:7)

42 US Native American agency

45 "Over these _____ have buried here" (Jeremiah 43:10 NIV) (2 words)

49 "As he that feareth _____" (Ecclesiastes 9:2) (2 words)

52 Ashcroft, e.g. (abbr.)

53 Part of **QUOTE**

54 Part of **QUOTE**

55 Part of **QUOTE**

56 "Immediately the cock _____" (Matthew 26:74)

57 Rizpah's mother, Saul's concubine (2 Samuel 3:7)

59 "The wall of the city shall fall down _____" (Joshua 6:5)

60 Colorful tropical fish

62 Quantity of paper

63 Taj Mahal site

64 Having pedal digits

66 "In just a _____" (very shortly)

58

ACROSS

1 Caused to go to a destination
5 Shammai's son (1 Chronicles 2:45)
9 "_____, and Magog, to gather them together to battle" (Revelations 20:8)
12 A son of Zabad (1 Chronicles 7:21)
14 Fever
15 Young female
16 "Which he _____ of me is true" (John 5:32)
18 "Of Harim, _____" (Nehemiah 12:15)
19 The border went to here from Remmonmethoar (Joshua 19:13)
20 "_____ and Medad" (Numbers 11:27)
21 "I will not _____ them" (Amos 5:22)
24 "When he should have _____" (Acts 28:6)
27 Periods of time 60 minutes long
28 "And God wrought _____ miracles by the hands of Paul" (Acts 19:11)
29 Are (arch.)
30 Verbalize
31 "And _____ greedily after the error of Balaam" (Jude 1:11)
32 "They have _____ themselves ill in their doings" (Micah 3:4)
35 Quickest
39 Transgression
40 Word preceding Psalm 119:121
41 Untruth
42 "Returned from _____ after the Philistines" (1 Samuel 17:53)
44 Adina's father (1 Chronicles 11:42)
46 "Thou _____ up the sum" (Ezekiel 28:12)
47 Owner of the hill, Samaria (1 Kings 16:24)
48 "Who layeth the _____ of his chambers" (Psalm 104:3)
49 "Say unto them which _____ it" (Ezekiel 13:11)
50 Otherwise
51 "We also have _____ you and testified" (1 Thessalonians 4:6)
57 Lack
58 "And Ahijah, Hanan, _____" (Nehemiah 10:26)
59 "Not to _____ thee" (Ruth 1:16)
60 Strange
61 Current events
62 At a certain time

DOWN

1 Stitch
2 Hophni's father (1 Samuel 4:4)
3 Rope web
4 "He lodgeth with one Simon a _____" (Acts 10:6)
5 Crush
6 Get older
7 Absent
8 Cupbearer and rebuilder (abbr.)
9 "The children of _____, the children of Gahar" (Ezra 2:47)
10 Solomon's temple was built on his threshing floor (2 Chronicles 3:1)
11 "Ye may be _____ also with exceeding joy" (1 Peter 4:13)
13 "Praise the LORD from the earth, ye dragons, and all _____" (Psalm 148:7)
15 "Neither shall _____ ship pass thereby" (Isaiah 33:21)
17 What Lot did in the gate of Sodom (Genesis 19:1)
20 Elijah (Romans 11:2)
21 Jezebel's husband
22 Center
23 "The men of _____ made Nergal" (2 Kings 17:30)
24 Caleb was one (Numbers 13)
25 "That _____ command" (Luke 9:54)
26 Pagiel's father (Numbers 1:13)
28 Unhappy
30 Hearing is one
33 "They may be _____ that falsely accuse" (1 Peter 3:16)
34 The prayers of the saints are in these
35 Jesus cursed this tree
36 The fifth encampment (Numbers 33:9)
37 Dimensions
38 Rip
40 Tiny insect
42 Desisted
43 Ellis _____ (abbr.)
44 District in Benjamin (1 Samuel 13:17)
45 Abraham was the first
46 A son of Nadab (1 Chronicles 2:30)
47 Sharp-toothed tool
48 Shoham's brother (1 Chronicles 24:27)
49 Homes of wild animals
51 Disperse
52 Single

by N. Teri Grottke

53 Not cooked
54 After Micah (abbr.)
55 Adam's wife
56 "As a lion in his _____"
    (Psalm 10:9)

59

ACROSS

1 Applaud
5 Question
8 "Awake, ye drunkards, and weep; and _____" (Joel 1:5)
12 "_____ name was Mordecai" (Esther 2:5)
13 Buzzing stinger
14 This priest rebuilt the temple
15 Curses
16 Dehydrated
17 "Mint and _____" (Matthew 23:23)
19 Letter to the church at Ephesus (abbr.)
20 You (arch.)
22 "My tongue is the pen of a ready _____" (Psalm 45:1)
23 Robbing
25 An altar (Joshua 22:34)
26 "Give _____, O heavens, and let me speak" (Deuteronomy 32:1 NASB)
27 "_____ mouth is smoother than oil" (Proverbs 5:3)
28 Salah's son (Genesis 10:24)
30 Get older
33 Well of strife (Genesis 26:20)
36 Impressed stamps
40 "By faith the _____ of Jericho fell down" (Hebrews 11:30)
43 Big hatchet
44 A son of Jehaleleel (1 Chronicles 4:16)
45 A son of Elam (Ezra 10:26)
46 Rahab let this down through her window (Joshua 2:15)
48 Capable
49 7 days
51 Male sheep
54 King Hezekiah's mother (2 Kings 18:2)
57 A Moabite border city (Numbers 21:15)
58 "In bondage under the _____ of the world" (Galatians 4:3)
63 Go to sleep
65 "Rain upon the _____ grass" (Psalm 72:6)
66 A son of Bela (1 Chronicles 7:7)
67 "Of _____ was taken" (1 Samuel 10:21)
68 Amos (abbr.)
69 "Sound of the _____" (Job 21:12)
71 Son of Shammai (1 Chronicles 2:45)
72 Hosea (abbr.)
73 "And he must _____ go through Samaria" (John 4:4)
74 Vocalize in song
75 "_____ there yet the treasures" (Micah 6:10)
76 Certain

DOWN

1 Dried out (arch.)
2 "The Egyptians shall _____ to drink of the water of the river" (Exodus 7:18)
3 Type of tree (Isaiah 44:14)
4 "Wheat with a _____" (Proverbs 27:22)
5 Son of Hillel (Judges 12:15)
6 Reu's son (Genesis 11:20)
7 The fifth angel was given this
8 "And thou _____ my voice" (Jonah 2:2)
9 A child of Gad (Numbers 26:16–18)
10 Communicate on paper
11 A city on Crete (Acts 27:8)
12 "There come two _____ more hereafter" (Revelation 9:12)
18 Make a mistake
21 Employ
22 Spider's art
24 "Say in their hearts, _____" (Psalm 35:25)
28 A son of Ram (1 Chronicles 2:27)
29 "Shimei, and _____" (1 Kings 1:8)
30 Reverent fear
31 Girl (slang)
32 Hophni's father (1 Samuel 4:4)
34 Bag
35 Second book (abbr.)
37 Jether's son (1 Chronicles 7:38)
38 "The _____ of truth shall be established for ever" (Proverbs 12:19)
39 "Now Rachel had taken the images. . .and _____ upon them" (Genesis 31:34)
41 "Sin is the transgression of the _____" (1 John 3:4)
42 Cutting wool off sheep
47 "And _____ away much people after him" (Acts 5:37)
50 Before (arch.)
52 Belonging to David's incestuous son
53 Maine (abbr.)
54 Attached to the shoulder

55 "Who layeth the _____ of his chambers" (Psalm 104:3)

56 Ribai's son (2 Samuel 23:29)

58 The father of Sychem (Genesis 7:16)

59 "And they _____ him" (Mark 11:4)

60 Simeon was called this (Acts 13:1)

61 Commerce

62 Iniquities

64 Strong metal

68 "Against Jerusalem, _____" (Ezekiel 26:2)

70 Peleg's son (Genesis 11:18)

by N. Teri Grottke

ACROSS

1 "Now the serpent was more subtil _____ any beast" (Genesis 3:1)

5 "Hundred and _____ years old" (Joshua 24:29)

8 Kill

12 "Habor, and _____" (1 Chronicles 5:26)

13 Esau's father-in-law (Genesis 26:34)

15 Dwelling

16 "With the _____" (Deuteronomy 28:27)

17 Travel other than on foot

18 "Shall I make thee as _____?" (Hosea 11:8)

20 To place

21 "_____ verily, their sound" (Romans 10:18)

22 Staff

24 A son of Bela (1 Chronicles 7:7)

25 Makes use of

27 Belonging to Jacob

29 Huri's father (1 Chronicles 5:14)

31 "If _____ he might find any thing thereon" (Mark 11:13)

32 A judge of Israel (Judges 3:15)

33 "They zealously _____ you" (Galatians 4:17)

36 "God saw that it _____ good" (Genesis 1:21)

37 "And Rekem, and Irpeel, and _____" (Joshua 18:27)

39 Became acquainted

42 "Destruction and _____ are in their ways" (Romans 3:16)

43 "That dippeth with me in the _____" (Mark 14:20)

44 People who inherit

46 "Make up beforehand your _____" (2 Corinthians 9:5)

48 Peter cut off his ear (John 18:10)

50 "Day of _____ birth" (Ecclesiastes 7:1)

51 Get older

52 Are (arch.)

53 "_____ wings of a great eagle" (Revelation 12:14)

54 Opposite of *bottom*

57 "Filled his holes with prey, and his dens with _____" (Nahum 2:12)

59 Encampment with 12 fountains and 70 palm trees (Numbers 33:9)

61 Steward of the house in Tirzah (1 Kings 16:9)

62 King of Sodom (Genesis 14:2)

63 Not female

64 Viewed

65 Zibeon's daughter (Genesis 36:2)

66 "As a lion in his _____" (Psalm 10:9)

67 Charity

DOWN

1 "Mordecai for _____?" (Esther 6:3)

2 Detest

3 "Which maketh _____, Orion" (Job 9:9)

4 Nahum (abbr.)

5 A conspirator against Esther's husband (Esther 2:21)

6 Belonging to Eli (poss.)

7 East of Eden (Genesis 4:16)

8 Hananiah (Daniel 1:7)

9 "_____, Hadid, and Ono" (Ezra 2:33)

10 A son of Gemalli (Numbers 13:12)

11 Annually

14 Salathiel's father (Luke 3:27)

19 Opposite of *hers*

21 Exclamation of affirmation

23 "And Moses called _____ the son of Nun Jehoshua" (Numbers 13:16)

26 "And Jacob _____ pottage" (Genesis 25:29)

28 Capable

29 "But he is a _____" (Romans 2:29)

30 "Against Jerusalem, _____" (Ezekiel 26:2)

33 "_____ there yet the treasures" (Micah 6:10)

34 Opposite of *near*

35 Birds do this

37 A son of Maachah (1 Chronicles 2:48)

38 Esarhaddon was king here (Ezra 4:2)

39 "But now bring me a _____" (2 Kings 3:15)

40 Jewish queen (abbr.)

41 "So shall _____ seed be" (Romans 4:18)

42 He was from mount Ephraim (Judges 17:1) (abbr.)

43 Payment

44 Nethinims (Nehemiah 7:46, 48)

45 Disciples left after death of Judas

46 Archers (arch.)

47 Japanese musician Yoko _____

48 Disfigure

49 Originate

by N. Teri Grottke

53 "Thou also, son of man, take thee a _____" (Ezekiel 4:1)

55 A brother of David (1 Chronicles 2:15)

56 "Baked it in _____" (Numbers 11:8)

58 "Helez the Paltite, _____" (2 Samuel 23:26)

60 Boy

61 Solomon's great-grandson (1 Kings 15:8)

61

Biblical Warriors

There were giants in the earth in those days;
. . .the same became mighty men which were of old, men of renown.

GENESIS 6:4

ACROSS

1 San _____, Italian resort city
5 "Eli _____ unto her" (1 Samuel 1:14)
9 "This man is a _____" (Acts 22:26)
14 Famous cookie
15 Madrid paintings
16 "To _____ harnessed" (Song of Songs 1:9 NIV) (2 words)
17 "At that day shall the heart of the _____ be as the heart of a woman in her pangs" (Jeremiah 49:22) (4 words)
20 City SW of Honshu, Japan
21 "They _____ my path" (Job 30:13)
22 Decorate again
23 This creature should be the sluggard's role model (Proverbs 6:6)
25 "Eat not of it _____" (Exodus 12:9)

27 "Wake up _____ all the men of war draw near" (Joel 3:9) (4 words)
36 "Lest he _____ thee to the judge" (Luke 12:58)
37 "_____, I have no man" (John 5:7)
38 Amoz's son (2 Kings 20:1)
39 Blue pencils
41 Old horse
43 Lowest deck of seats in a stadium
44 Where Jethro lived (Exodus 3:1)
46 Spanish sun
48 "I cast my _____ against them" (Acts 26:10 NIV)
49 "He had slain Gedaliah the son of Ahikam, _____ war" (Jeremiah 41:16) (4 words)
52 "One beka _____ person" (Exodus 38:26 NIV)

53 "I am as _____ mocked" (Job 12:4)
54 "Passeth through the paths of the _____" (Psalm 8:8)
58 "To a point below Beth _____" (1 Samuel 7:11 NIV)
60 "Thou didst _____ the earth with rivers" (Habbakuk 3:9)
65 "Pass before your brethren armed, _____ of valour" (Joshua 1:14) (4 words)
68 Proportion
69 Sit for an artist
70 "_____ your heart, and not your garments" (Joel 2:13)
71 Inactive
72 "I will give him the morning _____" (Revelation 2:28)
73 Cainan's father (Genesis 5:9)

DOWN

1 Tomato variety
2 Composer Satie
3 Vast
4 _____ and aahs
5 "Their dark _____" (Proverbs 1:6)
6 "As a seal upon thine _____" (Song of Solomon 8:6)
7 Object
8 Tenfold

9 UK fliers (abbr.)
10 "An _____ for every man" (Exodus 16:16)
11 "All things were _____ by him" (John 1:3)
12 "It became _____ in his hand" (Exodus 4:4) (2 words)
13 Captain of the Nautilus
18 Formerly Siamese
19 "_____ trying to please men?" (Galatians 1:10 NIV) (3 words)

24 "Behold, seven _____ ears and blasted" (Genesis 41:6)
26 "This shall be your _____ border" (Numbers 34:6)
27 Student paper
28 If Ovid had II eggs for breakfast and Nero had II, together they _____ (2 "words")
29 Skip or slur over a syllable, as "ma'am"

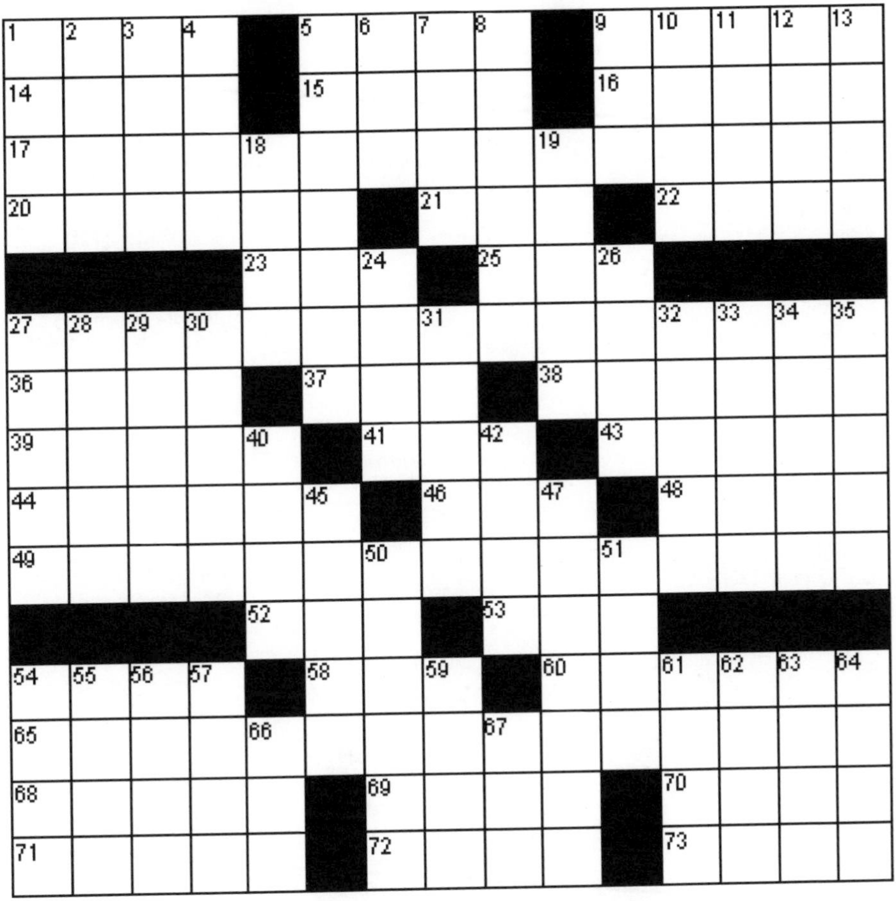

30 "The law might be fully _____ us" (Romans 8:4 NIV) (2 words)

31 Worthless stuff

32 "They deceive the minds of _____ people" (Romans 16:18 NIV)

33 "The camps that _____ the east" (Numbers 10:5) (2 words)

34 "Give _____ my words" (Psalm 5:1) (2 words)

35 "The _____ cometh in" (Hosea 7:1)

40 Cornmeal mush in New England

42 "_____ the pool of Siloam" (John 9:11) (2 words)

45 Dinah, to Esau (Genesis 25:25–26 and Genesis 34:1)

47 Illegal hangman

50 Daddy's dad

51 "Our hearts did _____" (Joshua 2:11)

54 Rani's gown

55 Enthusiasm

56 Old ones (Ger.)

57 "Grievous words _____ up anger" (Proverbs 15:1)

59 "Children not accused of _____ or unruly" (Titus 1:6)

61 Jane _____

62 "These things saith the _____" (Revelation 3:14)

63 _____-vein

64 "The four _____ of the grate of brass" (Exodus 38:5)

66 "When it is _____" (Job 6:17)

67 Organization founded by Juliette Gordon Low (abbr.)

ACROSS

1 Deborah was the only woman of them (abbr.)

4 "Son of _____" (Nehemiah 11:12)

8 "It shall not be lawful to impose _____" (Ezra 7:24)

12 "Pitched in the valley of _____" (Numbers 21:12)

14 "About like _____" (Psalm 118:12)

15 Palal's father (Nehemiah 3:25)

16 Jesus did this at the resurrection

17 "And with the _____" (Deuteronomy 28:27)

18 Circle

19 A son of Jehaleleel (1 Chronicles 4:16)

21 "The half tribe of Manasseh, _____" (Joshua 21:25)

23 David's traitorous son

25 Spinning toy

26 To place

27 Hadar's wife (Genesis 36:39)

30 Saul's grandfather (1 Chronicles 8:33)

33 Shaving tool

34 Abram's wife

38 Bela's father (1 Chronicles 5:8)

40 "The son of Dekar, in _____" (1 Kings 4:9)

42 "The linen _____ at a price" (1 Kings 10:28)

43 Chopped (arch.)

45 One of the wives of Ashur, the father of Tekoa (1 Chronicles 4:5)

47 Adam was the first

48 Rebekah was from here (Genesis 25:20)

51 "Against Jerusalem, _____" (Ezekiel 26:2)

54 Spider's art

55 "The children of Neziah, the children of _____" (Ezra 2:54)

59 A family of exiles (Nehemiah 7:48)

61 Tikvath's father (2 Chronicles 34:22)

62 "Thee in this _____" (2 Kings 9:26)

63 "Now the serpent was more subtil _____ any beast" (Genesis 3:1)

67 Rebuke

68 "_____, and Ivah?" (Isaiah 37:13)

69 The king's chamberlain (Esther 2:3)

70 A son of Ishmael (Genesis 25:15–16)

71 "Alammelech, and _____" (Joshua 19:26)

72 White precipitation

73 Commanded militarily

DOWN

1 "For Elnathan, and for _____" (Ezra 8:16)

2 Rain comes in this form

3 A son of Jahdai (1 Chronicles 2:47)

4 King Hezekiah's mother (2 Kings 18:2)

5 Became acquainted

6 Zechariah (abbr.)

7 "And of _____ twelve thousand men" (2 Samuel 10:6)

8 "_____ away thine eyes" (Song of Solomon 6:5)

9 Joram's son (Matthew 1:8)

10 Spear

11 "Ye are the _____ of the world" (Matthew 5:14)

12 "And the sons of Jonathan; Peleth, and _____" (1 Chronicles 2:33)

13 "The treacherous _____" (Isaiah 21:2)

20 King of Hebron (Joshua 10:3)

22 Larger than monkeys

24 "Matred, the daughter of _____" (Genesis 36:39)

25 "And Rekem, and Irpeel, and _____" (Joshua 18:27)

28 "Shew me a _____ for good" (Psalm 86:17)

29 Set down

30 Prophet to Nineveh (abbr.)

31 Before Daniel (abbr.)

32 Not cooked

35 A male sheep

36 A son of Jether (1 Chronicles 7:38)

37 Motel

39 Before Haggai (abbr.)

41 Pharez's twin brother (Genesis 38:28–30)

44 Sunrise

46 One of the king's chamberlains (Esther 4:5)

49 Paul said he was in these oft (2 Corinthians 11:23)

50 "And out of the tribe of Asher, _____" (Joshua 21:30)

51 First letter of the Greek alphabet

52 "To _____, and to Tobijah" (Zechariah 6:14)

53 A river of Damascus (2 Kings 5:12)

56 This goes before a fall

57 Bedad's son (Genesis 36:35)

58 "Sons of _____"
(1 Chronicles 7:12)

60 Joseph mourned for Jacob at his
threshing floor (Genesis 50:10)

64 Zephaniah's son (Zechariah 6:14)

65 Time past

66 "Behold, I make all things
_____" (Revelation 21:5)

by N. Teri Grottke

63

ACROSS

1 "Then Samuel took a _____ of oil" (1 Samuel 10:1)

5 One of Shaharaim's wives (1 Chronicles 8:8)

10 Saul's grandfather (1 Chronicles 8:33)

13 Island

14 We have five of these

15 Hophni's father (1 Samuel 4:4)

16 "But the water is _____, and the ground barren" (2 Kings 2:19)

18 Zibeon's son (1 Chronicles 1:40)

19 Also

20 "Whether is it _____ to say to the sick" (Mark 2:9)

21 Sleeping place

22 Bit (arch.)

23 Good student

25 Seller of purple

27 "Adami, _____, and Jabneel" (Joshua 19:33)

29 Jehosaphat's chief captain of Judah (2 Chronicles 17:14)

32 "_____ there yet the treasures" (Micah 6:10)

35 A king of Midian (Judges 8:5)

37 "The _____ of a whip" (Nahum 3:2)

38 "Cords of vanity, and sin as it were with a cart _____" (Isaiah 5:18)

40 Before (arch.)

41 Cry loudly

42 "Look from the top of _____" (Song of Solomon 4:8)

44 Father of Rachel and Leah (Genesis 29:16)

47 "Between Bethel and _____" (Genesis 13:3)

48 "And he must _____ go through Samaria" (John 4:4)

49 "The children of _____, the children of Siaha" (Ezra 2:44)

51 Belonging to Shem's father

54 Isaac's wife

58 Arad's brother (1 Chronicles 8:15)

60 Petroleum product

62 "And thou shalt make fifty _____ of gold" (Exodus 26:6)

63 Used to control a horse

64 Temple prophetess in Jesus' time (Luke 2:36–37)

65 Aholibah's sister (Ezekiel 23:4)

66 Last book of the Pentateuch (abbr.)

67 "And the _____ of them and of the chief priests prevailed" (Luke 23:23)

69 Smelling orifice

70 Possessive pronoun

71 "When a strong man _____ keepeth his palace" (Luke 11:21)

72 "The fallow _____" (Deuteronomy 14:5)

DOWN

1 Pumpkins grow on these

2 Abraham's heir

3 Encampment in the wilderness (Numbers 33:13)

4 "Had the _____, sitting, and clothed, and in his right mind" (Mark 5:15)

5 Beryllium (sym.)

6 Canaanite city (Joshua 11:21)

7 Jehu's great-grandfather (1 Chronicles 4:35)

8 Fit

9 A type of tree (Isaiah 44:14)

10 A son of Asaph (1 Chronicles 25:2)

11 Jesus cried this on the cross (Mark 15:34)

12 "The same excess of _____" (1 Peter 4:4)

14 "_____ sail, and so were driven" (Acts 27:17)

17 Eleasah's father (1 Chronicles 2:39)

22 Wife of a dead husband

24 "They _____ against me" (Hosea 7:14)

26 One of Jacob's sons

28 Military commander under Deborah (Judges 4:6–9)

30 Largest continent

31 Jesus' grandfather (Luke 3:23)

32 Son of Dishan (Genesis 36:28)

33 Center of New Testament politics

34 The firstfruits of Achaia unto Christ (Romans 16:5)

36 A grandson of Asher (Genesis 46:17)

39 Saul's witch was from here

43 Solomon's great-grandson (1 Kings 15:8)

45 King of Damascus (2 Corinthians 11:32)

46 This man named a village after himself (Numbers 32:42)

50 Gihon was this river coming out of Eden (Genesis 2:13)

52 Glory

53 "Land of _____" (Isaiah 49:12)

55 Her household reported contentions in the church (1 Corinthians 1:11)

56 Stop

57 One of Jacob's sons
(Genesis 35:26)

58 Ethan's grandfather
(1 Chronicles 6:44)

59 "There was a continual _____
given him of the king of Babylon"
(Jeremiah 52:34)

61 "_____ of blue" (Exodus 39:31)

64 Area near Babylon (2 Kings 17:24)

68 An altar (Joshua 22:34)

ACROSS

1 Saul's father (1 Samuel 9:3)
5 Hophni's father (1 Samuel 4:4)
8 "Where thou _____, I will die" (Ruth 1:17)
13 Jesus cried this on the cross (Mark 15:34)
14 A son of Zerah (1 Chronicles 2:6)
16 One of David's wives (2 Samuel 3:5)
17 "_____ of the earth?" (Ephesians 4:9)
19 Thirty-seventh encampment (Numbers 33:45)
20 "They that _____ networks" (Isaiah 19:9)
21 Bind
22 Opposite of *hers*
24 Ontario (abbr.)
26 So be it
27 "That dippeth with me in the _____" (Mark 14:20)
28 Petroleum product

30 "And _____, and Kedemoth" (Joshua 13:18)
33 First place
35 Type of tree (Isaiah 44:14)
38 Enan's son (Numbers 1:15)
39 "Make thee bonds and _____" (Jeremiah 27:2)
40 "And _____ lay at his feet until the morning" (Ruth 3:14)
41 One of the four Gospels
42 Skin wounds
43 "Nevertheless _____ heart" (1 Kings 15:14)
44 Deceived by the serpent
45 The butler's cell mate
46 Commerce
47 Unhappy
48 Was indebted to
49 "Now when Ezra had _____, and when he had confessed" (Ezra 10:1)

50 "The _____ of their God was upon the Jews" (Ezra 5:5)
51 A duke of Edom (Genesis 36:43)
52 A son of Helem (1 Chronicles 7:35)
55 Accomplish
57 "When _____ king" (2 Samuel 8:9)
58 Capable
61 Observe (arch.)
63 Utilize
65 A son of Manasseh (Numbers 32:39–42)
67 A city on Crete (Acts 27:8)
68 Arabian city (Job 6:19)
70 After eight
71 "At the _____ of the city" (Proverbs 8:3)
72 Book named for a queen (abbr.)
73 Effortless

DOWN

1 Retained
2 "_____ the Ahohite" (1 Chronicles 11:29)
3 Very (arch.)
4 Strike
5 An altar (Joshua 22:34)
6 Phaltiel's father (2 Samuel 3:15)
7 A son of Bela (1 Chronicles 7:7)
8 Ground moisture
9 "_____, and Bariah" (1 Chronicles 3:22)
10 A son of Shem (Genesis 10:22)
11 Rescue
12 "See _____ that ye walk circumspectly" (Ephesians 5:15)
15 Amos (abbr.)

18 Adina's father (1 Chronicles 11:42)
23 "And _____ the prophet cried unto the LORD" (2 Kings 20:11) (abbr.)
25 "_____ have they, but they smell not" (Psalm 115:6)
27 Evil
29 Possessive pronoun
30 One of the sons of thunder
31 Ezra proclaimed a fast there (Ezra 8:21)
32 Employed
33 "The priest took a chest, and _____ a hole in the lid of it" (2 Kings 12:9)
34 A son of Ram (1 Chronicles 2:27)
35 Analysis of an ore

36 Jonah appreciated this
37 "The son of _____" (1 Kings 4:10)
39 Wooden collar (arch.)
42 Used a saw
43 A son of Shem (Genesis 10:22)
45 Lad
46 "_____ up a child" (Proverbs 22:6)
49 Professional (abbr.)
50 One who consumes food
51 Things
52 Island
53 "What _____ ye to weep" (Acts 21:13)
54 Bird home
56 Three strikes and you're _____

by N. Teri Grottke

58 Asa's father (1 Chronicles 3:10)

59 "Baked it in _____"
(Numbers 11:8)

60 "_____ shall see God"
(Matthew 5:8)

62 Livestock feed

64 "_____ that ye refuse"
(Hebrews 12:25)

66 Single

69 Astatine (sym.)

65

Biblical Pairs

So he went out and caught three hundred foxes and tied them tail to tail in pairs. He then fastened a torch to every pair of tails.

JUDGES 15:4 NIV

ACROSS

1 "If an ox _____ a man or a woman" (Exodus 21:28)

5 "With the _____ facing Joppa" (Joshua 19:46 NIV)

9 Olympic gymnast Comaneci

14 "An _____ for every man" (Exodus 16:16)

15 "Or clothe his neck with a flowing _____?" (Job 39:19 NIV)

16 "One for _____" (Matthew 17:4)

17 **BIBLICAL PAIR** from 1 Samuel 17 (3 words)

20 "At whom do you _____" (Isaiah 57:4 NIV)

21 "No one _____ a patch" (Matthew 9:16 NIV)

22 "Passed to the _____ of Cyprus" (Acts 27:4 NIV)

23 "Thou anointest my head with _____" (Psalm 23:5)

24 "Saddled his _____" (Numbers 22:21)

27 A very long time

29 **BIBLICAL PAIR** from Ruth 1

34 "In wrath they _____ me" (Psalm 55:3)

37 "Thou art _____ sister" (Genesis 24:60)

38 "I will break off a tender _____" (Ezekiel 17:22 NIV)

39 Memo notation, meaning to hurry (abbr.)

40 Greek philosopher

43 "With a _____ of blue" (Exodus 28:28)

44 Violin forerunner

46 "Judas had the _____" (John 13:29)

47 Israeli Red Sea port

48 **BIBLICAL PAIR** from Acts 15–17 (3 words)

52 Blackthorn

53 Moon explorer (abbr.)

54 "The _____ isn't there! Where can I turn now? (Genesis 37:30 NIV)

57 Father of Cush (Genesis 10:6)

60 "In the cities of the _____" (Jeremiah 33:13)

62 "Fine linen, and coral, and _____" (Ezekiel 27:16)

64 **BIBLICAL PAIR** from 2 Kings 2 (3 words)

68 Ocean vessel

69 "No, _____ you will be condemned" (James 5:12 NIV) (2 words)

70 Sterling (abbr.)

71 First to reach the North Pole

72 "As he saith also in _____" (Romans 9:25)

73 "Restore all that was _____" (2 Kings 8:6)

DOWN

1 "For _____ loved the world" (John 3:16) (2 words)

2 Man from Muscat

3 Jump for joy

4 One of the Great Lakes

5 "I _____ brother to dragons" (Job 30:29) (2 words)

6 "He _____ before, and climbed up into a sycomore tree" (Luke 19:4)

7 "All the _____ of the earth shall see the salvation of our God" (Isaiah 52:10)

8 Sea between Greece and Turkey

9 Wrestling holds

10 Mr. Baba

11 "By which it had gone down in the _____ of Ahaz" (2 Kings 20:11)

12 "When your words came, _____ them" (Jeremiah 15:16 NIV) (2 words)

13 "Now _____ was speaking with me" (Daniel 8:18) (2 words)

18 Danube feeder (Ger.)

19 "Fellowservants, which _____ him an hundred pence" (Matthew 18:28)

25 "Get thee down, that the rain _____ thee not" (1 Kings 18:44)

26 Synagogue, to a Jew

28 Major Italian port

29 Wards off

30 "Cretans and _____—we hear them" (Acts 2:11 NIV)

31 Type of exam

by David K. Shortess

32 "_____, Rehob, Hashabiah" (Nehemiah 10:11 NIV)

33 "Where can _____ meat for all these people?" (Numbers 11:13 NIV) (2 words)

34 "David took an _____" (1 Samuel 16:23)

35 "I saw as it were _____ of glass" (Revelation 15:2) (2 words)

36 Prohibition (var.)

41 "He is the _____" (Isaiah 9:15)

42 Stare amorously

45 "Which is called _____" (Luke 23:33)

49 Father of Shem (Genesis 5:32)

50 Part of FDR

51 A son of Helem (1 Chronicles 7:35)

54 Sew temporarily

55 "Worship no _____ god" (Exodus 34:14)

56 "A thousand _____ as one day" (2 Peter 3:8)

57 "A very present _____ in trouble" (Psalm 46:1)

58 "That they should believe _____" (2 Thessalonians 2:11) (2 words)

59 "Here is your _____" (Luke 19:20 NIV)

61 Grandson of Adam (Genesis 5:6)

63 Silent star Lillian

65 Follows Isaiah (abbr.)

66 "A loving _____" (Proverbs 5:19 NIV)

67 "Between their teeth, _____ it was chewed" (Numbers 11:33)

ACROSS

1 "My bowels were _____ for him" (Song of Solomon 5:4)

6 "A _____ language" (Zephaniah 3:9)

10 Son of Eliphaz (Genesis 36:11)

14 A river of Damascus (2 Kings 5:12)

15 Greek form of *Asher* (Revelation 7:6)

16 Birth till death

17 Rule

18 Having to do with the priesthood

20 "Of Harim, _____" (Nehemiah 12:15)

21 Possessive pronoun

22 "Prepared unto _____ good work" (2 Timothy 2:21)

23 Salathiel's father (Luke 3:27)

25 Construct

27 Governor on this side of the river (Ezra 5:3)

30 Belonging to me

31 Boy

34 Expect

35 Type of tree (Genesis 30:37)

36 "Out of whose womb came the _____?" (Job 38:29)

37 Hurt

38 Josaphat's son (Matthew 1:8)

39 Furious driver (2 Kings 9:20)

40 Jether's son (1 Chronicles 7:38)

41 Nethinim (Ezra 2:47)

42 Father to eight sons (1 Samuel 17:12)

43 Nehemiah (abbr.)

44 Jabal's mother (Genesis 4:20)

45 Able to die

46 A duke of Edom (Genesis 36:43)

47 Samson slew one thousand Philistines here (Judges 15:12–16)

48 A gem on the third row of the ephod (Exodus 28:19)

51 Winged mammal

52 How the earth was watered before the flood (Genesis 2:6)

56 "The waters unto _____ and Jordan" (Judges 7:24)

59 "This is the sixth _____ with her, who was called barren" (Luke 1:36)

60 Salah's son (Genesis 10:24)

61 A duke of Sihon (Joshua 13:21)

62 Abijah's brother (2 Chronicles 11:20)

63 Phares's brother (Matthew 1:3)

64 Bound

65 Rose sticker

DOWN

1 Feminine name that means "bitter" (Ruth 1:20)

2 Ruth's son (Ruth 4:13–17)

3 Conceited

4 "_____ with her suburbs; four cities" (Joshua 21:29)

5 Rachel's son, whose name means "He has vindicated" (Genesis 30:6 NIV)

6 Son of Raphu (Numbers 13:9)

7 Makes use of

8 Bible's final book (abbr.)

9 A son of Gad (Genesis 46:16)

10 Oily fruit

11 Quick rodents

12 A great distance

13 Depend

19 Means "Thou art weighed in the balances, and art found wanting" (Daniel 5:27)

21 A son of Bela (1 Chronicles 7:7)

24 Consume food

25 "Of the Hermonites, from the hill _____" (Psalm 42:6)

26 "Suburbs, and _____" (1 Chronicles 6:73)

27 A son of Ephraim (Numbers 26:35)

28 Cognizant

29 "Pitched at _____" (Numbers 33:27)

30 Name of bitter spring that Moses sweetened (Exodus 15:23–25)

31 Recline (arch.)

32 Daughter of Caleb (1 Chronicles 2:49)

33 Eliasaph's father (Numbers 1:14)

35 King of Hebron (Joshua 10:3)

38 The brother of Shammai (1 Chronicles 2:28)

39 A son of Bela (1 Chronicles 7:7)

41 "Ira an Ithrite, _____ an Ithrite, Uriah the Hittite: thirty and seven in all" (2 Samuel 23:38–39)

42 Dutch for "you"

45 Became acquainted

46 Amasa's father (2 Samuel 17:25)

47 Jahath's son (1 Chronicles 4:2)

48 "Kishion, and _____" (Joshua 19:20)

49 A priestly city of Benjamin (Joshua 21:17)

50 "_____, Hizkijah, Azzur" (Nehemiah 10:17)

by N. Teri Grottke

51 "The ______ lying in a manger" (Luke 2:16)

53 "______ the waters" (Exodus 15:25)

54 Night sky illuminator

55 "The seven ______ ears devoured the seven rank" (Genesis 41:7)

57 Are (arch.)

58 "Shimei, and ______" (1 Kings 1:8)

59 Floor cover

67

ACROSS

1 Ground moisture
4 "Cheeks, and the _____"
(Deuteronomy 18:3)
7 Before (arch.)
10 Daniel had a vision by this river
(Daniel 8:1–2)
12 At once (Mark 1:30)
14 Married a foreign wife in exile
(Ezra 10:34)
15 "_____ the Son, lest he be
angry" (Psalm 2:12)
16 "Habor, and _____"
(1 Chronicles 5:26)
17 Jesus raised a young man from
the dead here (Luke 7:11)
19 "To _____ you, and to comfort
you" (1 Thessalonians 3:2)
21 A son of Saul (1 Samuel 14:49)
23 Zibeon's son (1 Chronicles 1:40)
24 Number

25 A rebuilder of the wall
(Nehemiah 3:25)
29 "Have renounced the _____
things" (2 Corinthians 4:2)
32 A city in Naphtali
(Joshua 19:32–38)
34 "His city was _____"
(Genesis 36:39)
35 Talmai's father (Numbers 13:22)
39 "The same vail _____ away"
(2 Corinthians 3:14)
41 "As _____ babes, desire the
sincere milk of the word"
(1 Peter 2:2)
43 Eliasaph's father (Numbers 3:24)
44 Summit
46 "Mary the mother of James, and
_____" (Mark 16:1)
47 Abraham bought the cave of
Machpelah from him
(Genesis 23:16–18)

50 Hearing is one
51 "Nor _____ my love, until he
please" (Song of Solomon 8:4)
54 "As he that lieth upon the top of a
_____" (Proverbs 23:34)
56 Chelub's son (1 Chronicles 4:11)
57 "And I answered him, I am an
_____" (2 Samuel 1:8)
62 Horses are steered with these
63 King of Sodom (Genesis 14:2)
64 Enoch's son (Genesis 4:18)
65 "Shimei, and _____" (1 Kings 1:8)
66 "_____ the Ahohite"
(1 Chronicles 11:29)
67 Claudius commanded all Jews to
depart from here (Acts 18:2)
68 King Baasha fought with him all
their days (1 Kings 15:32)
69 Transgression
70 Saul's grandfather
(1 Chronicles 8:33)

DOWN

1 Esau's sons held this title
(Genesis 36:15)
2 Belonging to Eli (poss.)
3 "Even thou _____ as one of
them" (Obadiah 1:11)
4 A son of Merari (Numbers 3:20)
5 "Mattithiah, and Shema, and
_____" (Nehemiah 8:4)
6 Adoration
7 Timothy's mother (2 Timothy 1:5)
8 "A living sacrifice, holy,
acceptable unto God, which
is your _____ service"
(Romans 12:1)
9 Elkanah's grandfather
(1 Samuel 1:1)
11 Isaiah (abbr.)
13 Nahum (abbr.)

18 Joshua's father (Numbers 11:28)
20 King of Moab (Numbers 22:4)
22 Italy (abbr.)
25 Apostle to the Gentiles
26 "Of Harim, _____"
(Nehemiah 12:15)
27 Not on time
28 The Lord told Saul to destroy
these people (1 Samuel 15:1–3)
30 One of Jacob's sons
(Exodus 1:1–4)
31 "Render therefore to all their
_____" (Romans 13:7)
33 A son of Canaan (Genesis 10:15)
36 12:00 p.m.
37 Weapons
38 "Every _____ should bow"
(Philippians 2:10)

40 "_____ was an hair of their
head" (Daniel 3:27)
42 Garbage
45 "To cover the two _____ of the
chapiters" (2 Chronicles 4:13)
48 Cyrus was king here
(2 Chronicles 36:22)
49 Ezbai's son (1 Chronicles 11:37)
51 "Before Abraham was, I _____"
(John 8:58)
52 Spider's art
53 Enan's son (Numbers 1:15)
55 Killed
57 King Hezekiah's mother
(2 Kings 18:2)
58 The people of Syria were to go
into captivity here (Amos 1:5)
59 Strong metal

60 Gentle

61 "Mahli, and _____"
(1 Chronicles 23:23)

68

ACROSS

1 Adam was the first
4 "He is a _____, which is one inwardly" (Romans 2:29)
7 Area near Babylon (2 Kings 17:24)
10 Lotan's son (1 Chronicles 1:39)
12 Ahira's father (Numbers 1:15)
14 Manna was measured in this unit (Exodus 16:15–16)
15 Disciples did this to Jesus in the storm
16 In this place
17 "One to his _____, another to his merchandise" (Matthew 22:5)
18 Inside
19 "Your brethren, _____" (Hosea 2:1)
20 Birds do this
21 "Destitute of _____ food" (James 2:15)
23 Son of Gad (Genesis 46:16)

25 Prophet to the Edomites (abbr.)
28 "But the wheat and the _____ were not smitten" (Exodus 9:32)
29 Crop-destroying insect
33 After Zechariah (abbr.)
34 Micaiah's father (1 Kings 22:8)
37 Paul and Silas were sent by night here (Acts 17:10)
38 Esau's father-in-law (Genesis 26:34)
40 Before (arch.)
41 Wealthy
42 Entrances to cities
44 Big
47 "Against Jerusalem, _____" (Ezekiel 26:2)
48 "Who is the firstfruits of _____ unto Christ" (Romans 16:5)
50 "Altogether for _____ sakes?" (1 Corinthians 9:10)

51 Biggest star in our solar system
52 Male sheep
53 "Up and down in _____" (Acts 27:27)
55 Twenty-first letter of the Greek alphabet
57 Rephaiah's father (1 Chronicles 4:42)
59 Commerce
63 Dog parasite
64 Heber's father (Luke 3:35)
65 "Ran greedily after the _____ of Balaam for reward" (Jude 1:11)
66 Strong promise
67 Breadth
68 Not drunk
69 Right hand (abbr.)
70 "Canaan shall be _____ servant" (Genesis 9:26)
71 Fight between countries

DOWN

1 "Rain upon the _____ grass" (Psalm 72:6)
2 Manasseh's son (2 Kings 21:18)
3 Not clothed
4 Azariah's father (2 Chronicles 29:12)
5 Foe
6 "The flesh of the child waxed _____" (2 Kings 4:34)
7 "Shelesh, and _____" (1 Chronicles 7:35)
8 "That the Lord is _____ pitiful, and of tender mercy" (James 5:11)
9 Attached to the shoulder
10 "Between Bethel and _____" (Genesis 13:3)
11 Brother of Gershon (Genesis 46:11)

13 "_____, and goeth out" (Joshua 19:27)
14 Comissioned soldier
22 Thirty-seventh encampment (Numbers 33:45)
24 Steal
25 Ending
26 "Who taught _____ to cast a stumblingblock" (Revelation 2:14)
27 "In Asher and in _____" (1 Kings 4:16)
30 Greek form of *Uriah* (Matthew 1:6)
31 "Great well that is in _____" (1 Samuel 19:22)
32 Son of Ephraim (Numbers 26:35)
35 Jether's son (1 Chronicles 7:38)
36 "Took counsel with the _____ against him" (Mark 3:6)

39 Shemaiah's son (1 Chronicles 3:22)
43 "The children of _____" (Nehemiah 7:47)
45 "Going up to _____, which is by Ibleam" (2 Kings 9:27)
46 Descendants of Eri
49 Wrong
53 Sheshan's daughter (1 Chronicles 2:31)
54 "_____ cannot make him flee" (Job 41:28)
55 "I will requite thee in this _____" (2 Kings 9:26)
56 A son of Caanan (Genesis 10:15)
58 Giant (2 Samuel 21:18)
60 Father of Anak (Joshua 15:13)
61 "Rewardeth the proud _____" (Psalm 31:23)

62 Make a mistake

63 "Who gave himself _____ our sins" (Galatians 1:4)

by N. Teri Grottke

69

Prepaid

But because of his great love for us, God, who is rich in mercy, made us alive with Christ even when we were dead in transgressions.

Ephesians 2:4–5 NIV

ACROSS

1 Cellular blueprints

5 Buncos

10 "Fools, yea, children of _____ men" (Job 30:8)

14 "The harvest is _____" (Joel 3:13)

15 "As for Saul, he made _____ of the church" (Acts 8:3 NKJV)

16 "The sons of Dishan; Uz, and _____" (1 Chronicles 1:42)

17 "Even in laughter the heart may _____" (Proverbs 14:13 NIV)

18 Athenian market

19 "I am _____ also" (2 Corinthians 11:21)

20 Start of **QUOTE** from Romans 5:8 (4 words)

23 Passover feast

24 Racing craft

25 "Will live, even though he _____" (John 11:25 NIV)

28 "Below the _____ of Pisgah" (Deuteronomy 3:17 NIV)

32 "Ye shall eat the _____ of the land" (Genesis 45:18)

35 "One for _____" (Matthew 17:4)

38 "_____ went forth, and his sons" (Genesis 8:18)

39 "Let us make man in _____ image" (Genesis 1:26)

40 **QUOTE**, cont'd

43 "When ye pray, _____ not vain repetitions" (Matthew 6:7)

44 "No _____ will pitch his tent there" (Isaiah 13:20 NIV)

46 "Will you not _____ them?" (Isaiah 48:6 NIV)

47 "_____ skins of rams" (Exodus 35:23)

48 "That thou _____ the burden of all this people upon me?" (Numbers 11:11)

51 "What profit is _____ we slay our brother" (Genesis 37:26) (2 words)

53 "Thou shalt not _____" (Exodus 20:15)

56 "His wrath can _____ up in a moment" (Psalm 2:12 NIV)

60 End of **QUOTE** (4 words)

65 "Whither have ye made a _____ to day?" (1 Samuel 27:10)

66 Type of musical composition

67 Gypsy men

68 Sheriff Andy's boy

69 "They _____ gods?" (Jeremiah 16:20) (2 words)

70 "I was blind, now _____" (John 9:25) (2 words)

71 "He who _____ souls is wise" (Proverbs 11:30 NIV)

72 Four-door auto

73 "His _____ with ravin" (Nahum 2:12)

DOWN

1 "Now the reaper _____ his wages" (John 4:36 NIV)

2 Hole in the wall

3 Plant pest

4 Stitched closed the eyes of a falcon

5 *Pygmalion* writer

6 "As a _____ is full of birds" (Jeremiah 5:27)

7 Asserts

8 "Sichem, unto the plain of _____" (Genesis 12:6)

9 Shakes up

10 Cyrus's domain (Ezra 5:13)

11 "My beloved is like _____" (Song of Solomon 2:9) (2 words)

12 "Nibshan, and the city of _____" (Joshua 15:62)

13 "What is mine _____" (Job 6:11)

21 The canal, the lake, and its port

22 Right-angle pipe fitting

26 "He ran unto _____, and said" (1 Samuel 3:5)

27 "Made them _____ great sin" (2 Kings 17:21) (2 words)

29 "In those days will I _____ out my spirit" (Joel 2:29)

by David K. Shortess

30 "I was at _____" (Job 16:12)

31 "Which is _____ for you" (Luke 22:20)

32 "Binding his _____ unto the vine" (Genesis 49:11)

33 Emanation

34 Serving aid

36 "_____ it came to pass" (Exodus 1:21)

37 Highway rig

41 Home dye brand

42 "Speak not with a _____ neck" (Psalm 75:5)

45 "Hast thou here any _____?" (Genesis 19:12)

49 Avenue crossers (abbr.)

50 Tropical fish

52 Quite flushed

54 "How right they are to _____ you!" (Song of Songs 1:4 NIV)

55 "He _____ its interior walls with cedar boards" (1 Kings 6:15 NIV)

57 "Jesus _____" (Matthew 9:19)

58 Cud reservoir

59 Slalom tracks

60 "The cock shall not _____" (John 13:38)

61 Arizona tribe

62 "That there be no _____" (Deuteronomy 11:17)

63 Author Ferber

64 "To _____ the sabbath days?" (Luke 6:2) (2 words)

70

ACROSS

1 Be indebted to (arch.)
6 "Wilderness of _____" (Exodus 15:22)
10 Only New Testament history book
14 Moza's son (1 Chronicles 8:37)
15 Comfort
16 Specific one
17 Nearly extinct
19 Type of weed
20 "_____ verily, their sound" (Romans 10:18)
21 Bird homes
22 King of Tyre (1 Chronicles 14:1)
23 "And forgive us our _____" (Matthew 6:12)
24 Mizzah's brother (Genesis 36:13)
25 June (abbr.)

27 "Helez the Paltite, _____" (2 Samuel 23:26)
28 Bottom layer on shoes
29 The earth was destroyed by a flood this many times
31 Son of Ribai (1 Chronicles 11:31)
33 Habakkuk (abbr.)
36 "Ye shall point out for you mount _____" (Numbers 34:7)
37 "Which maketh Arcturus, _____, and Pleiades" (Job 9:9)
38 Caleb's son (1 Chronicles 4:15)
39 Solomon's great-grandson (1 Kings 15:8)
40 "Bodily _____ like a dove" (Luke 3:22)
41 Son of Eliphaz (Genesis 36:11)
42 "For he that is dead is _____ from sin" (Romans 6:7)
44 Spider's art

46 Near
47 Rob
48 A river of Damascus (2 Kings 5:12)
50 Takes a break
51 Celebratory meal
52 Which person?
55 "Your brethren, _____" (Hosea 2:1)
56 Set apart for service
58 "Moses drew _____" (Exodus 20:21)
59 "Sallu, _____, Hilkiah" (Nehemiah 12:7)
60 Realm
61 Cattle
62 "Captains over _____, and officers among your tribes" (Deuteronomy 1:15)
63 Finished

DOWN

1 To carry out directions
2 Intoxicating grape juice
3 "In the two _____ of the mercy seat" (Exodus 25:18)
4 Large lake
5 "He lodgeth with one Simon a _____" (Acts 10:6)
6 "What thou _____, write in a book" (Revelation 1:11)
7 "_____ that find no pasture" (Lamentations 1:6)
8 Makes use of
9 Scarlet
10 Clothing
11 "The father of the valley of _____" (1 Chronicles 4:14)
12 "Pitched at _____" (Numbers 33:27)
13 Originate

18 A priestly city of Benjamin (Joshua 21:17)
22 Jesus' grandfather (Luke 3:23)
23 Pass away
24 "Surely the princes of _____ are fools" (Isaiah 19:11)
25 Jediael's brother (1 Chronicles 11:45)
26 Seth's son (Genesis 4:26)
28 Foot covering
30 "And no _____, of whatsoever craft he be" (Revelation 18:22)
31 Enoch's son (Genesis 4:18)
32 "Dip the _____ of his finger in water" (Luke 16:24)
34 "_____, and Dumah" (Joshua 15:52)
35 "Suffer me first to go and _____ my father" (Luke 9:59)

37 A son of Zerubbabel (1 Chronicles 3:19–20)
40 "And falling into a place where two _____ met" (Acts 27:41)
41 This man found King Ahab for Elijah (1 Kings 18) (abbr.)
43 Go to sleep
44 "Even thou _____ as one of them" (Obadiah 1:11)
45 Whole
47 A son of Joseph (Luke 3:26)
48 A baptismal site of John the Baptist (John 3:23)
49 "When Israel turneth their _____ before their enemies!" (Joshua 7:8)
50 "That could keep _____, came with a perfect heart" (1 Chronicles 12:38)

by N. Teri Grottke

51 Renown

52 "Driven with the _____ and tossed" (James 1:6)

53 The king's chamberlain (Esther 2:3)

54 Azariah's father (2 Chronicles 15:1)

56 "Moses. . ._____ down by a well" (Exodus 2:15)

57 Disperse

71

ACROSS

1 Tear
4 Adam and Eve's book (abbr.)
7 Poisonous snakes
11 This man had visions about wheels (abbr.)
12 "Helkath, and _____" (Joshua 19:25)
13 A son of Beriah (1 Chronicles 8:16)
14 "_____ there yet the treasures" (Micah 6:10)
15 Esau's father-in-law (Genesis 26:34)
16 "Suddenly there _____ round about him a light" (Acts 9:3)
18 "The harvest is _____" (Joel 3:13)
20 Untruth
21 Vocalist
22 Twenty-first letter of the Greek alphabet
24 Total

25 Caleb was one (Numbers 13)
26 "The grace of the _____ of it perisheth" (James 1:11)
30 Rip
32 One of Jacob's sons (Genesis 35:26)
33 "_____ the Canaanite" (Numbers 21:1)
35 Enrollment in neighboring schools
39 "_____ every man to go out from me" (Genesis 45:1)
40 Jephthah fled to there (Judges 11:3)
41 "_____ of Judah" (2 Samuel 6:2)
42 Jacob's brother
43 "Thou shalt be for _____ to the fire" (Ezekiel 21:32)
44 Get up
45 Esau lived here
47 Came in

49 Jether's son (1 Chronicles 7:38)
52 Partook
53 She replaced Queen Vashti (abbr.)
54 "In that _____ thou truly" (John 4:18)
56 Knight
58 Corridor
62 Jesus' Roman judge
63 Farthest part
65 Buzzing stinger
66 A son of Zebulun (Genesis 46:14)
67 Male pig
68 King Hezekiah sought his advice (2 Kings 19:1–2) (abbr.)
69 "Mahli, and _____" (1 Chronicles 23:23)
70 "Destroy _____ kings and people" (Ezra 6:12)
71 Type of tree (Isaiah 44:14)

DOWN

1 Back guard
2 "The fourth to _____" (1 Chronicles 25:11)
3 "Wizards that _____, and that mutter" (Isaiah 8:19)
4 "And when _____ was the deputy of Achaia" (Acts 18:12)
5 Jesus cried this on the cross (Mark 15:34)
6 After eight
7 An idol of Hamath (2 Kings 17:30)
8 Turn quickly
9 Labor pains (arch.)
10 Fleecy ruminant
12 Masculine pronoun
13 Came forth
17 Parched

19 Place where Paul encountered disciples of John the Baptist (Acts 19)
23 Employ
24 Horse enclosure
26 Visage
27 "Nevertheless _____ heart" (1 Kings 15:14)
28 Hotham's sister (1 Chronicles 7:32)
29 "Setteth on fire the course of _____" (James 3:6)
31 "As when a lion _____" (Revelation 10:3)
34 Small deer
36 Couple
37 Otherwise

38 Lack
41 Winged mammals
43 "Vessels of wrath _____ to destruction" (Romans 9:22)
46 Resurrection holiday
48 "Cuth made _____" (2 Kings 17:30)
49 "And the sucking child shall play on the hole of the _____" (Isaiah 11:8)
50 Elevate
51 Was ill
55 "Even _____ to die" (Romans 5:7)
56 "_____ shall offer gifts" (Psalm 72:10)
57 Image

by N. Teri Grottke

59 Asa's father (1 Chronicles 3:10)

60 A smaller quantity

61 Rachel's sister

64 Judah's firstborn (Numbers 26:19)

72

ACROSS

1 "And _____ him" (Judges 16:16)
6 Boaz's wife
10 "Do not _____ the edge" (Ecclesiastes 10:10)
14 Stop
15 Priest during the reign of King Artaxerxes (Ezra 7:11)
16 Jesus' grandfather (Luke 3:23)
17 A son of Aaron (Exodus 6:23)
18 Hananiah's father (Jeremiah 28:1)
19 Manna was measured in this unit (Exodus 16:15–16)
20 Spear
21 Hasty
22 "Whosoever shall say to his brother, _____, shall be in danger of the council" (Matthew 5:22)
23 Elderly
25 "I will pay ten thousand _____ of silver" (Esther 3:9)
27 A son of Joktan (Genesis 10:27)

30 Son of Bani (Ezra 10:34)
33 Unhappy
34 Land east of Eden (Genesis 4:16)
35 Understand
37 Aaron's brother
41 Jesus raised a young man from the dead here (Luke 7:11-15)
43 One who consumes food
45 "As he that lieth upon the top of a _____" (Proverbs 23:34)
46 Inside
48 Naomi wanted to be called this (Ruth 1:20)
49 "Name of his city was _____" (1 Chronicles 1:50)
50 Deep hole
52 Rope web
53 "Wilderness of _____" (Exodus 15:22)
54 Shooters of arrows

58 A son of Benjamin (Genesis 46:21)
60 Close
61 Jezebel's husband (1 Kings 16:30–31)
64 Type of leaf the dove brought Noah (Genesis 8:11)
68 "The men of the other _____" (Nehemiah 7:33)
69 "That at the _____ of Jesus" (Philippians 2:10)
70 Rulers' nationality at Jesus' time
71 Largest continent
72 Clothed
73 Zebulun's border turned eastward from this city (Joshua 19:12)
74 "That which _____ been" (Ecclesiastes 6:10)
75 Type of trees
76 Belonging to _____ Pasha, German explorer (poss.)

DOWN

1 "Even unto Ithiel and _____" (Proverbs 30:1)
2 Prince slain with Evi, Rekem, Zur, and Hur (Numbers 31:8)
3 Increase
4 Mamre's brother (Genesis 14:13)
5 Eliasaph's father (Numbers 1:14)
6 Support
7 Shimei's son (1 Chronicles 6:29)
8 "I _____ that through your prayers I shall be given unto you" (Philemon 1:22)
9 Tikvah's father (2 Kings 22:14)
10 "O Ephraim, thou committest _____" (Hosea 5:3)
11 "_____, and Chalcol" (1 Kings 4:31)

12 Selected ones
13 A son of Japheth (Genesis 10:2)
24 Esau's sons held this title (Genesis 36:15)
26 Twenty-fifth book of the OT (abbr.)
27 "_____, their brethren" (Nehemiah 12:9)
28 "Surely the princes of _____ are fools" (Isaiah 19:11)
29 Returned exiles from Ezra 2:15
31 "Tappuah, and _____" (Joshua 15:34)
32 A son of Seir the Horite (Genesis 36:20)
36 "And _____ destroyed of the destroyer" (1 Corinthians 10:10)

38 A son of the giant (2 Samuel 21:18)
39 Jacob's brother
40 Mix
42 "Unto the fountain of the water of _____" (Joshua 15:9)
44 Charge
47 "The wheat and the _____ were not smitten" (Exodus 9:32)
51 "In a _____ I saw a vision" (Acts 11:5)
53 "Go, wash in the pool of _____" (John 9:7)
54 "The children of _____" (Ezra 2:50)
55 Son of Zorobabel (Luke 3:27)

56 "And which of you. . .can add to his stature one _____?" (Luke 12:25)

57 "The true worshippers _____ worship the Father in spirit and in truth" (John 4:23)

59 Steed

62 "_____, and Shema" (Joshua 15:26)

63 "_____ of spices" (Song of Solomon 6:2)

65 Zaccur's father (Nehemiah 3:2)

66 Conceited

67 "The Lᴏʀᴅ shall judge the _____ of the earth" (1 Samuel 2:10)

by N. Teri Grottke

73

There's Nothing Like This Present!

Every perfect gift is from above.

JAMES 1:17

ACROSS

1 "He _____ it" (Matthew 8:9 NIV)

5 "_____ prophets no harm" (1 Chronicles 16:22) (2 words)

9 "Shall lead _____ with the voice of doves" (Nahum 2:7) (2 words)

14 Formerly Christiana

15 Nabisco treat

16 "How right they are to _____ you!" (Song of Songs 1:4 NIV)

17 Start of a grateful **VERSE** from 2 Corinthians 9:15 (4 words)

20 "Bread _____ in secret is pleasant" (Proverbs 9:17)

21 "Zion: retire, _____ not" (Jeremiah 4:6)

22 Phoenix suburb

23 "I said unto him, _____, thou knowest" (Revelation 7:14)

25 "Rat-_____-tat"

27 "It had _____ horns" (Daniel 7:7)

28 "The foal of an _____" (Zechariah 9:9)

31 "Coated it with _____ and pitch" (Exodus 2:3 NIV)

33 "Their calls will _____ through the windows" (Zephaniah 2:14 NIV)

35 "Know that it is _____, even at the doors" (Matthew 24:33)

37 **VERSE**, cont'd

39 Aikido relative

43 "As Baalath Beer (Ramah in the _____)" (Joshua 19:8 NIV)

45 "Cast the _____ away" (Matthew 13:48)

47 Absalom's sister (2 Samuel 13:1)

48 Positive poles

50 **VERSE**, cont'd

52 Droop

53 "Out of the _____ of Jesse" (Isaiah 11:1)

55 Land east of Eden (Genesis 4:16)

57 "That they may _____ your good works" (Matthew 5:16)

58 Bit of current

61 Bravos in Baja

63 "Under your arms to _____ the ropes" (Jeremiah 38:12 NIV)

65 Constricting snakes

67 "They _____ man from Cyrene" (Matthew 27:32 NIV) (2 words)

69 "Then appeared the _____ also" (Matthew 13:26)

73 End of **VERSE** (2 words)

76 Sioux tribe branch

77 Stare amorously

78 Bony beginning (prefix)

79 "All my _____ shall Tychicus declare unto you" (Colossians 4:7)

80 "Go and _____ them" (Genesis 29:7)

81 "That he may set his _____ on high" (Habbakuk 2:9)

DOWN

1 "They shall _____" (Jeremiah 50:36)

2 US industrial safety watchdog

3 Israeli Red Sea port

4 Loudness units

5 Bill Gates created this while working for IBM

6 Sun and moon

7 "Her whelps _____ man" (Proverbs 17:12) (2 words)

8 "_____ no bread" (Deuteronomy 29:6 NIV) (2 words)

9 Fedora, for example

10 "Esau, who is _____" (Genesis 36:1)

11 Thesaurus man

12 "When they _____ early" (1 Samuel 5:4)

13 Kind of Ford

18 "Mine heart shall be _____ unto you" (1 Chronicles 12:17)

19 Village on the Hudson

24 Opposite of *plaintiff* (abbr.)

26 "In the corners of the streets, (26) they may be (29) of men" (Matthew 6:5)

28 Daughter of Phanuel (Luke 2:36)

29 See 26 Down

30 Starch-bearing palm

32 "Will a man _____ God?" (Malachi 3:8)

34 Speech-related

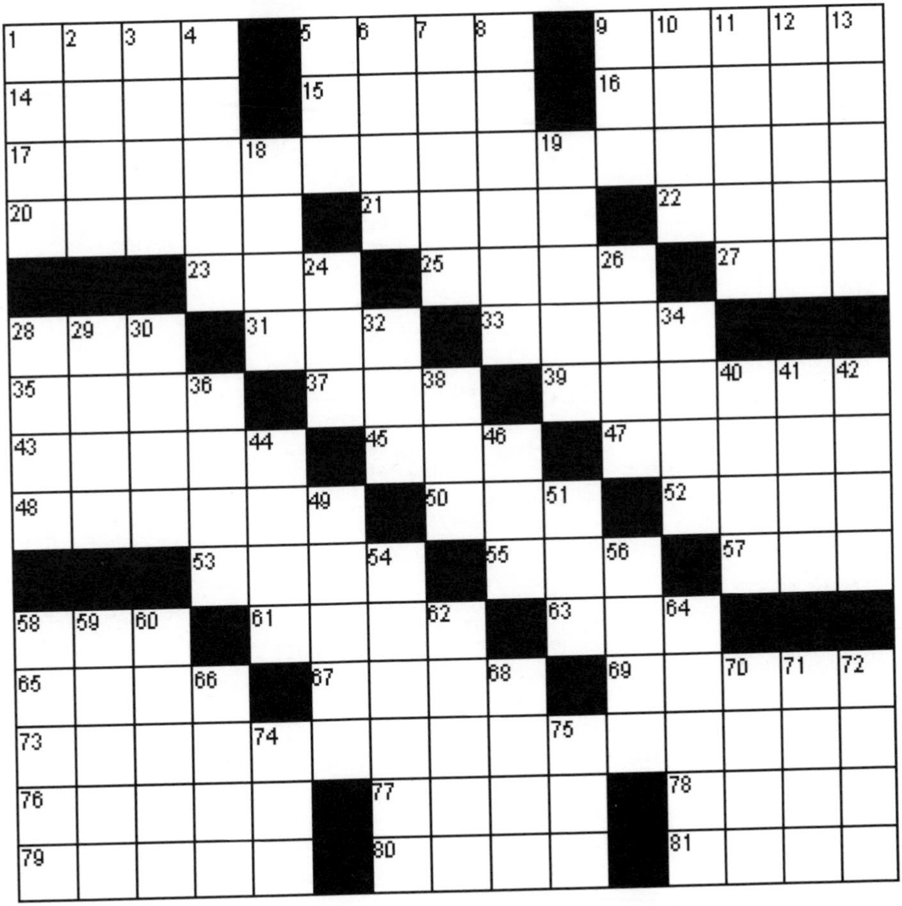

by David K. Shortess

36 Carmine and cinnabar

38 Stadium cry

40 Follows Joel

41 "The _____ of the bricks" (Exodus 5:8)

42 Agatha's colleague

44 Put the kibosh on

46 "He will silence her noisy _____" (Jeremiah 51:55 NIV)

49 Alabama civil rights march town

51 "He it is, to whom I shall give a _____" (John 13:26)

54 "All ye _____ the earth" (Zephaniah 2:3) (2 words)

56 "Son of man, record this _____" (Ezekiel 24:2 NIV)

58 Adjoins

59 Impressionism founder

60 "In times _____ people great" (Deuteronomy 2:10) (2 words)

62 "Ran at flood _____ as before" (Joshua 4:18 NIV)

64 "Set it by _____" (1 Samuel 5:2)

66 "There is no _____ in thee"

(Song of Solomon 4:7)

68 "I have wounded them that they were not (68) to (70)" (Psalm 18:38)

70 See 68 Down

71 Small newts

72 "Let it stand!"

74 Compass point midway northeast and east

75 "Even as ye were _____" (1 Corinthians 12:2)

ACROSS

1 Eshcol's brother (Genesis 14:13)
5 Larger than monkeys
9 "Her _____ was to light" (Ruth 2:3)
12 A son of Gad (Genesis 46:16)
13 Another name for *Zoar* (Genesis 14:2)
14 "_____ shall offer gifts" (Psalm 72:10)
15 Zebulun's border turned eastward from this city (Joshua 19:12)
16 A son of Caleb (1 Chronicles 4:15)
17 A son of Joktan (Genesis 10:27)
18 Belonging to Abimelech
20 Stakes
21 Not easily found
22 A bird forbidden to eat (Deuteronomy 14:12)
24 Jerusalem (Joshua 18:28)

28 "_____ the waters" (Exodus 15:25)
29 "Children of _____" (Ezra 2:15)
30 Amos' father (Luke 3:25)
33 King David's music leader
37 David did this before the ark
39 Cain and Abel's book (abbr.)
40 Ithai's father (1 Chronicles 11:31)
41 A son of Caleb (1 Chronicles 2:18)
42 A son of Shem (Genesis 10:22)
44 "And straightway they forsook their _____" (Mark 1:18)
45 "And in the _____" (Deuteronomy 1:7)
47 "They shall mount up with wings as _____" (Isaiah 40:31)
49 "That which was spoken by _____ the prophet" (Matthew 2:17)
52 Jezebel's husband

54 "Mahli, and _____" (1 Chronicles 23:23)
55 "He that hateth _____ is sure" (Proverbs 11:15)
61 "_____ him vehemently" (Luke 11:53)
62 "The fourth to _____" (1 Chronicles 25:11)
63 Unbaked bread
64 Descendants
65 Sadoc's father (Matthew 1:14)
66 Moses' father (Exodus 6:20)
67 "The world through _____ might be saved" (John 3:17)
68 "Put them under _____, and under harrows of iron" (2 Samuel 12:31)
69 This will be cast into the lake of fire

DOWN

1 "_____, and Dumah" (Joshua 15:52)
2 Salathiel's father (Luke 3:27)
3 Fifth encampment (Numbers 33:9)
4 "The horses and their _____ shall come down" (Haggai 2:22)
5 Saul's first cousin (1 Samuel 14:50)
6 Jesus is the Prince of this
7 King Hoshea's father (2 Kings 15:30)
8 Nazarite judge
9 Seventeenth order of the priesthood (1 Chronicles 24:15)
10 A river of Damascus (2 Kings 5:12)
11 "Say to the sick of the _____" (Mark 2:9)

12 Solomon's great-grandson (1 Kings 15:8)
14 "_____ that gain is godliness" (1 Timothy 6:5)
19 "I have _____ still" (Job 3:13)
23 Night sky illuminator
24 The brother of Shammai (1 Chronicles 2:28)
25 "Tower of _____" (Genesis 35:21)
26 "To _____ all that call on thy name" (Acts 9:14)
27 "They _____ the roof where he was" (Mark 2:4)
28 A son of Helem (1 Chronicles 7:35)
31 Shammah's father (2 Samuel 23:11)
32 A son of Bani (Ezra 10:34)

34 Cain's victim
35 Scalp
36 Snake sound
38 "Tappuah, and _____" (Joshua 15:34)
43 Flesh food
46 Chief captain (Acts 24)
48 A son of Midian (Genesis 25:4)
49 Aholibamah's son (Genesis 36:5)
50 "Og the king of Bashan, which dwelt at Astaroth in _____" (Deuteronomy 1:4)
51 A son of Jahdai (1 Chronicles 2:47)
52 "The _____ cannot" (Job 41:28)
53 People who inherit
56 Shimei's son (1 Chronicles 6:29)

57 "Let fall also _____ of the handfuls" (Ruth 2:16)

58 Throw

59 Son of Nathan of Zobah (2 Samuel 23:36)

60 Philemon (abbr.)

by N. Teri Grottke

75

ACROSS

1 Saul's father (1 Samuel 14:51)
5 Flavor
10 "_____ there yet the treasures" (Micah 6:10)
13 Rephaiah's father (1 Chronicles 4:42)
14 A son of David (1 Chronicles 3:5–6)
15 Esau's father-in-law (Genesis 26:34)
16 A son of Caleb (1 Chronicles 4:15)
17 "They were much perplexed _____" (Luke 24:4)
19 A son of Jacob (Genesis 35:26)
20 By yourself
21 "Ye also, as lively stones, are built up a spiritual _____, an holy priesthood" (1 Peter 2:5)
22 "Reprove not a _____" (Proverbs 9:8)

24 Impede
25 "Any of his _____" (Job 34:27)
26 "Out of the _____ clay" (Psalm 40:2)
27 Lean
29 "_____, and Ivah?" (Isaiah 37:13)
30 Sharp-toothed tool
33 Suspend
34 Kings (abbr.)
35 A son of Jehiel (1 Chronicles 9:35–37)
36 Chicken product
37 Prevent
39 "And _____ about" (Revelation 1:13)
40 _____ Lee, maker of bakery products
41 "A _____, and a sword, and a sharp arrow" (Proverbs 25:18)

43 "Destruction and _____ are in their ways" (Romans 3:16)
46 "The _____ of God do set themselves in array against me" (Job 6:4)
49 Ribai's son (2 Samuel 23:29)
50 "By the breath of God _____ is given" (Job 37:10)
52 Rope web
53 "Then came he out of the land of the _____" (Acts 7:4)
55 After eight
56 Weapons
57 Esli's father (Luke 3:25)
58 "_____, Hizkijah, Azzur" (Nehemiah 10:17)
59 "Her _____ was to light" (Ruth 2:3)
60 Clothe
61 Chopped

DOWN

1 Monarchs
2 Abraham's heir
3 "Woe to the land _____ with wings" (Isaiah 18:1)
4 "But Solomon built _____ an house" (Acts 7:47)
5 "Neither let me give flattering _____ unto man" (Job 32:21)
6 Despise
7 "Set it between Mizpeh and _____" (1 Samuel 7:12)
8 Type of weed
9 Before (arch.)
10 Audible
11 Wake up
12 Come in
15 "Ivory and _____" (Ezekiel 27:15)
18 Enan's son (Numbers 1:15)

20 No matter which
23 Resounded
24 Liquid measure (Leviticus 23:13)
26 Maine (abbr.)
27 "And Ezra opened _____ book" (Nehemiah 8:5)
28 Third to last book of the OT (abbr.)
29 Your thigh is connected to this
30 "He spake by his servant Ahijah the _____" (1 Kings 15:29)
31 "To meet the Lord in the _____" (1 Thessalonians 4:17)
32 "_____ ye not what" (Romans 11:2)
34 Kona, Hawaii (airport code)
35 Son of Jakeh (Proverbs 30:1)

37 Zebulun's border turned eastward from this city (Joshua 19:12)
38 Test
40 Impressed stamps
41 "Sent _____ unto them" (Genesis 43:34)
42 Are (arch.)
43 "The word of the Lord that came to _____ the Morasthite" (Micah 1:1)
44 Amasa's father (2 Samuel 17:25)
45 Mail requires this
46 Used to take a live coal off the altar (Isaiah 6:6)
47 "To _____ them again unto repentance" (Hebrews 6:6)
48 "They cast four anchors out of the _____, and wished for the day" (Acts 27:29)

by N. Teri Grottke

50 "God hath not given us the spirit of _____" (2 Timothy 1:7)

51 Uncontrolled anger

54 "Garments, _____ stood" (Zechariah 3:3)

55 Book after Micah (abbr.)

76

ACROSS

1 A son of Zophah
(1 Chronicles 7:36)

5 Garbage

10 Seminary (abbr.)

13 This priest rebuilt the temple

14 "Man named _____" (Acts 9:33)

15 A king of Midian (Numbers 31:8)

16 "Found at _____" (Acts 8:40)

18 Bird home

19 Make angry

20 Load down (arch.)

21 Are (arch.)

22 Gave a loan

23 "And shall water the valley of
_____" (Joel 3:18)

25 Six, _____, eight

27 A child of Lotan (Genesis 36:22)

29 Curses

32 Bottom edge of a garment

35 Ulam's brother (1 Chronicles 7:16)

37 Small bread grain

38 "And _____, and Parah"
(Joshua 18:23)

40 Fuss

41 "Land from _____ to the
wilderness" (Isaiah 16:1)

42 "To _____ them again unto
repentance" (Hebrews 6:6)

44 A son of Ezer (1 Chronicles 1:42)

47 Saul's grandfather
(1 Chronicles 8:33)

48 This goes before destruction

49 "Name of _____" (Judges 1:11)

51 Eleventh Hebrew month
(Zechariah 1:7)

54 Sickness

58 "Used curious _____"
(Acts 19:19)

60 Male sheep

62 King of Lachish (Joshua 10:3)

63 Pass away

64 Land measurement

65 "_____ the most Holy"
(Daniel 9:24)

66 "Borders of _____" (Joshua 11:2)

67 "Put up thy sword into the
_____" (John 18:11)

69 Endurance test

70 Possessive pronoun

71 "Come to _____" (Isaiah 10:28)

72 "See _____ that ye walk
circumspectly" (Ephesians 5:15)

DOWN

1 Impressed stamps

2 Ahio's brother (2 Samuel 6:3)

3 A son of Gad (Genesis 46:16)

4 Despise (arch.)

5 "That _____ command"
(Luke 9:54)

6 Temple prophetess in Jesus' time
(Luke 2:36–37)

7 Prophets (arch.)

8 Flavor

9 Purim's originator (Esther 9:26)

10 Rehoboam the son of Solomon
reigned this many years in Judah
(1 Kings 14:21)

11 "_____ the death of the cross"
(Philippians 2:8)

12 Mixed (arch.)

14 An idol of Hamath (2 Kings 17:30)

17 Complete

22 Belonging to Jacob's first wife
(poss.)

24 "The son of Dekar, in _____"
(1 Kings 4:9)

26 Oath

28 "Eldad and _____ do prophesy
in the camp" (Numbers 11:27)

30 "Lest he _____ thee to the
judge" (Luke 12:58)

31 Night sky illuminator

32 "The joy of the _____ ceaseth"
(Isaiah 24:8)

33 Always

34 "Who maketh his angels spirits,
and his _____ a flame of fire"
(Hebrews 1:7)

36 "My bowels were _____ for him"
(Song of Solomon 5:4)

39 Darius was of the seed of these
(Daniel 9:1)

43 Spider's art

45 Jeroboam's son (1 Kings 14:1)

46 First Hebrew month (Esther 3:7)

50 "Whatsoever things are of good
_____" (Philippians 4:8)

52 "Borders of _____ to Ataroth"
(Joshua 16:2)

53 A son of Micah
(1 Chronicles 8:35)

55 Ahitub's son (1 Samuel 14:3)

56 "For _____ the fathers fell
asleep" (2 Peter 3:4)

57 Consumed

58 Melchi's father (Luke 3:28)

59 "The same excess of _____"
(1 Peter 4:4)

61 Flesh food

64 Solomon's great-grandson
(1 Kings 15:8)

68 Thorium (sym.)

by N. Teri Grottke

77

How God Works

For my thoughts are not your thoughts,
neither are your ways my ways, saith the LORD.
ISAIAH 55:8

ACROSS

1 "I watched the _____ he charged" (Daniel 8:4 NIV) (2 words)
6 Numerical science
10 Josip Broz
14 One-celled animal (var.)
15 Ta-ta in Rome
16 "Neither pray _____ these alone" (John 17:20) (2 words)
17 Start of **QUOTE** from Zechariah 4:6 (3 words)
19 "For her grapes are fully _____" (Revelation 14:18)
20 Tempe, Arizona school (abbr.)
21 Major ingredient of air
23 "And she took a _____" (2 Samuel 13:9)
26 Mork's home
28 Speaker of **QUOTE**
29 Very small matter

31 "Give yourself no_____" (Lamentations 2:18 NIV)
33 "Lord, I am ready _____ with thee" (Luke 22:33) (2 words)
34 "As _____ my fathers were" (Psalm 39:12)
35 "Teachers, having itching _____" (2 Timothy 4:3)
39 **QUOTE**, cont'd (4 words)
43 A son of Mushi (1 Chronicles 23:23)
44 Hankering
45 "This drove which _____?" (Genesis 33:8) (2 words)
47 "I warn you, _____ before" (Galatians 5:21 NIV) (3 words)
50 "Do violence _____ man" (Luke 3:14) (2 words)
51 "The LORD _____" (Isaiah 54:5) (2 words)

55 "The name of the wicked shall _____" (Proverbs 10:7)
57 "Set them in two rows, six on a _____" (Leviticus 24:6)
58 "Then _____ soon as she heard that Jesus was coming" (John 11:20) (2 words)
60 "To _____, Jerusalem" (Jeremiah 25:18)
62 It maintains highways in the Grand Canyon State (abbr.)
63 End of **QUOTE** (3 words)
68 Whirlybird (abbr.)
69 "The singers sang _____" (Nehemiah 12:42)
70 "Leave not thy _____" (Ecclesiastes 10:4)
71 Pooch's remarks
72 Locomotive drivers (abbr.)
73 "_____ of Athens" (Acts 17:22) (2 words)

DOWN

1 "He _____ and worshipped him" (Mark 5:6)
2 Latin 101 word
3 "The LORD _____ Balaam" (Numbers 23:16)
4 "He said, _____ Father" (Mark 14:36)
5 "Let not the king _____" (2 Chronicles 18:7) (2 words)
6 AT&T rival
7 "Champ" or "camp" conclusion

8 One of the Society Islands
9 "Exceeding _____ flame of the fire" (Daniel 3:22) (2 words)
10 A scenic region of the Alps
11 "_____ and prepare a place for you" (John 14:3) (3 words)
12 Sot
13 "Beginning of days _____ of life" (Hebrews 7:3 NIV) (2 words)
18 Washington's Senator Patty

22 "I _____ to those whose sin" (1 John 5:16 NIV)
23 Singer Boone
24 "He slew _____ time" (2 Samuel 23:8) (2 words)
25 "There is _____ beside me" (Isaiah 45:5) (2 words)
27 Brown seaweed
30 "He giveth _____ grace" (James 4:6)
32 Frank _____ Wright

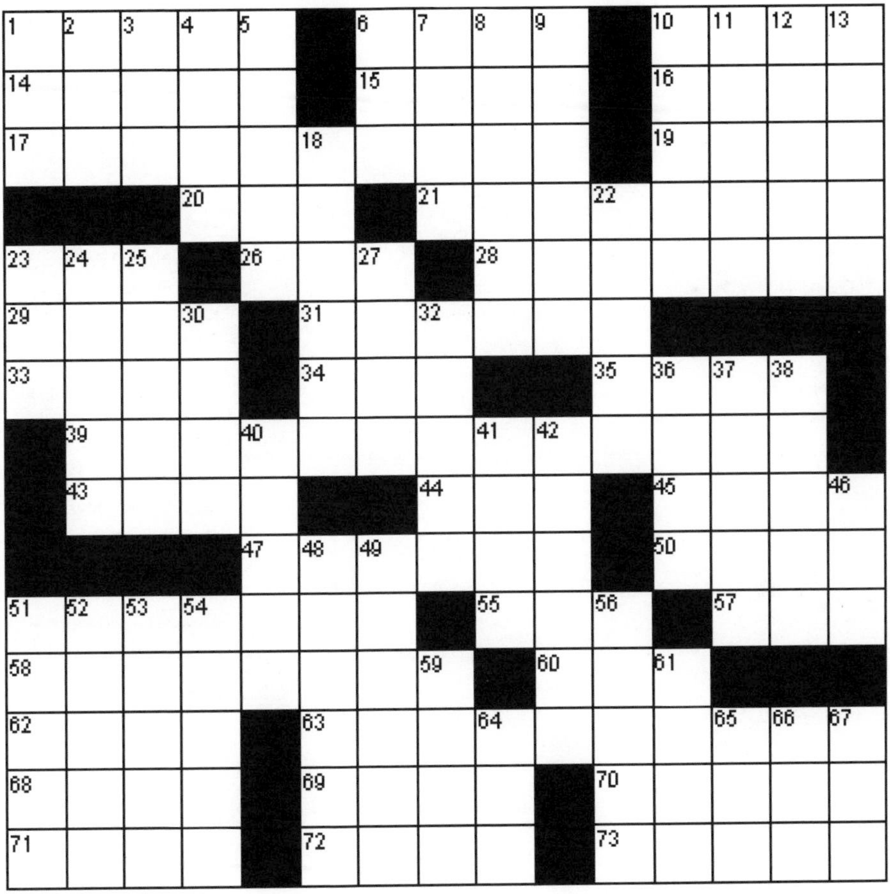

by David K. Shortess

36 "The jaws of the peoples _____ that leads them astray" (Isaiah 30:28 NIV) (2 words)

37 "One _____ comes this year" (Jeremiah 51:46 NIV)

38 Dictation taker (abbr.)

40 Audacious

41 Kind of dam

42 Bestows

46 "As a thread of _____ is broken" (Judges 16:9)

48 "The world also shall be _____" (1 Chronicles 16:30)

49 "Wait, _____ the LORD" (Psalm 27:14) (3 words)

51 City on the Missouri River

52 Volume control

53 First duke of Normandy

54 Preminger and namesakes

56 Like some canoes

59 Narcissistic

61 "Take thee a _____, and lay it before thee" (Ezekiel 4:1)

64 Gridiron gains (abbr.)

65 "A _____ without blemish" (Ezekiel 46:4)

66 "Out of whose womb came the _____?" (Job 38:29)

67 "It came to pass after _____ days" (Jeremiah 42:7)

78

ACROSS

1 "Ye also, as lively stones, are built up a spiritual _____, an holy priesthood" (1 Peter 2:5)

6 Type of tree (Isaiah 44:14)

9 Gave a loan

13 David's incestuous son (2 Samuel 13:1–14)

14 Bite repeatedly

16 "Mahli, and _____" (1 Chronicles 23:23)

17 "Possessors of _____ or houses sold them" (Acts 4:34)

18 Lotan's son (1 Chronicles 1:39)

19 Anak's father (Joshua 15:13)

20 A son of Bela (1 Chronicles 7:7)

21 Problems

23 "_____ before the king" (Esther 6:1)

24 "An he _____ also" (Proverbs 30:31)

25 "The same was Adino the _____" (2 Samuel 23:8)

27 "Hodijah, Bani, _____" (Nehemiah 10:13)

31 Chelub's son (1 Chronicles 27:26)

33 Azariah's father (2 Chronicles 15:1)

34 Load (arch.)

36 Employs

41 Have need of (arch.)

43 He came with Zerubbabel (Nehemiah 7:7)

45 Saul's witch was from here

46 "And _____, and Parah" (Joshua 18:23)

48 Smelling orifice

49 Levite grandfather of Ethan (1 Chronicles 6:44)

51 "The waters were _____ from off the earth" (Genesis 8:11)

53 "Salute _____, our helper in Christ" (Romans 16:9)

57 Not any

59 "Moses drew _____" (Exodus 20:21)

60 King of Damascus (2 Corinthians 11:32)

62 Jether's son (1 Chronicles 7:38)

65 A son of Merari (1 Chronicles 24:27)

66 "Draw _____ to God, and he will draw" (James 4:8)

67 "The children of Sisera, the children of _____" (Nehemiah 7:55)

69 "Captains over _____, and officers among your tribes" (Deuteronomy 1:15)

70 Breadth

71 Idol

72 Otherwise

73 A son of Gad (Genesis 46:16)

74 "The horse and his _____ hath he thrown into the sea" (Exodus 15:1)

DOWN

1 "Helkath, and _____" (Joshua 19:25)

2 Son of Eliphaz (Genesis 36:11)

3 "_____, their brethren" (Nehemiah 12:9)

4 "And Jacob _____ pottage" (Genesis 25:29)

5 "Lifted up as an _____ upon his land" (Zechariah 9:16)

6 Caleb's daughter (1 Chronicles 2:49)

7 Yelled

8 In this place

9 "This only would I _____ of you" (Galatians 3:2)

10 "Og the king of Bashan, which dwelt at Astaroth in _____" (Deuteronomy 1:4)

11 Jeroboam's father (1 Kings 11:26)

12 Commerce

15 "The foolishness of God is _____ than men" (1 Corinthians 1:25)

22 "Even the salvation of your _____" (1 Peter 1:9)

26 "_____ and Gispa were over the Nethinims" (Nehemiah 11:21)

27 Skeletal component

28 First garden

29 Lack

30 Zechariah's father (Ezra 5:1)

32 "Gedaliah, and _____" (1 Chronicles 25:3)

35 Joseph mourned for Jacob at his threshing floor (Genesis 50:10)

37 A son of Helem (1 Chronicles 7:35)

38 "The same excess of _____" (1 Peter 4:4)

39 Comfort

40 Structure built for storage

42 "Shuthelah: of _____" (Numbers 26:36)

44 "Look from the top of _____" (Song of Solomon 4:8)

47 "And offering him _____" (Luke 23:36)

50 "Barley, and _____, and lentiles" (Ezekiel 4:9)

52 "Thou shalt _____ thyself: for then shall the Lᴏʀᴅ go" (2 Samuel 5:24)

53 Bring together

54 "_____ against me" (Hosea 7:14)

55 Farm buildings

56 Get up

58 Shemaiah's son (1 Chronicles 26:7)

61 "The harvest is _____" (Joel 3:13)

62 "Alammelech, and _____" (Joshua 19:26)

63 Uncontrolled anger

64 "Sons of _____" (1 Chronicles 7:12)

68 "Children of _____" (Ezra 2:57)

by N. Teri Grottke

79

ACROSS

1 Deep-water vehicle
5 "Dominion and power, _____ now and ever" (Jude 1:25)
9 "Here am I; _____ art thou, my son?" (Genesis 27:18)
12 Employs
14 Jesus cried this on the cross (Mark 15:34)
15 Team
16 Adrammelech and Sharezer's brother (2 Kings 19:37)
18 Recover
19 Iniquities
20 "And the chief _____ in the synagogues" (Mark 12:39)
21 Divested of honors (var.)

24 "_____ them out of the church" (3 John 1:10)
27 Greek form of *Uriah* (Matthew 1:6)
28 "They are _____ children" (Jeremiah 4:22)
29 Drinking vessel
30 A son of Bani (Ezra 10:34)
31 "_____ there yet the treasures" (Micah 6:10)
32 "Walkest orderly, and _____ the law" (Acts 21:24)
35 Snake sound
39 Single
40 First book (abbr.)
41 "Shimei, and _____" (1 Kings 1:8)
42 Male sibling

44 "Or crookbackt, or a _____" (Leviticus 21:20)
46 "The _____ of whose shoes" (Mark 1:7)
47 Allow
48 "Plains of _____?" (Deuteronomy 11:30)
49 Tibetan monk
50 Above
51 Uzziah's son (1 Chronicles 27:25)
57 Not as much
58 Tree chopping tools
59 Remove hair
60 Mordecai's charge (abbr.)
61 Dwelling
62 Past tense of *spit*

DOWN

1 "_____ held court under the Palm of Deborah" (Judges 4:5 NIV)
2 "_____ heart was filled with pain" (Genesis 6:6 NIV)
3 "Helez the Paltite, _____" (2 Samuel 23:26)
4 Cyrus was king here (2 Chronicles 36:22)
5 "_____ of spices" (Song of Solomon 6:2)
6 Elderly
7 Also
8 Liquid measure (Leviticus 23:13)
9 "Pomegranates on each _____" (2 Chronicles 4:13)
10 "For he shall be like the _____ in the desert" (Jeremiah 17:6)
11 "I am a brother to dragons, and a companion to _____" (Job 30:29)
13 "And there were also with him other little _____" (Mark 4:36)
15 "Carry these ten _____ unto the captain" (1 Samuel 17:18)

17 Tiny insect
20 "Thou that art full of _____" (Isaiah 22:2)
21 "He made him to _____ honey out of the rock" (Deuteronomy 32:13)
22 Not false
23 "The harvest is _____" (Joel 3:13)
24 Twelfth book of the NT (abbr.)
25 Astatine (sym.)
26 Blemish
28 To place
30 Utilize (arch.)
33 "The singers, and the _____" (Ezra 7:7)
34 Methuselah's father (Genesis 5:21)
35 Female objective pronoun
36 A duke of Edom (Genesis 36:43)
37 Salathiel's father (Luke 3:27)
38 Present
40 Acquire

42 "To whom thou _____ witness" (John 3:26)
43 "_____ lifted his eyes and looked" (Joshua 5:13)
44 He forsook Paul (2 Timothy 4:10)
45 "Debates, envyings, _____, strifes" (2 Corinthians 12:20)
46 "There will I give thee my _____" (Song of Solomon 7:12)
47 Cooking vessel
48 Underground rodent
49 "We _____ not" (2 John 1:8)
51 "By his name _____" (Psalm 68:4)
52 One of the books authored by Moses (abbr.)
53 Edge of a garment
54 "Her _____ was to light" (Ruth 2:3)
55 Area near Babylon (2 Kings 17:24)
56 Rope web

by N. Teri Grottke

80

ACROSS

1 Cow's moo
4 "I shall seem to him _____ deceiver" (Genesis 27:12) (2 words)
7 Night flier
10 Mighty man of David (2 Samuel 23:36)
11 "Stand in the _____" (Ezekiel 22:30)
12 Azaziah's son (1 Chronicles 27:20)
15 The field of blood (Acts 1:19)
17 "Things...seen were not made of things which do _____" (Hebrews 11:3)
18 "Otherwise it is of no strength at all while the _____ liveth" (Hebrews 9:17)
19 "The hollow of Jacob's thigh in the sinew that _____" (Genesis 32:32)
20 Bird homes
22 Consume food
23 "Who taught _____ to cast a stumblingblock" (Revelation 2:14)
27 Pure
29 "Three days _____ I fell sick" (1 Samuel 30:13)
30 Arrow ejector
31 "A _____ of dove's dung" (2 Kings 6:25)
34 "Not fulfil the _____ of the flesh" (Galatians 5:16)
35 Eating surface
37 Comfort
38 Allow
39 Verbalize
40 "The children of _____" (Ezra 2:12)
41 "Surely the princes of _____ are fools" (Isaiah 19:11)
43 Clothe
44 Sharp-toothed tool
45 "She _____ upon the Assyrians" (Ezekiel 23:12)
49 "Land of _____" (Genesis 36:34)
52 "And at Bethbirei, and at _____" (1 Chronicles 4:31)
57 Mountain where Jesus liked to go
58 "I have seen an _____ thing in the house of Israel" (Hosea 6:10)
59 "Thence unto _____" (Acts 21:1)
60 Before (arch.)
61 Resting place
62 Gathers her chickens under her wings (Matthew 23:37)
63 "Garments, _____ stood" (Zechariah 3:3)
64 Hophni's father (1 Samuel 1:3)

DOWN

1 "_____ of blue" (Exodus 39:31)
2 "Day of _____ birth" (Ecclesiastes 7:1)
3 "Knowing that thou _____ also do more than I say" (Philemon 1:21)
4 A gem on the third row of the ephod (Exodus 28:19)
5 "Arrived at _____" (Acts 20:15)
6 Separate
7 A bird forbidden to eat (Leviticus 11:13)
8 Small bread grain
9 "_____ not unto thine own understanding" (Proverbs 3:5)
10 This hits a ball
12 Possesses
13 "Moreover the Nethinims dwelt in _____" (Nehemiah 3:26)
14 It "dwelleth between the cherubims" (1 Chronicles 13:6)
16 David liked to _____ before the ark (2 Samuel 6:14)
21 "And the archers _____ at king Josiah" (2 Chronicles 35:23)
23 "Toss thee like a _____ into a large country" (Isaiah 22:18)
24 "The burning _____, that shall consume the eyes" (Leviticus 26:16)
25 Failed to win
26 Tiny insect
28 To be indebted
30 Color of a horse
31 "As a _____ is full of birds" (Jeremiah 5:27)
32 "Nevertheless _____ heart" (1 Kings 15:14)
33 "_____ of spices" (Song of Solomon 6:2)
35 Goodwill message broadcast to a wide audience (abbr.)
36 Real estate
37 Ezra (abbr.)
40 A son of Bela (1 Chronicles 8:3)
41 A child of Ezer (Genesis 36:27)
42 "Believed the master and the _____ of the ship" (Acts 27:11)
44 "_____ a scorner" (Proverbs 19:25)
46 "And Moses called _____ the son of Nun Jehoshua" (Numbers 13:16)
47 Rose sticker
48 "_____ nor sown" (Deuteronomy 21:4)
49 Highest point

50 Hoshea's father (2 Kings 15:30)
51 Book after Solomon's song (abbr.)
53 Upward slope
54 Cain's victim
55 "_____ the Ahohite"
   (1 Chronicles 11:29)
56 Became acquainted

by N. Teri Grottke

81

ACROSS

1 Rephaiah's father
(1 Chronicles 4:42)

5 Opposite of *females*

10 "And Ahijah, Hanan, _____"
(Nehemiah 10:26)

14 "See _____ that ye walk
circumspectly" (Ephesians 5:15)

15 "_____, and Accad"
(Genesis 10:10)

16 Gadite who was one of David's
mighty men (2 Samuel 23:36)

17 "Collar of my _____" (Job 30:18)

18 "To another _____ of spirits"
(1 Corinthians 12:10)

20 "Wrath, strife, seditions, _____"
(Galatians 5:20)

22 One of the wives of Ashur, the
father of Tekoa (1 Chronicles 4:5)

23 The border went to here from
Remmonmethoar (Joshua 19:13)

24 Entrance

26 Toughen

29 Noisy

30 Obese

33 Shammah's father
(2 Samuel 23:11)

34 "As vinegar upon _____"
(Proverbs 25:20)

35 King Hezekiah's mother
(2 Kings 18:1–2)

36 This goes before destruction

38 Single

39 Ophrah was in the land of
_____ (1 Samuel 13:17)

41 Writing tool

42 Watched secretly

44 Too

45 "_____ verily, their sound"
(Romans 10:18)

46 Snake sound

47 "And I will _____ him as a nail in
a sure place" (Isaiah 22:23)

49 Measure (arch.)

50 "The dung _____, and
viewed the walls of Jerusalem"
(Nehemiah 2:13)

51 "Down in _____" (Acts 27:27)

54 Clothing

58 "Teaching, and _____ toward
Jerusalem" (Luke 13:22)

61 The eighth person (2 Peter 2:5)

62 "Eshtemoh, and _____"
(Joshua 15:50)

63 "They came to _____ in
Pamphylia" (Acts 13:13)

64 Nagge's son (Luke 3:25)

65 "_____, and Ivah?" (Isaiah 37:13)

66 Did have (arch.)

67 Not shallow

DOWN

1 "The scab, and with the _____"
(Deuteronomy 28:27)

2 Foot covering

3 "_____, O Israel: The LORD our
God is one LORD"
(Deuteronomy 6:4)

4 "For they _____ evil against
thee" (Psalm 21:11)

5 "And Darius the _____ took the
kingdom" (Daniel 5:31)

6 "Argob and _____"
(2 Kings 15:25)

7 A smaller amount

8 Ecclesiastes (abbr.)

9 "_____ hid the spies we sent"
(Joshua 6:17 NIV)

10 Saul's first cousin
(1 Samuel 14:50)

11 Crucifixion instrument

12 Temple prophetess in Jesus' time

13 "Draw _____ to God, and he will
draw nigh to you" (James 4:8)

19 "Unto _____, and from thence
unto Patara" (Acts 21:1)

21 "_____ that ye refuse not him"
(Hebrews 12:25)

24 "She _____ upon the Assyrians"
(Ezekiel 23:12)

25 "Altogether for _____ sakes?"
(1 Corinthians 9:10)

26 Joyful

27 "_____ with thine adversary
quickly" (Matthew 5:25)

28 "Into my _____"
(Lamentations 3:13)

29 Battles are drawn on these

30 "If a man be overtaken in a
_____" (Galatians 6:1)

31 To humble

32 "Benhanan, and _____"
(1 Chronicles 4:20)

34 "The _____ of a whip"
(Nahum 3:2)

37 A city of Judah (Joshua 15:52)

40 Hurried

43 There is one at the center of a
peach

47 Didn't remember (arch.)

48 This is attached to the shoulder

49 "And Jeuz, and Shachia, and
_____" (1 Chronicles 8:10)

50 Piercing spasms of pain

51 A son of Zibeon (Genesis 36:24)

52 "For he hath _____ marvellous
things" (Psalm 98:1)

by N. Teri Grottke

53 "The _____ of that house was great" (Luke 6:49)

54 "Wherefore _____ up the loins of your mind" (1 Peter 1:13)

55 Smelling orifice

56 Story

57 Deep-water vehicle

59 After the Corinthians (abbr.)

60 Exclamation of affirmation

82

Biblical Waters

[Jesus said,] "Whoever believes in me, as the Scripture has said, streams of living water will flow from within him."

JOHN 7:38 NIV

ACROSS

1 "Whereby we cry, _____, Father" (Romans 8:15)

5 "Shouted _____ if they were thieves" (Job 30:5 NIV) (2 words)

9 "When I looked, behold _____ in the wall" (Ezekiel 8:7) (2 words)

14 Liquid food

15 "A dead _____ flea?" (1 Samuel 24:14 NIV) (2 words)

16 "You were the _____ of perfection" (Ezekiel 28:12 NIV)

17 **BIBLICAL WATER:** "Go, wash in _____" (John 9:7) (4 words)

20 "Thy want as an _____ man" (Proverbs 6:11)

21 "The land of Nod, on the east of _____" (Genesis 4:16)

22 Bond foe (2 words)

23 "The twelfth month, which is the month _____" (Esther 8:12)

25 Follows Monday (abbr.)

27 "For this _____ is mount Sinai in Arabia" (Galatians 4:25)

30 **BIBLICAL WATER:** "Now _____ was there" (John 4:6) (2 words)

35 Halfway

36 "Reprove _____ scorner, lest he hate thee" (Proverbs 9:8) (2 words)

37 Paper fastener

38 "Save the beast that _____ upon" (Nehemiah 2:12) (2 words)

40 Reputed sixth sense

42 "In a moment, in the twinkling of an _____ the last trump" (1 Corinthians 15:52) (2 words)

43 "He saw the _____ of linen lying there" (John 20:6 NIV)

45 Greek god of love

47 British record label

48 **BIBLICAL WATER:** "Their south border was from the shore of _____" (Joshua 15:2) (3 words)

50 "For, behold, the day cometh, that shall burn _____ oven" (Malachi 4:1) (2 words)

51 "Pitched by the valley of _____" (1 Samuel 17:2)

52 "Don't change it" (on a manuscript)

54 Davenport location

57 Malayan sailing outrigger

59 "Who will _____ the battle?" (1 Kings 20:14 NIV)

63 **BIBLICAL WATER:** "Jesus, walking by _____" (Matthew 4:18) (4 words)

66 Tangy apple juice

67 "He hath spread _____ for my feet" (Lamentations 1:13) (2 words)

68 "They put on him a purple _____" (John 19:2)

69 "The _____, and the vails" (Isaiah 3:23)

70 "Temple of Baal and _____ it down" (2 Chronicles 23:17 NIV)

71 "Dwelt in the top of the rock _____" (Judges 15:8)

DOWN

1 Nick and Nora's pooch

2 Danish physics Nobelist Niels

3 Ethnic group in Ghana whose language is Lelemi

4 "He shall _____ in his glory" (Psalm 102:16)

5 "Why make ye this _____, and weep?" (Mark 5:39)

6 "You cannot _____ wrong" (Habbakuk 1:13 NIV)

7 "Am I _____ at hand" (Jeremiah 23:23) (2 words)

8 "They escaped all _____ land" (Acts 27:44) (2 words)

9 "He answered, Here _____" (1 Samuel 3:4) (2 words)

10 "To _____ over the trees?" (Judges 9:9 NIV) (2 words)

11 "By this time there is a bad _____" (John 11:39 NIV)

12 "Yet will they _____ upon the LORD" (Micah 3:11)

13 Sesame Street character

18 "The _____ number of them is to be redeemed" (Numbers 3:48)

19 Ignores

24 Town in SW Arizona

26 _____ Park, Colorado

27 "But there went up _____ from the earth" (Genesis 2:6) (2 words)

by David K. Shortess

28 Circumference

29 "How right they are to _____ you!" (Song of Songs 1:4 NIV)

31 "Is not under bondage in such _____" (1 Corinthians 7:15)

32 Pointless weapons

33 Andean ruminant

34 Admit (2 words)

36 Its capital is Katmandu

39 "He was _____ in his feet" (1 Kings 15:23)

41 Prophet of doom

44 "_____ fine on" (to hand down an abrupt sentence)

46 Cereal grain plant

49 "Took him by the _____" (Matthew 18:28)

50 "Or a bride her _____?" (Jeremiah 2:32)

53 Immigrants' class (abbr.)

54 "Hair has grown in it, the _____ is healed" (Leviticus 13:37 NIV)

55 Mississippi feeder

56 "What shall _____ then?" (Luke 3:10) (2 words)

58 "To speak evil _____ man" (Titus 3:2) (2 words)

60 "There was also _____ for the rest" (Joshua 17:2) (2 words)

61 "_____, five kings of Midian" (Numbers 31:8)

62 "The Nile will _____ with frogs" (Exodus 8:3 NIV)

64 Hesitation sounds

65 "_____ it up" (Revelation 10:10)

83

ACROSS

1 "And the fenced cities are Ziddim, _____, and Hammath" (Joshua 19:35)
4 Descendants of Jacob
8 "First the _____, then the ear" (Mark 4:28)
13 Largest continent
15 King Hoshea's father (2 Kings 15:30)
16 King of Zobah (2 Samuel 8:3)
17 Winged mammals
18 Dig
19 Away
20 "Render therefore to all their _____" (Romans 13:7)
21 "But they _____ not that saying" (Mark 9:32)
23 Problems

25 "_____ thee out of my mouth" (Revelation 3:16)
26 Revile
28 Trapped
33 "And they set the altar upon his _____" (Ezra 3:3)
36 Sister of a parent
39 Underground rodent
40 Dwelling place
41 A son of Bela (1 Chronicles 7:7)
42 Jesus did this at the resurrection
43 Young female
44 This man had 454 children (Ezra 2:15)
45 "House, _____ Rahab" (Joshua 2:1)
46 "_____ shall dance there" (Isaiah 13:21)

48 "The rock _____" (Judges 15:11)
50 Person who inherits
53 "Ashbelites: of _____" (Numbers 26:38)
57 Console (arch.)
62 Exhaust
63 "But _____ foolish questions" (Titus 3:9)
64 A son of Seir (1 Chronicles 1:38)
65 Always
66 Wait on
67 "Shall compel thee to go a _____" (Matthew 5:41)
68 "Land from _____" (Isaiah 16:1)
69 "_____ whose fruit" (Jude 1:12)
70 Heber's father (Luke 3:35)
71 Barbecued pork

DOWN

1 Micha's father (Nehemiah 11:17)
2 Belonging to Jacob's brother
3 "The _____ of it" (Numbers 9:3)
4 Jerusalem (Joshua 18:28)
5 Esau's father-in-law (Genesis 26:34)
6 "Appointed the _____ of the priests and the Levites" (Nehemiah 13:30)
7 Fleecy ruminant
8 Made of brass (arch.)
9 "_____ ye be condemned" (James 5:9)
10 A son of Abinadab (2 Samuel 6:3)
11 Father of Puah (Judges 10:1)
12 Gaal's father (Judges 9:26)
14 "Let all the house of Israel know _____" (Acts 2:36)
22 Decomposing metal

24 Comfort
27 "Have _____ a wound" (Obadiah 1:7)
29 Family of Kohath (Numbers 3:27)
30 There was none at the inn
31 Otherwise
32 Act
33 "Bound two talents of silver in two _____" (2 Kings 5:23)
34 Asa's father (1 Chronicles 3:10)
35 Classify
37 "Shallum, and Telem, and _____" (Ezra 10:24)
38 Before ten
42 Zibeon's daughter (Genesis 36:2)
44 Greek form of *Asher* (Revelation 7:6)
47 "Unto _____, and from thence unto Patara" (Acts 21:1)

49 "And the sons of Micah were, Pithon, and Melech, and _____" (1 Chronicles 9:41)
51 Things
52 A son of Ulla (1 Chronicles 7:39)
54 The Jordan is the main one in Israel
55 A son of Gad (Genesis 46:16)
56 King Saul's eldest daughter (1 Samuel 14:49)
57 Throw out
58 Across
59 A greater amount
60 After four
61 Having great height

by N. Teri Grottke

84

ACROSS

1 Jump

5 "Destroy _____ kings and people" (Ezra 6:12)

8 "Though ye have _____" (Psalm 68:13)

12 A child of Gad (Numbers 26:15–16)

13 "Between Bethel and _____" (Genesis 13:3)

14 "The houses _____, and the women ravished" (Zechariah 14:2)

16 "I _____ unto you in an epistle" (1 Corinthians 5:9)

18 "Which _____ took" (1 Chronicles 4:18)

20 "_____ there yet the treasures" (Micah 6:10)

21 "Did yield fruit that sprang up and _____" (Mark 4:8)

23 Large lake

24 Possesses

25 Stannum

26 "Praise the Lord. . .and _____ him" (Romans 15:11)

27 Mourn aloud

30 "And the shekel shall be twenty _____" (Ezekiel 45:12)

32 "_____ the office" (1 Timothy 3:13)

33 "_____ for all" (1 Timothy 2:6)

35 Dibri was of this tribe (Leviticus 24:11)

36 "Thou _____ near in the day that I called upon thee" (Lamentations 3:57)

38 One of Jether's sons (1 Chronicles 7:38)

41 "Be _____ from this bond on the sabbath day?" (Luke 13:16)

42 "Before _____ by the way" (2 Samuel 2:24)

43 Resting place of Noah's ark (Genesis 8:4)

45 Chuza's wife (Luke 8:3)

47 Slough off

48 "_____, and the mighty men which belonged to David" (1 Kings 1:8)

50 Night flier

51 Strike

52 "To _____ you, and to comfort you" (1 Thessalonians 3:2)

56 A son of Bela (1 Chronicles 7:7)

57 Complete

58 Jesus said He would be this (Luke 9:22)

60 Ramiah's father (Ezra 10:25)

62 "Cheeks, and the _____" (Deuteronomy 18:3)

64 Otherwise

65 Means "God hath numbered thy kingdom, and finished it" (Daniel 5:26)

66 "_____ hath been a succourer of many" (Romans 16:2)

67 Wise men came from here

DOWN

1 "Condescend to men of _____ estate" (Romans 12:16)

2 Chelub's son (1 Chronicles 27:26)

3 At once (Mark 1:30)

4 "Which the Lord _____, and not man" (Hebrews 8:2)

5 "Say in their hearts, _____" (Psalm 35:25)

6 Tibetan monk

7 "When thou _____ down, thou shalt not be afraid" (Proverbs 3:24)

8 "Bored a hole in the _____ of it" (2 Kings 12:9)

9 "_____ ye abide in me, and my words abide in you" (John 15:7)

10 A son of Pashur (Ezra 10:22)

11 "Salute Philologus, and Julia, _____" (Romans 16:15)

14 "Who hath _____ of eyes?" (Proverbs 23:29)

15 Christians believe in the resurrection of the _____

17 "Shuthelah: of _____" (Numbers 26:36)

19 "Ye have _____ as kings without us" (1 Corinthians 4:8)

22 Time on the Atlantic coast (abbr.)

26 Fleeing "on the _____"

27 A child of Shem (Genesis 10:22)

28 This king removed the sodomites out of the land (1 Kings 15:11–12)

29 "The _____ of Sodom were wicked and sinners" (Genesis 13:13)

31 "The name of the wicked shall _____" (Proverbs 10:7)

33 "_____ in the law, and makest thy boast of God" (Romans 2:17)

34 Reverent fear

36 "Borders of _____" (Joshua 11:2)

37 "As when a lion _____" (Revelation 10:3)

38 Sixteenth letter of the Hebrew alphabet (precedes Psalm 119:121)

39 "And _____ greedily after the error of Balaam" (Jude 1:11)

40 "Against Jerusalem, _____" (Ezekiel 26:2)

41 Boy

42 "Nathanael of Cana in _____" (John 21:2)

43 "Ashbelites: of _____" (Numbers 26:38)

44 Go to sleep

45 "The patience of _____"

46 "I am a brother to dragons, and a companion to _____" (Job 30:29)

47 Deep-water vehicle

49 Things

53 A sibling to Haniel and Rezia (1 Chronicles 7:39)

54 Heber's father (Luke 3:35)

55 Snake sound

57 Utilize

59 Rope web

61 God sits _____ high

63 "That _____ command fire to come down" (Luke 9:54)

85

The Hall of Faith

Now faith is the substance of things hoped for,
the evidence of things not seen.

HEBREWS 11:1

ACROSS

1 London transport
5 Tall ornamental grasses
10 "Horns of ivory and _____" (Ezekiel 27:15)
15 "Saw that their _____ was dead" (1 Samuel 17:51 NIV)
16 "A blind man, or _____" (Leviticus 21:18) (2 words)
17 Fracas
18 "Cast him into _____" (Genesis 37:24) (2 words)
19 "_____ flood stage as before" (Joshua 4:18 NIV) (2 words)
20 "If I make my _____ hell" (Psalm 139:8) (2 words)
21 Three names from the biblical **HALL OF FAITH** (see Hebrews 11) (3 words)
24 Plant trunks
25 Painted metalware
26 "Such as he _____ get" (Leviticus 14:30)
29 GI's duds (abbr.)
30 Cuckoo pint genus
31 Sauce or bean
34 "There was _____" (Luke 8:24) (2 words)
36 "Lying on _____" (Matthew 9:2 NIV) (2 words)
37 "_____ ghost" (Matthew 14:26 NIV) (2 words)
38 Three more from the **HALL OF FAITH** (3 words)
42 Chow
43 Alamo rival
44 "_____ like stallions" (Jeremiah 50:11 NIV)
45 GM or IBM (abbr.)
46 "Ye _____ chosen generation" (1 Peter 2:9) (2 words)
47 "As though I shot _____ mark" (1 Samuel 20:20) (2 words)
49 "As a wild bull in a _____" (Isaiah 51:20)
50 Middle Eastern chief (var.)
51 "Behold a great _____" (Daniel 2:31)
53 Three more from the **HALL OF FAITH** (3 words)
59 Kind of energy
60 "With eyes _____" (Psalm 17:11 NIV)
61 "I will give unto _____, and to thy seed" (Genesis 17:8)
62 Japanese port
63 Rachel, to Rebekah (Genesis 27:42–43; 29:10)
64 "Both the _____ of it" (Ezekiel 15:4)
65 German city NW of Essen
66 "Azal: _____ shall flee" (Zechariah 14:5) (2 words)
67 "By the _____, and by the hinds" (Song of Solomon 2:7)

DOWN

1 "More _____ the first" (Revelation 2:19)
2 Result of payment default (abbr.)
3 La Scala solo
4 "The _____ will eat them up" (Isaiah 50:9 NIV)
5 Dressed (poetic)
6 Tocsins
7 "Should such a _____ I flee?" (Nehemiah 6:11) (2 words)
8 Oriental nanny
9 "They _____, they catch men" (Jeremiah 5:26) (3 words)
10 "To _____ his father" (Genesis 50:2)
11 Bathysphere man
12 Ye _____ Shoppe
13 First moon walker _____ Armstrong
14 Appetite
22 "Laid it in _____" (Mark 6:29) (2 words)
23 "Out of the _____ of God" (Matthew 4:4)
26 "Our ship was to unload its _____" (Acts 21:3 NIV)
27 "Those who pass by without _____" (Micah 2:8 NIV) (2 words)
28 Book after Micah
30 Iowa State locale
31 "I will _____ all my raiment" (Isaiah 63:3)
32 Native American tribe originally from Missouri
33 Pleasure craft
35 Assaying place

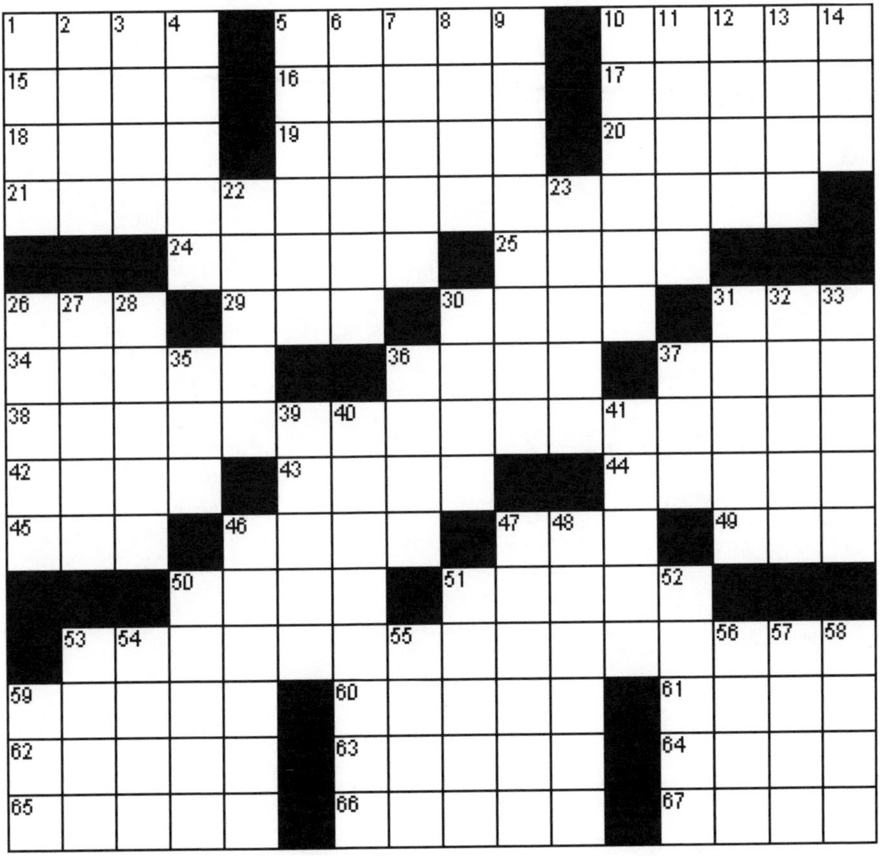

by David K. Shortess

36 Location of the seven churches (see Revelation 1:11)

37 Follows "expert" (suffix)

39 A leader under Ezra's direction (Ezra 8:16)

40 "Cause them to rule _____" (Daniel 11:39) (2 words)

41 "Stricken _____" (Joshua 23:1) (2 words)

46 Espousing neither the upright nor the debauched

47 "Thou shalt make _____ seat of pure gold" (Exodus 25:17) (2 words)

48 Soft ice cream franchise: _____-Freez

50 "To every one _____ of bread" (2 Samuel 6:19) (2 words)

51 "As he came, and said, _____ company" (2 Kings 9:17) (3 words)

52 "_____ into the rock" (Isaiah 2:10)

53 Son of Eliezer (Luke 3:29)

54 "_____ for the day!" (Joel 1:15)

55 Rolie Polie _____ (children's television show)

56 Cry of disbelief (2 words)

57 Yield

58 Noted pianist Dame Myra

59 "They _____ not, neither do they reap" (Matthew 6:26)

86

ACROSS

1 "_____ ye well" (Acts 15:29)
5 "Curse ye _____, said the angel of the LORD" (Judges 5:23)
10 Obnoxious
14 Son of Nathan of Zobah (2 Samuel 23:36)
15 By yourself
16 Micaiah's father (2 Chronicles 18:7)
17 "The _____ of that house was great" (Luke 6:49)
18 "Some which walk among you _____" (2 Thessalonians 3:11)
20 "Unto them repaired _____ the Gibeonite" (Nehemiah 3:7)
22 Greek form of *Uriah* (Matthew 1:6)
23 Zuph's son (1 Chronicles 6:34–35)
24 High-energy foods
26 A son of Seir (Genesis 36:20–21)

29 A son of Zophah (1 Chronicles 7:36)
30 "And _____ had a sister called Mary" (Luke 10:39)
33 A son of Helem (1 Chronicles 7:35)
34 "First the _____, then the ear" (Mark 4:28)
35 Fussy middle-aged woman
36 "Look from the top of _____" (Song of Solomon 4:8)
38 "To meet the Lord in the _____" (1 Thessalonians 4:17)
39 Light smell
41 Saul's grandfather (1 Chronicles 8:33)
42 "If by any _____ I may provoke" (Romans 11:14)
44 Endurance test
45 "_____ there yet the treasures" (Micah 6:10)

46 Without hair
47 "If I _____ not Jerusalem above my chief joy" (Psalm 137:6)
49 Make well
50 "Thee in this _____" (2 Kings 9:26)
51 He forsook Paul (2 Timothy 4:10)
54 "Family of the _____" (Numbers 26:36)
58 Adrammelech and Sharezer's brother (2 Kings 19:37)
61 Steward of the house in Tirzah (1 Kings 16:9)
62 Otherwise
63 Strain
64 Salathiel's father (Luke 3:27)
65 Deep holes
66 "The Amorites would dwell in mount _____" (Judges 1:35)
67 Closure

DOWN

1 "Rejoicing of the hope _____ unto the end" (Hebrews 3:6)
2 Fever
3 Revile
4 Nehushta's father (2 Kings 24:8)
5 "In the land of _____, where he begat two sons" (Acts 7:29)
6 A son of Elam (Ezra 10:26)
7 A son of Benjamin (Genesis 46:21)
8 Elpaal helped to build it (1 Chronicles 8:12)
9 "And the fenced cities are Ziddim, _____, and Hammath" (Joshua 19:35)
10 "And their _____ in wait on the west of the city" (Joshua 8:13)
11 Ahab's father (1 Kings 16:28)
12 Haniel's father (1 Chronicles 7:39)

13 Weeks are made of these
19 "Doeth not any of those _____, but even hath eaten upon the mountains" (Ezekiel 18:11)
21 Also
24 "Delivered me from all my _____" (Psalm 34:4)
25 A son of Bela (Numbers 26:40)
26 Pagan goddess of the Ephesians
27 Pashur's father (Jeremiah 20:1)
28 Trap
29 Sightless
30 "Lo, my _____ arose" (Genesis 37:7)
31 "Come they not _____, even of your lusts" (James 4:1)
32 Come in
34 "_____ of Judah" (2 Samuel 6:2)

37 Trap
40 "The _____ are alway liars" (Titus 1:12)
43 "For the barley was in the _____" (Exodus 9:31)
47 "He fitteth it with _____" (Isaiah 44:13)
48 "And _____ greedily after the error of Balaam" (Jude 1:11)
49 Concerns
50 "_____ all things; hold fast that which is good" (1 Thessalonians 5:21)
51 Obscure, mysterious
52 Nagge's son (Luke 3:25)
53 "As he that lieth upon the top of a _____" (Proverbs 23:34)
54 "Mahli, and _____" (1 Chronicles 23:23)

by N. Teri Grottke

55 "Take also of the _____ of life, and eat" (Genesis 3:22)

56 This priest wrote a book of the Bible

57 "God hath given thee all them that _____ with thee" (Acts 27:24)

59 Soot

60 Pass away

87

ACROSS

1 "_____, and Shema" (Joshua 15:26)
5 Bear hand
8 King Hoshea's father (2 Kings 15:30)
12 "For this cause left I thee in _____" (Titus 1:5)
13 Before (arch.)
14 Tibetan monk
15 Employed
16 Eve was made from Adam's
17 Idol
19 Utilize
20 Farthest part
22 "We have no king but _____" (John 19:15)
23 A son of Jeconiah (1 Chronicles 3:17–18)
25 "Whose seed _____ in itself" (Genesis 1:11)
26 King Hezekiah's mother (2 Kings 18:1–2)
27 "And _____ greedily after the error of Balaam" (Jude 1:11)
28 "Nevertheless _____ heart" (1 Kings 15:14)
30 A contemporary of Jeroboam (1 Kings 15:9)
33 "The rock _____" (Judges 15:11)
36 Servant of the church at Cenchrea (Romans 16:1)
40 Humpbacked animal
43 To be indebted
44 One of the wives of Ashur (1 Chronicles 4:5)
45 "Before the cock crow _____, thou shalt deny me thrice" (Mark 14:72)
46 "Their sound _____ into all the earth" (Romans 10:18)
48 A brother of Jerimoth of Bela (1 Chronicles 7:7)
49 Ear grain
51 Queen of the Persian Empire (abbr.)
54 "Lod, and _____" (Nehemiah 11:35)
57 Physical education (abbr.)
58 Tehinnah's son (1 Chronicles 4:12)
63 "_____ the madness of the prophet" (2 Peter 2:16)
65 First place
66 "Of Keros, the children of _____" (Nehemiah 7:47)
67 "There shall come forth a vessel for the _____" (Proverbs 25:4)
68 "Against Jerusalem, _____" (Ezekiel 26:2)
69 "Libnah, and _____" (Joshua 15:42)
71 Beach surface
72 "Between Bethel and _____" (Genesis 13:3)
73 Machbenah's father (1 Chronicles 2:49)
74 Tips
75 "Helez the Paltite, _____" (2 Samuel 23:26)
76 "And Herod was highly displeased with them of _____ and Sidon" (Acts 12:20)

DOWN

1 Get up
2 "Which _____ took" (1 Chronicles 4:18)
3 Partook
4 "Nebo, and over _____" (Isaiah 15:2)
5 "They came to _____ in Pamphylia" (Acts 13:13)
6 "Argob and _____" (2 Kings 15:25)
7 Spider's art
8 Deuel's son (Numbers 1:14)
9 Crippled
10 Absalom's captain (2 Samuel 17:25)
11 "The children of _____, the children of Shalmai" (Ezra 2:46)
12 A city of Hadarezer (1 Chronicles 18:8)
18 A son of Gad (Genesis 46:16)
21 Eat formally
22 King Saul's father (Acts 13:21)
24 Moabite border city (Numbers 21:15)
28 So be it
29 "_____ gave me of the tree, and I did eat" (Genesis 3:12)
30 Take action
31 Not see, but _____
32 "The children of _____" (Ezra 2:57)
34 Small city
35 Reverent fear
37 Hophni's father (1 Samuel 1:3)
38 To be an attorney, one must pass the _____
39 A son of Benjamin (Genesis 46:21)
41 Ecclesiastes (abbr.)
42 Large spotted cats
47 "Captains over _____, and officers among your tribes" (Deuteronomy 1:15)
50 Color of blood

52 "Thou _____ in the throne judging right" (Psalm 9:4)

53 Thorium (sym.)

54 "And the waters returned from _____ the earth continually" (Genesis 8:3)

55 "The _____ of a whip" (Nahum 3:2)

56 Solomon's temple was built on his threshing floor (2 Chronicles 3:1)

58 A son of David (1 Chronicles 3:1, 5–6)

59 "Micah his son, _____ his son" (1 Chronicles 5:5)

60 One of Zilpah's sons (Genesis 35:26)

61 Strain

62 "Habor, and _____" (1 Chronicles 5:26)

64 "The wicked _____" (Psalm 11:2)

68 Abdiel's son (1 Chronicles 5:15)

70 "So shall _____ seed be" (Romans 4:18)

by N. Teri Grottke

ACROSS

1 "A _____ of dove's dung" (2 Kings 6:25)
4 "Hundred and _____ years old" (Joshua 24:29)
7 Till
11 King Hezekiah's mother (2 Kings 18:1–2)
12 Brother of James (Jude 1:1)
13 "Not to _____ thee" (Ruth 1:16)
14 Untruth
15 Manna was measured in this unit
16 "For what _____ he spake" (John 13:28)
18 One of the four Gospels
20 "Shallum, and Telem, and _____" (Ezra 10:24)
21 Put out the flame
22 Sick
24 Take to court
25 "This woman was full of good works and almsdeeds which _____ did" (Acts 9:36)

26 "Even till thou come to _____" (Judges 11:33)
30 "Seeth the _____ coming, and leaveth the sheep" (John 10:12)
32 Jesus did this at the resurrection
33 A son of Seir (1 Chronicles 1:38)
35 Father (Galatians 4:6)
39 "Dwelt in their _____" (1 Chronicles 4:41)
40 "To meet the Lord in the _____" (1 Thessalonians 4:17)
41 Killed
42 Temple prophetess in Jesus' time (Luke 2:36–37)
43 A son of Shem (Genesis 10:22)
44 "Every _____, which my heavenly Father hath not planted, shall be rooted up" (Matthew 15:13)
45 Bird home
47 "All _____ of mighty men" (Song of Solomon 4:4)

49 "Against Jerusalem, _____" (Ezekiel 26:2)
52 "So many as the stars of the _____ in multitude" (Hebrews 11:12)
53 Possessive pronoun
54 "And the Hivite, and the Arkite, and the _____" (Genesis 10:17)
56 "Zechariah, _____" (1 Chronicles 15:18)
58 Take care of
62 Resting place of Noah's ark
63 Uncontrolled anger
65 Small deer
66 Shamgar's father (Judges 3:31)
67 Greek form of *Asher* (Revelation 7:6)
68 Partook
69 Pelt
70 "_____ verily, their sound" (Romans 10:18)
71 Saul's uncle (1 Samuel 14:50)

DOWN

1 Peaceful
2 Asa's father (1 Chronicles 3:10)
3 "Touched the _____" (Luke 7:14)
4 "Therefore shall a _____ arise" (Hosea 10:14)
5 "Mahli, and _____" (1 Chronicles 23:23)
6 Salathiel's father (Luke 3:27)
7 Father of Gedor (1 Chronicles 4:4)
8 "Master, the Jews of _____ sought to stone thee" (John 11:8)
9 Bread bakes in these
10 Young woman
12 Book of Moses' successor (abbr.)
13 "_____ of grapes" (Numbers 6:3)

17 "God created _____ heaven" (Genesis 1:1)
19 "Salute Herodion my _____" (Romans 16:11)
23 Untruths
24 "I will send _____ of flies upon thee" (Exodus 8:21)
26 Naomi wanted to be called this (Ruth 1:20)
27 Strong metal
28 12:00 p.m.
29 "The sweetness of a man's friend by _____ counsel" (Proverbs 27:9)
31 "Thou _____ away to the Chaldeans" (Jeremiah 37:13)

34 A brother of Jachan (1 Chronicles 5:13)
36 "Remnant of _____" (Zephaniah 1:4)
37 "To _____ all that call on thy name" (Acts 9:14)
38 Picnic pests
41 "Did _____ upon him" (Mark 15:19)
43 Inquire (arch.)
46 "Who remembered us in our low _____" (Psalm 136:23)
48 "As the door turneth upon his _____" (Proverbs 26:14)
49 One of David's sons (1 Kings 15:11)
50 "A certain Adullamite, whose name was _____" (Genesis 38:1)

by N. Teri Grottke

51 A son of Elioenai
   (1 Chronicles 3:24)

55 Enoch's son (Genesis 4:18)

56 Donkey sound

57 Comfort

59 "Shuthelah: of _____"
   (Numbers 26:36)

60 "_____ that man, and have no
   company with him"
   (2 Thessalonians 3:14)

61 "The fallow _____"
   (Deuteronomy 14:5)

64 Judah's firstborn (Genesis 38:3)

89

Blessed Assurance

Again the high priest asked him, and said unto him,
Art thou the Christ, the Son of the Blessed? And Jesus said, I am.
MARK 14:61–62

ACROSS

1 He wrote, "Never send to know for whom the bell tolls; it tolls for thee"
6 Actor who played the title role in *The Thief of Baghdad*
10 Verne's captain
14 Love in Lyon (Fr.)
15 Ku Klux _____
16 Withdraw (abbr.)
17 Beginning of some assuring **WORDS** of Jesus (John 14:1) (4 words)
20 Historical period
21 "And after that also King of _____" (Hebrews 7:2)
22 Singer Fisher
23 Swiss speciality chemical company
24 Least active
25 **WORDS**, cont'd (3 words)
30 "I have been an _____ in a strange land" (Exodus 18:3)
31 "For to come to him with _____" (Acts 17:15) (2 words)
35 "Have I _____ of mad men" (1 Samuel 21:15)
36 _____-Davis, pharmaceutical company
38 River in France
39 Ridiculing
41 Wash cycle
42 **WORDS**, cont'd (3 words)
45 Pre-Roman Italian
48 Formerly (arch.)
49 PhD hurdle
50 "Make thy face to _____ upon thy servant" (Psalm 31:16)
52 "Finally, brothers, good-by. _____ for perfection" (2 Corinthians 13:11 NIV)
55 End of **WORDS** (4 words)
58 "A man that flattereth his neighbour spreadeth _____ for his feet" (Proverbs 29:5) (2 words)
59 One of the Guthrie boys
60 "Was there _____ the death of Herod" (Matthew 2:15)
61 Small fishing boat
62 Adolescent
63 Contaminate

DOWN

1 "The valley of Shaveh, which is the king's _____" (Genesis 14:17)
2 "Now an _____ is the tenth part of an ephah" (Exodus 16:36)
3 "For there is _____ just man upon earth" (Ecclesiastes 7:20) (2 words)
4 Joshua's father (Exodus 33:11)
5 Farmer's bane
6 First US space station
7 It's good for burns
8 Author of *The Wonderful Wizard of Oz*, L. Frank _____
9 Reno school (abbr.)
10 Grandma's fine, decorative stitchery
11 Get out of through clever deceit
12 Slugger Roger
13 Double quartet
18 Superstitious or social prohibition (var.)
19 Actress Lamarr and namesakes
23 A good reputation depends on it
24 "And their words seemed to them as _____ tales" (Luke 24:11)
25 "Against the _____ of the rovers" (1 Chronicles 12:21)
26 Civil War general Robert _____ (2 words)
27 Layer of a wedding cake
28 "Now the city was _____ and great" (Nehemiah 7:4)
29 Wapiti
32 Follows *ti* or *ty*
33 Amoco rival, once upon a time
34 "What _____ is this that ye have done?" (Genesis 44:15)
36 "I will even make the _____ for fire great" (Ezekiel 24:9)
37 Black cuckoos in warmer parts of America

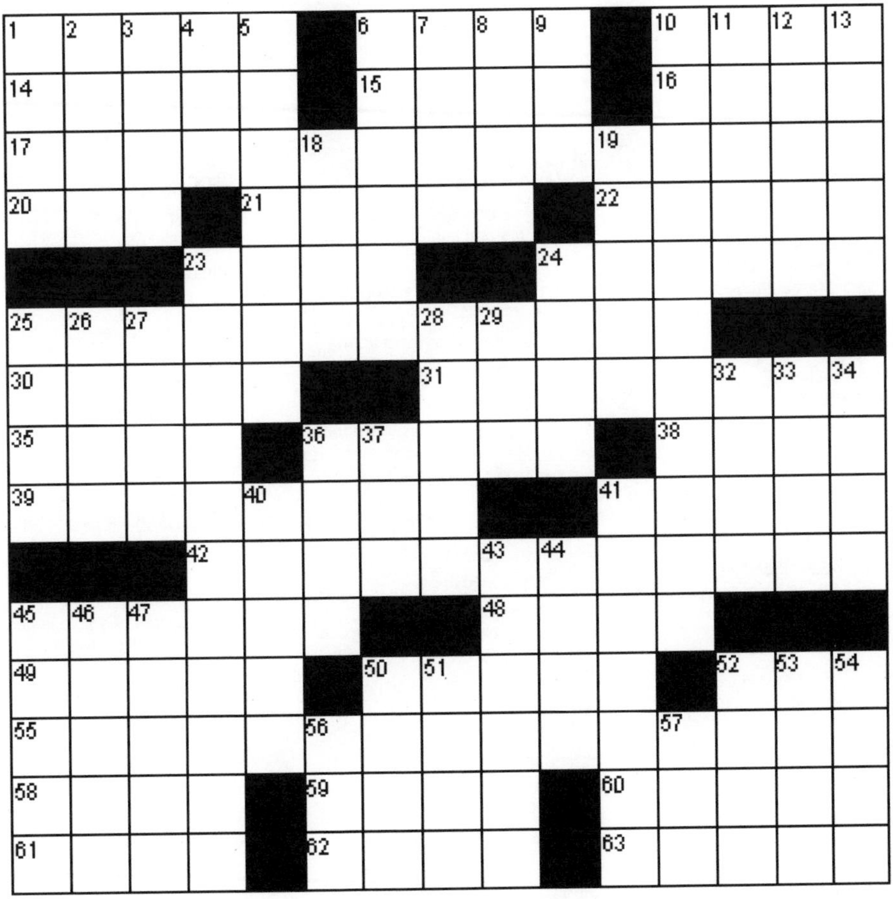

by David K. Shortess

40 "Wail, oaks of Bashan; the _____ forest has been cut down!" (Zechariah 11:2 NIV)

41 "When ye see a cloud _____ of the west" (Luke 12:54) (2 words)

43 "He would put the _____ again" (Exodus 34:33 NLT) (2 words)

44 European sea eagles

45 "Could not be eaten, they were _____" (Jeremiah 24:2) (2 words)

46 "Now therefore ye _____ more strangers" (Ephesians 2:19) (2 words)

47 Piece of farm equipment

50 Withered and dry

51 "Lest he _____ thee to the judge" (Luke 12:58)

52 Opposed to (prefix)

53 "_____ love with Tamar" (2 Samuel 13:4 NIV) (2 words)

54 "All the hills shall _____" (Amos 9:13)

56 "When anyone went to a wine _____ to draw fifty" (Haggai 2:16 NIV)

57 "And by night _____ pillar of fire" (Exodus 13:21) (2 words)

90

ACROSS

1 A son of Joktan (Genesis 10:28–29)

5 Not female

9 "He is a _____, which is one inwardly" (Romans 2:29)

12 Jesus did this at the resurrection

13 "_____ for the day!" (Joel 1:15)

14 Jesus' first miracle was here

15 "Micah his son, _____ his son" (1 Chronicles 5:5)

16 Multitude

17 A son of Ram (1 Chronicles 2:27)

18 "No man that warreth _____ himself" (2 Timothy 2:4)

20 Green citrus

21 Belonging to Eli (poss.)

22 Belonging to the adversary

24 "The children of Bazluth, the children of _____" (Ezra 2:52)

28 "Brought the heads of _____" (Judges 7:25)

29 At once (Mark 1:30)

30 "What _____ the LORD require of thee" (Micah 6:8)

33 Another name for *Hebron* (Genesis 35:27)

37 Palti's father (Numbers 13:9)

39 Greek form of *Noah* (Luke 17:26)

40 Increase in salary

41 Some people do this when they pray

42 "While the earth remaineth. . . _____ and heat. . .shall not cease" (Genesis 8:22)

44 Rip

45 Uncontrolled anger

47 "Securely as men _____ from war" (Micah 2:8)

49 An idol of Hamath (2 Kings 17:29–30)

52 Nagge's son (Luke 3:25)

54 Make acquaintance

55 Jacob's descendants

61 Too

62 Salathiel's father (Luke 3:27)

63 The son of Zerah (1 Chronicles 6:41)

64 Prophet (arch.)

65 Esau's father-in-law (Genesis 26:34)

66 "And there were seven sons of one _____, a Jew" (Acts 19:14)

67 Increase

68 Move quickly

69 "Blessed are the pure in heart: for _____ shall see God" (Matthew 5:8)

DOWN

1 Jerahmeel's son (1 Chronicles 2:25)

2 "None other _____ there" (John 6:22)

3 Forms a single land mass with Europe

4 "Which also _____ on his breast at supper" (John 21:20)

5 A son of Merari (Numbers 3:20)

6 "Myrrh and _____" (Song of Solomon 4:14)

7 Final

8 Ahasuerus's wife (Esther 2:17)

9 A son of Shimhi (1 Chronicles 8:19)

10 Foe

11 Goods

12 "_____ there yet the treasures" (Micah 6:10)

14 "Shall ye _____ your sabbath" (Leviticus 23:32)

19 "Ye may be _____ also with exceeding joy" (1 Peter 4:13)

23 Not far

24 One of the four Gospels

25 Ahira's father (Numbers 1:15)

26 Expect

27 "Out of Judah an _____ of my mountains" (Isaiah 65:9)

28 A son of Zerubbabel (1 Chronicles 3:19–20)

31 The earth was destroyed by a flood this many times

32 Also

34 "Touched the _____" (Luke 7:14)

35 "Nevertheless _____ heart was perfect" (1 Kings 15:14)

36 In this place

38 A son of Sheresh (1 Chronicles 7:16)

43 Valley

46 "Thou hast _____ thy brother" (Matthew 18:15)

48 Most contemptible

49 Absalom's captain (2 Samuel 17:25)

50 A son of Nadab (1 Chronicles 2:30)

51 "The son of _____" (1 Kings 4:10)

52 Blunder

53 Child of God

56 "Land from _____ to the wilderness" (Isaiah 16:1)

57 What you scratch

58 You (arch.)

59 "The spirit that dwelleth
in us lusteth to _____?"
(James 4:5)

60 "Of Keros, the children of _____"
(Nehemiah 7:47)

91

ACROSS

1 Gained a victory
4 Chopped
8 Unhappy
11 Abdiel's son (1 Chronicles 5:15)
12 "Did stand the queen in gold of _____" (Psalm 45:9)
14 A son of Gad (Genesis 46:16)
15 _____, Exodus, Leviticus (abbr.)
16 Particular ones
17 This is eaten on birthdays
18 Appendage
20 "And what _____ soever he rideth upon" (Leviticus 15:9)
23 "Which maketh Arcturus, _____, and Pleiades" (Job 9:9)
26 Staff
27 Walls of shrubs

30 The devil
32 Adam's wife
33 South Africa (abbr.)
34 Sharp-toothed tool
35 Decay
37 Partner of the false prophet
39 To place
40 "Hammoleketh bare _____" (1 Chronicles 7:18)
42 Right hand (abbr.)
43 Great sorrow
44 Moabite border city (Numbers 21:15)
45 "To meet the Lord in the _____" (1 Thessalonians 4:17)
46 Baanah's son (1 Chronicles 11:30)
48 "Do nothing _____" (Acts 19:36)

50 Small deer
51 Susi's son (Numbers 13:11)
53 Plea
55 "_____ there yet the treasures" (Micah 6:10)
58 "I _____ above all things" (3 John 1:2)
61 Similar
64 Doctor of optometry (abbr.)
65 A son of Bela (1 Chronicles 7:7)
66 "Filled his holes with prey, and his dens with _____" (Nahum 2:12)
67 The "First State" (abbr.)
68 Joshua's father (Exodus 33:11)
69 Give for temporary use
70 Erbium (sym.)

DOWN

1 "Shall be astonished, and _____ his head" (Jeremiah 18:16)
2 A son of Zerubbabel (1 Chronicles 3:20)
3 After eight
4 "For I was afraid of the anger and _____ displeasure" (Deuteronomy 9:19)
5 Galatians, _____, Philippians (abbr.)
6 "But _____ keepeth his word" (1 John 2:5)
7 First Jewish month
8 Large lake
9 Where the mercy seat is
10 Pass away
13 Scarlet
17 "His countenance is as Lebanon, excellent as the _____" (Song of Solomon 5:15)

19 "_____, and Magog, to gather them together to battle" (Revelation 20:8)
21 "Ran again unto the well to _____ water" (Genesis 24:20)
22 Haran's son (Genesis 11:31)
24 "Give thyself no _____" (Lamentations 2:18)
25 _____, Jeremiah, Lamentations (abbr.)
27 Titus, Philemon, _____ (abbr.)
28 Always
29 "Isaac was comforted after his mother's _____" (Genesis 24:67)
30 "Eli _____ upon a seat by the wayside" (1 Samuel 4:13)
31 A son of Benjamin (1 Chronicles 8:1–2)
34 "_____that ye refuse" (Hebrews 12:25)
36 Work

38 Ephraim's daughter (1 Chronicles 7:24)
39 "And Jacob _____ pottage" (Genesis 25:29)
40 Enoch's son (Genesis 4:18)
41 "And every meat offering, mingled with oil, and _____" (Leviticus 7:10)
43 Cry
44 A son of Bela (Numbers 26:40)
47 Cut
49 "Of Keros, the children of _____" (Nehemiah 7:47)
51 Jeduthun's son (Nehemiah 11:17)
52 Not dead
54 "The LORD would not. . . give _____ unto you" (Deuteronomy 1:45)
56 "And he _____ upon a cherub" (Psalm 18:10)

[Crossword puzzle grid]

57 "Mahli, and _____"
(1 Chronicles 23:23)

58 "That I may _____ Christ"
(Philippians 3:8)

59 Caleb's son (1 Chronicles 4:15)

60 Transgression

62 Relatives

63 "The latter _____" (Ruth 3:10)

by N. Teri Grottke

92

ACROSS

1 Perverse
5 Ruth's mother-in-law
10 Male red deer
14 Jesus cried this on the cross
(Mark 15:34)
15 A son of Shemidah
(1 Chronicles 7:19)
16 Carry out directions
17 Jesus came to _____ the world
(John 12:47)
18 "Benhanan, and _____"
(1 Chronicles 4:20)
19 "Touched the _____" (Luke 7:14)
20 Elizur's father (Numbers 1:5)
22 Renowned
24 Jether's son (1 Chronicles 7:38)
25 Taxi
26 "Blessed is the man to whom the
Lord will not _____ sin"
(Romans 4:8)

30 "The fallow _____"
(Deuteronomy 14:5)
32 "Against Jerusalem, _____"
(Ezekiel 26:2)
35 "God hath given thee all them
that _____ with thee"
(Acts 27:24)
36 Sons of thunder (Mark 3:17)
38 Daughter of Phanuel (Luke 2:36)
39 "What thou _____, write in a
book" (Revelation 1:11)
40 Son of Dishan (1 Chronicles 1:42)
41 "Thou _____ my head with oil"
(Psalm 23:5)
43 A son of Benjamin
(Genesis 46:21)
44 Is able
45 Sister of a parent
46 Opposite of find (arch.)
48 "Bored a hole in the _____ of it"
(2 Kings 12:9)

49 "Came to Joel the _____"
(Joel 1:1)
50 "_____; and from Mahanaim"
(Joshua 13:26)
54 "Filled the _____ to water their
father's flock" (Exodus 2:16)
59 Always
60 "_____ nor sown"
(Deuteronomy 21:4)
62 Ark builder
63 Tear apart
64 "That the _____ of your faith"
(1 Peter 1:7)
65 "Even _____ to die"
(Romans 5:7)
66 Picnic pests
67 "If _____ he might find any
thing thereon" (Mark 11:13)
68 Azariah's father
(2 Chronicles 15:1)

DOWN

1 "The children of Israel. . .gathered,
some more, some _____"
(Exodus 16:17)
2 King Hoshea's father
(2 Kings 15:30)
3 "The women _____ hangings
for the grove" (2 Kings 23:7)
4 Perished
5 "Setteth on fire the course of
_____" (James 3:6)
6 Enan's son (Numbers 1:15)
7 "The _____ of gladness"
(Psalm 45:7)
8 Shammai's son
(1 Chronicles 2:45)
9 Without guilt
10 Moses' brother-in-law
(Numbers 10:29)

11 This month corresponds to Nisan
(Deuteronomy 16:1)
12 "They _____ to and fro"
(Psalm 107:27)
13 "And Herod was highly
displeased with them of _____
and Sidon" (Acts 12:20)
21 Consume food
23 Type of weed
26 Abraham's heir
27 Bread from heaven
28 A duke of Edom (Genesis 36:41)
29 Daniel had a vision by this river
(Daniel 8:1–2)
30 "_____ thou well to be angry?"
(Jonah 4:4)
31 Opposite of west

32 "_____ with thine adversary
quickly" (Matthew 5:25)
33 Blood pumper
34 "The children of _____"
(Ezra 2:50)
36 "Ye have _____ rebellious
against the LORD"
(Deuteronomy 31:27)
37 Worn out clothing
39 "For their heart _____
destruction" (Proverbs 24:2)
42 Jesus raised a young man from
the dead here (Luke 7:11)
46 "She brought forth butter in a
_____ dish" (Judges 5:25)
47 "The children of Lod, Hadid, and
_____" (Ezra 2:33)
48 "Made a supper to his _____"
(Mark 6:21)

49 Rob

50 King of Sodom (Genesis 14:2)

51 "_____ the death of the cross" (Philippians 2:8)

52 Cloth shelter

53 Naomi wanted to be called this (Ruth 1:20)

55 "I will _____ all that afflict thee" (Zephaniah 3:19)

56 Prod

57 Rabbit

58 Slough off

61 Tear

93

A Reason to Love

*A new commandment I give unto you,
That ye love one another; as I have loved you.*
JOHN 13:34

ACROSS

1 Philippine island

6 "Why should _____ with thee?" (2 Samuel 13:26) (2 words)

10 "Or if he _____ for a fish" (Matthew 7:10 NIV)

14 "The wind swept them away without leaving a _____" (Daniel 2:35 NIV)

15 Enthusiasm

16 Japheth's father (Genesis 6:10)

17 "Have _____ day!" (2 words)

18 Rich vein

19 "Jesus saith unto them, Come and _____" (John 21:12)

20 Start of **QUOTE** from 1 John 4:11 (4 words)

23 Actor Harrison

24 Company symbol

25 Airport abbreviation

27 "Lord, not my feet _____" (John 13:9)

30 **QUOTE**, cont'd

34 Middle-Eastern Arab group (abbr.)

35 "It was not my _____" (Numbers 16:28 NIV)

36 San _____, a tiny country within Italy

37 **QUOTE**, cont'd (5 words)

40 Demons

41 "To preach the word in _____" (Acts 16:6)

42 Moon buggy (abbr.)

43 "Then _____ down upon my face" (Ezekiel 11:13) (2 words)

44 Alum

45 "Shut the doors, and _____ them" (Nehemiah 7:3)

46 "Ye have done evil _____ doing" (Genesis 44:5) (2 words)

48 *Logue* or *center* prefix

50 End of **QUOTE** (3 words)

57 "Thou art my _____" (Psalm 71:5)

58 "Let down your _____ for a draught" (Luke 5:4)

59 "_____ him away while we slept" (Matthew 28:13)

60 "Even so, _____" (Revelation 1:7)

61 "He shall come _____ dead body" (Numbers 6:6) (2 words)

62 "Who can _____ man what shall be" (Ecclesiastes 6:12) (2 words)

63 "A _____ heart deviseth his way" (Proverbs 16:9)

64 "Like fullers' _____" (Malachi 3:2)

65 "At whom do you _____ and stick out your tongue?" (Isaiah 57:4 NIV)

DOWN

1 "His own parents will _____ him" (Zechariah 13:3 NIV)

2 "Rule Britannia" composer

3 "He armed him with a coat of _____" (1 Samuel 17:38)

4 "They were all with one _____ in one place" (Acts 2:1)

5 He played Superman

6 "I _____ my peace, even from good" (Psalm 39:2)

7 "Jesus cried with a loud voice, saying, _____" (Mark 15:34)

8 "A _____ is coming against her from the north" (Jeremiah 46:20 NIV)

9 "Can _____ upon hot coals" (Proverbs 6:28) (2 words)

10 "Set bars _____" (Job 38:10) (2 words)

11 "_____ good news from a far country" (Proverbs 25:25) (2 words)

12 Nigerian industrial city

13 "_____ saith unto him" (John 11:27)

21 Book after Genesis

22 South Dakota native

25 Bordon's ad bovine

26 "Took a _____" (John 13:4)

28 Opposite of *positive* (abbr.)

29 Volcanic mudflow

31 One of the string instruments

32 "_____ into his gates with thanksgiving" (Psalm 100:4)

33 "In one hour your _____ has come!" (Revelation 18:10 NIV)

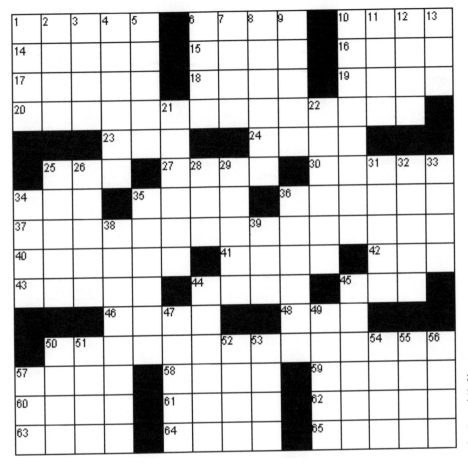

by David K. Shortess

34 Huff's partner

35 Old-time antiseptic

36 "The _____ pleased him" (Esther 2:9)

38 Peps up

39 IRA relative (abbr.)

44 "Was _____ Padanaram" (Genesis 28:7) (2 words)

45 "If a serpent had _____ any man" (Numbers 21:9)

47 "My _____ for me" (1 Chronicles 22:7) (2 words)

49 "Write them upon the _____ of thy house" (Deuteronomy 6:9)

50 Juan's hill

51 "To _____ the blind eyes" (Isaiah 42:7)

52 Sicilian volcano

53 "To whom I shall give _____" (John 13:26) (2 words)

54 "Behold a _____ in the wall" (Ezekiel 8:7)

55 Fashion magazine

56 "Wilt thou _____ it up in three days?" (John 2:20)

57 Father of Canaan (Genesis 9:18)

94

ACROSS

1 "Children of _____"
(Ezra 2:57)

4 Joshua cut off the Anakims from
here (Joshua 11:21)

8 "And Zechariah, and _____"
(1 Chronicles 15:20)

13 "My belly is as wine which
hath no _____" (Job 32:19)

15 "And he _____ upon a cherub"
(Psalm 18:10)

16 "_____ also and the villages
thereof: and they dwelt there"
(2 Chronicles 28:18)

17 "The scab, and with the _____"
(Deuteronomy 28:27)

18 "We cannot speak unto thee
_____ or good" (Genesis 24:50)

19 "His _____ over me was love"
(Song of Solomon 2:4)

20 "I proved thee at the waters of
_____" (Psalm 81:7)

22 Acquire

23 A son of Bela (Numbers 26:40)

24 Refuse to admit

25 Rocks

28 Ground moisture

29 Amos, _____, Jonah (abbr.)

30 "Sallu, _____, Hilkiah"
(Nehemiah 12:7)

34 King Hezekiah's mother
(2 Kings 18:2)

36 Often (arch.)

39 "The _____ of truth shall be
established for ever"
(Proverbs 12:19)

41 A son of Gad (Genesis 46:16)

42 "The hinder end of the spear
smote him under the fifth
_____" (2 Samuel 2:23)

43 "Let her be as the. . .pleasant
_____" (Proverbs 5:19)

44 "The barley was in the _____"
(Exodus 9:31)

45 Female chicken

46 "Destroy _____ kings and
people" (Ezra 6:12)

47 "Borders of _____" (Joshua 11:2)

48 "God created _____ heaven"
(Genesis 1:1)

49 Omega

50 What the wind did at the parting
of the Red Sea

52 Allow

54 Are (arch.)

56 Elijah's successor

59 "The collar of my _____"
(Job 30:18)

61 "Against Jerusalem, _____"
(Ezekiel 26:2)

64 Tree of the olive family

65 A son of Mizraim (Genesis 10:13)

68 Toi was king of this country
(2 Samuel 8:9)

70 Own (Scot.)

71 "_____ shall offer gifts"
(Psalm 72:10)

72 Brother of Shuni and Ezbon
(Genesis 46:16)

73 Joseph mourned for Jacob at his
threshing floor (Genesis 50:7–10)

74 Cloth shelter

75 Basin (arch.)

76 "Captains over _____, and
officers among your tribes"
(Deuteronomy 1:15)

77 Untruth

DOWN

1 "And _____, and Parah"
(Joshua 18:23)

2 Measured (arch.)

3 "Why should it be thought a
thing _____ with
you" (Acts 26:8)

4 A great man among the Anakims
(Joshua 15:13)

5 Belonging to Shem's father

6 Increase

7 Beryllium (sym.)

8 A size of type approximately 5½
points

9 A desert through which the
children of Israel traveled
(Numbers 20:1)

10 A son of Helem
(1 Chronicles 7:35)

11 Jeshua's son (Nehemiah 3:19)

12 Master

14 Yours (arch.)

19 The son of Jehoiada (1 Kings 4:4)

21 "Thou makest us a _____
among the heathen"
(Psalm 44:14)

22 "Thy navel is like a round
_____" (Song of Solomon 7:2)

26 Turn over (abbr.)

27 South Africa (abbr.)

31 Delaiah's father (Nehemiah 6:10)

32 A son of Jerahmeel
(1 Chronicles 2:25)

33 Nice

34 Member of the Semitic people of
the Arabian Peninsula

35 Invoice

37 Stupid

38 One of the conspirators against
Esther's husband (Esther 2:21)

by N. Teri Grottke

40 "And he sent them to _____ the kingdom of God" (Luke 9:2)

51 "That _____ command" (Luke 9:54)

53 After Wednesday (abbr.)

55 Cook

57 Dead language

58 One of Shephi's brother (1 Chronicles 1:40)

60 Ginath's son (1 Kings 16:21)

61 Jezebel's husband

62 "Habor, and _____" (1 Chronicles 5:26)

63 Book after Joel (abbr.)

66 Stops

67 Breed

69 Fuss

70 Daniel _____ no pleasant bread (Daniel 10:3)

73 Astatine (sym.)

95

ACROSS

1 Beryllium (sym.)

3 Disfigure

6 "Building the rebellious and the _____ city" (Ezra 4:12)

9 Adam was the first

10 "Brought the heads of _____" (Judges 7:25)

12 A son of Eliphaz (Genesis 36:11)

14 Seventeenth book (abbr.)

15 Ammihud's son (1 Chronicles 9:4)

17 Before (arch.)

18 "And he must _____ go through Samaria" (John 4:4)

20 Hophni's father (1 Samuel 1:3)

21 The butler's cell mate (Genesis 40:1–3)

22 "For ye tithe mint and _____" (Luke 11:42)

23 Gemalli's son (Numbers 13:12)

25 Capable

26 Judah's firstborn (1 Chronicles 2:3)

27 Hanun's father (Nehemiah 3:30)

31 Weep

32 Joab's brother (1 Chronicles 2:16)

35 "But the wheat and the _____ were not smitten" (Exodus 9:32)

36 Abdiel's son (1 Chronicles 5:15)

37 Abraham's father (Genesis 11:26)

38 Motel

39 Faithful husband and prophet (abbr.)

40 "Nebo, and over _____" (Isaiah 15:2)

41 Book before Obadiah (abbr.)

42 King of Damascus (2 Corinthians 11:32)

44 "Children of _____" (1 Chronicles 7:12)

45 One of Jacob's sons (Genesis 30:1–6)

46 "Thou _____ the deeds of the Nicolaitanes" (Revelation 2:6)

49 "Go to the _____, thou sluggard" (Proverbs 6:6)

50 "_____, and Calneh, in the land of Shinar" (Genesis 10:10)

53 Jachan's brother (1 Chronicles 5:13)

54 She hid the Hebrew spies (Joshua 2:1–6)

57 A son of Hothan the Aroerite (1 Chronicles 11:44)

58 Naarai's father (1 Chronicles 11:37)

60 Jether's son (1 Chronicles 7:38)

61 "_____ of the brooks of Gaash" (1 Chronicles 11:32)

62 Otherwise

63 Consume food

64 This man led the rebuilding of Jerusalem (abbr.)

65 NT church people in Asia (abbr.)

66 "Forasmuch as _____ excellent spirit" (Daniel 5:12)

DOWN

1 "In presence am _____ among you" (2 Corinthians 10:1)

2 Venture

3 Animal unclean for eating (Leviticus 11:29)

4 Are (arch.)

5 "But Peter _____ the matter from the beginning" (Acts 11:4)

6 "Not knowing the things that shall _____ me there" (Acts 20:22)

7 "Sallu, _____, Hilkiah" (Nehemiah 12:7)

8 "Even _____ to die" (Romans 5:7)

9 "Save only that which the young _____ have eaten" (Genesis 14:24)

11 "A little _____, and a little honey" (Genesis 43:11)

12 "Son of _____" (Isaiah 7:6)

13 Saul's grandfather (1 Chronicles 8:33)

16 "They departed from _____, and pitched in Dibongad" (Numbers 33:45)

19 "We have done that which was our _____ to do" (Luke 17:10)

24 A son of Kohath (Numbers 3:19)

25 Achan was stoned in this valley (Joshua 7:24–25)

26 Consumes (arch.)

28 "Joseph of _____, an honourable counsellor" (Mark 15:43)

29 A duke of Edom (1 Chronicles 1:52)

30 Zephaniah's son (Zechariah 6:14)

33 "_____ there yet the treasures" (Micah 6:10)

34 Livable

36 "Against Jerusalem, _____" (Ezekiel 26:2)

40 A son of Bani (Ezra 10:34)

41 "Of Harim, _____" (Nehemiah 12:15)

43 "The children of Sisera, the children of _____" (Ezra 2:53)

47 This prophet dreamed about wheels (abbr.)

48 Dimensions

49 "Argob and _____"
   (2 Kings 15:25)

50 Type of tree (Isaiah 44:14)

51 A city of Hadarezer
   (1 Chronicles 18:8)

52 Feel deeply about

55 Son of Dishan (Genesis 36:28)

56 Nocturnal, winged mammal

59 Type of snake

by N. Teri Grottke

96

ACROSS

1 "The king's _____"
(Genesis 14:17)

5 Heber's wife (Judges 4:17)

9 "If by any _____ I may provoke"
(Romans 11:14)

14 Son of Nathan of Zobah
(2 Samuel 23:36)

15 "The land was not _____ to
bear them" (Genesis 13:6)

16 Another name for *Hebron*
(Genesis 35:27)

17 A son of Shemaiah
(1 Chronicles 26:7)

19 "_____ them out from before
you" (Judges 6:9)

20 "Traitors, _____, highminded,
lovers of pleasures"
(2 Timothy 3:4)

21 A son of Jehiel
(1 Chronicles 9:35–37)

23 The _____ of Galilee

24 A son of Ulla (1 Chronicles 7:39)

26 The fruit tree had seed in _____
(Genesis 1:11)

29 "Choosing _____ to suffer
affliction" (Hebrews 11:25)

32 David _____ Goliath

33 Hebrew women were delivered
_____ the midwives arrived
(Exodus 1:19)

34 Jeroboam's father (1 Kings 11:26)

37 "The son of Dekar, in _____"
(1 Kings 4:9)

41 "No more _____" (Hosea 2:16)

43 A son of Gad (Genesis 46:16)

44 "Mint and _____"
(Matthew 23:23)

45 "Down in _____" (Acts 27:27)

46 Moses' brother

48 "Of Keros, the children of _____"
(Nehemiah 7:47)

49 "Being _____ together"
(Colossians 2:2)

51 A son of Japhlet
(1 Chronicles 7:33)

53 Despise

56 Abhor

57 Right hand (abbr.)

58 Rescue

61 Older person

65 "Letters in _____ name"
(1 Kings 21:8)

68 "Rejoice not thou, whole _____"
(Isaiah 14:29)

70 The waters of _____ were bitter
(Exodus 15:23)

71 Esau's father-in-law
(Genesis 26:34)

72 "Tappuah, and _____"
(Joshua 15:34)

73 Trap

74 "I will even _____ a curse upon
you" (Malachi 2:2)

75 Dwelling place of lions

DOWN

1 "That dippeth with me in the
_____" (Mark 14:20)

2 Shammah's father
(2 Samuel 23:11)

3 "Eli, Eli, _____ sabachthani?"
(Matthew 27:46)

4 Tahath's son (1 Chronicles 7:20)

5 "By his name _____"
(Psalm 68:4)

6 Hezron's wife (1 Chronicles 2:24)

7 King Hoshea's father
(2 Kings 15:30)

8 Samson slew 1,000 Philistines
here (Judges 15:14–15)

9 Insane

10 Make a mistake

11 To humble

12 Bellybutton

13 "Lo, my _____ arose"
(Genesis 37:7)

18 "The Libertines, and _____"
(Acts 6:9)

22 Petroleum product

25 "_____ there yet the treasures"
(Micah 6:10)

27 "Husham of the land of the
_____ reigned in his stead"
(1 Chronicles 1:45)

28 Graceful water bird

29 A king of Midian (Numbers 31:8)

30 "_____ the Canaanite"
(Numbers 21:1)

31 Rip

32 Mix

35 What you do to a drum

36 One of Pispah's brothers
(1 Chronicles 7:38)

38 One of Maachah's sons
(1 Chronicles 8:29–30)

39 The Holy Spirit forbade Paul to
preach here (Acts 16:6)

40 "Yea, what _____, yea, what
revenge!" (2 Corinthians 7:11)

42 "They shall enter in at the
windows _____ a thief"
(Joel 2:9)

47 This man found King Ahab for
Elijah (abbr.)

50 Possessive pronoun

52 "The hills _____ like wax"
(Psalm 97:5)

53 "_____ of gold" (Nehemiah 7:72)

54 One of Zerah's sons (1 Chronicles 2:6)

55 Abraham's father (Luke 3:34)

56 Eliab's father (Numbers 1:9)

59 Larger than monkeys

60 "And in the _____" (Deuteronomy 1:7)

62 Jesus invited Peter to "come and _____" (John 21:11–12)

63 Ahira's father (Numbers 1:15)

64 Male sheep

66 Prohibit

67 "Behold, _____ was leprous" (Numbers 12:10)

69 "The latter _____" (Ruth 3:10)

97

Happy Mother's Day!

Honor your father and your mother, so that you may live long.

EXODUS 20:12 NIV

ACROSS

1 Start of **VERSE** appropriate to the theme day (Proverbs 31:10)

4 "_____ vanity" (Ecclesiastes 1:2) (2 words)

9 "Arise, and go into the _____ which is called Straight" (Acts 9:11)

15 "That no _____ can come between them" (Job 41:16)

16 Is like a broken _____" (Proverbs 25:19)

17 It is time for you _____ LORD" (Psalm 119:126 NIV) (3 words)

18 "Looked out _____ window" (2 Kings 9:30) (2 words)

19 A whip for the _____" (Proverbs 26:3)

20 Ciphers

21 **VERSE**, cont'd (4 words)

24 "The foal of an _____" (Matthew 21:5)

25 "Their murders, their magic _____" (Revelation 9:21 NIV)

26 "Ye are the _____ of the earth" (Matthew 5:13)

29 "Judah _____ wife for Er, his first-born" (Genesis 38:6 NIV) (2 words)

31 "_____ him all ye people" (Romans 15:11)

35 Third son of Jether (1 Chronicles 7:38)

36 "Which is the king's _____" (Genesis 14:17)

38 Taos, for example

40 **VERSE**, cont'd (4 words)

44 "On _____ the time I punish him" (Jeremiah 49:8 NIV) (2 words)

45 Sandwich cookie

46 Derivative (abbr.)

47 Newspaper department

48 "Took _____ of him" (Luke 10:34)

50 "They were not _____" (Job 39:16)

51 "God saw _____ it was good" (Genesis 1:10)

53 Fort Worth school (abbr.)

55 End of **VERSE** (4 words)

64 On ice

65 Presidential candidate Ralph

66 Cry of surprise

67 State #49

68 "Of Zebulun; _____ the son of Helon" (Numbers 1:9)

69 "_____ the sacrifices of the dead" (Psalm 106:28)

70 "There shall be _____ of any man's life among you" (Acts 27:22) (2 words)

71 "Their _____ were evil" (John 3:19)

72 "His eyes were _____" (1 Samuel 4:15)

DOWN

1 Women's corp in WWII (abbr.)

2 "Fighting _____ pregnant woman" (Exodus 21:22 NIV) (2 words)

3 "But though we, _____ angel from heaven" (Galatians 1:8) (2 words)

4 "A woman lay _____ feet" (Ruth 3:8) (2 words)

5 Mournful water fowl

6 "The _____ is King for ever and ever" (Psalm 10:16)

7 "_____ ghost" (Matthew 14:26 NIV) (2 words)

8 Fifth Jewish month

9 "Let us _____ rebuilding" (Nehemiah 2:18 NIV)

10 Eagerly promotes

11 Pasta sauce brand

12 "The woodwork will _____ it" (Habbakuk 2:11 NIV)

13 Part of Caesar's last words (2 words)

14 "_____ thee like a ball" (Isaiah 22:18)

22 "First seven _____ kine" (Genesis 41:20)

23 "_____ the Ithrite" (1 Chronicles 11:40)

26 "They were _____ in two" (Hebrews 11:37 NIV)

27 "I _____ in the night" (Nehemiah 2:12)

28 Tibetan priests

29 Day-_____ dyes

30 "_____ the land of the free"

31 Follows *jugg* or *but*

32 "Her feet _____ not in her house" (Proverbs 7:11)

33 Stress result

34 "Be ye _____ of the word" (James 1:22)

36 Genetic stuff

by David K. Shortess

37 Sternward

38 It means "before" (prefix)

39 "Spring _____ well" (Numbers 21:17)

41 Arctic diver

42 "Came unto mount _____" (Numbers 20:22)

43 "_____ the messenger came to him" (2 Kings 6:32)

48 "The fourth part of a _____" (2 Kings 6:25)

49 "Your sin _____ for" (Isaiah 6:7 NIV)

50 Wheel center

51 Arduous journeys

52 "They _____ king over them" (Revelation 9:11 NIV) (2 words)

53 "_____ their winepresses, and suffer thirst" (Job 24:11)

54 Edges of streets

55 "_____ of mine own self do nothing" (John 5:30) (2 words)

56 Sing or fly alone

57 "A colt the _____ of an ass" (Matthew 21:5)

58 "The soldiers _____ mocked him" (Luke 23:36)

59 "The _____ of Siddim was full" (Genesis 14:10)

60 Film star Adams, Ernie Kovacs' wife

61 "Oh that _____ wings like a dove!" (Psalm 55:6) (2 words)

62 "Nothing to _____ was thirsty" (Matthew 25:42 NIV) (2 words)

63 "He shall dwell in the tents of _____" (Genesis 9:27)

98

ACROSS

1 "They drew to shore, and. . . cast the _____ away" (Matthew 13:48)
4 King of Sodom (Genesis 14:2)
8 "Valley of _____" (Psalm 84:6)
12 Darius was one of these
14 Sadoc's father (Matthew 1:14)
15 A son of Ulla (1 Chronicles 7:39)
16 Where the children of Israel pitched before Ijeabarim (Numbers 21:10–11)
17 "The companies of Sheba waited for the troops" (Job 6:19)
18 Salathiel's father (Luke 3:27)
19 Johanan's father (2 Kings 25:23)
21 Reviler
23 "Salute Herodion my _____" (Romans 16:11)
25 A son of Jacob (Genesis 30:11)
26 God's prophet to four kings of Judah (abbr.)
27 "Husham of the land of the _____ reigned in his stead" (1 Chronicles 1:45)
30 Buzzing stinger
33 "_____ weeping for her children" (Jeremiah 31:15)
34 He came with Zerubbabel (Ezra 2:2)
38 "_____, and Dumah" (Joshua 15:52)
40 "And their _____, and their felloes" (1 Kings 7:33)
42 Exhaust
43 "And the herdmen of _____" (Genesis 26:20)
45 Belonging to Jacob's first wife
47 Bowling target
48 "Plentifully _____ the proud doer" (Psalm 31:23)
51 Solomon's great-grandson (1 Chronicles 3:10)
54 A god of Babylon (Isaiah 46:1)
55 Tanhumeth's son (2 Kings 25:23)
59 "Maaziah, _____, Shemaiah: these were the priests" (Nehemiah 10:8)
61 "Wheat with a _____" (Proverbs 27:22)
62 Image
63 Small flying insect
67 Children of Israel left Succoth and pitched here (Numbers 33:6)
68 "_____, and Ivah?" (Isaiah 37:13)
69 A son of Caanan (Genesis 10:15)
70 Product of weeping
71 "_____ the office of a deacon" (1 Timothy 3:13)
72 "_____ shall see God" (Matthew 5:8)
73 Opposite of *bright*

DOWN

1 "The children of _____, six hundred twenty and three" (Ezra 2:11)
2 Decorate
3 Despise
4 This is used to hit a ball
5 He was a Zadokite priest (abbr.)
6 Sixth book of the NT (abbr.)
7 Resting place of Noah's ark
8 Uzzi's father; Hashabiah's son (Nehemiah 11:22)
9 A son of Gad (Genesis 46:16)
10 Concerns
11 Enan's son (Numbers 1:15)
12 Make fun of
13 Bani's father (1 Chronicles 6:46)
20 Mordecai's enemy
22 Arad's brother (1 Chronicles 8:15)
24 "Dimnah with her suburbs, _____ with her suburbs" (Joshua 21:35)
25 "And _____ wife bare him sons" (Judges 11:2)
28 "For if ye do these things, ye shall _____ fall" (2 Peter 1:10)
29 To place
30 Sack
31 Before (arch.)
32 "Will set them to _____ his ground" (1 Samuel 8:12)
35 Your thigh is connected to this
36 "Shallum, and Telem, and _____" (Ezra 10:24)
37 "The daughters of _____ were beautiful" (Genesis 6:2 NASB)
39 Barrier
41 Fleecy ruminant
44 A king of Midian (Numbers 31:8)
46 Lane
49 "A far more exceeding and eternal _____ of glory" (2 Corinthians 4:17)
50 "_____ to deceit" (Job 31:5)
51 A son of Aaron (Exodus 6:23)
52 "Jonah was gone down into the _____ of the ship" (Jonah 1:5)
53 By yourself
56 Ribai's son (1 Chronicles 11:31)
57 "_____ against the fenced cities" (Zephaniah 1:16)
58 Edges of garments
60 "Ye may be _____ also with exceeding joy" (1 Peter 4:13)

64 This man was badgered by Sanballat and Tobiah while rebuilding Jerusalem (abbr.)

65 Partook

66 "So shall _____ seed be" (Romans 4:18)

by N. Teri Grottke

99

ACROSS

1 Strike with the foot
5 North, south, east, _____
9 Brag
14 Jesus cried this on the cross (Mark 15:34)
15 "That which _____ been" (Ecclesiastes 6:10)
16 Ithai's father (1 Chronicles 11:31)
17 Hearing organs
18 "As he saith also in _____" (Romans 9:25)
19 A shade of green
20 Wins in wrestling
21 Turn away from sin
23 "God said, Let there _____ light" (Genesis 1:3)
24 Gaal's father (Judges 9:26)
26 A son of Benjamin (Genesis 46:21)
28 "_____, Zeboim, Neballat, Lod, and Ono" (Nehemiah 11:34–35)
30 "And Cain went _____ from the presence of the Lord" (Genesis 4:16)
32 Tubs
36 Steal
37 Accomplishers
39 "Shelesh, and _____" (1 Chronicles 7:35)
40 Talmai's father (Numbers 13:22)
42 "Shall be your _____" (Ezekiel 45:12)
44 "Hand by the _____ of the door" (Song of Solomon 5:4)
45 "I will put my hook in thy _____" (2 Kings 19:28)
46 Azor's son (Matthew 1:14)
48 "Delilah therefore took _____ ropes, and bound him therewith" (Judges 16:12)
49 "The beauty of old men is the _____ head" (Proverbs 20:29)
50 "Zechariah, _____" (1 Chronicles 15:18)
51 Birds fly with these
53 "_____ that ye refuse" (Hebrews 12:25)
55 Too
56 Maine (abbr.)
58 "Land of _____" (Genesis 36:34)
61 This is above the eye
65 "And Hazarshual, and _____, and Azem" (Joshua 19:3)
67 Brother of Uz (Genesis 36:28)
68 Dwell
69 Get up
70 "They _____ his praise" (Psalm 106:12)
71 Place of perfection
72 Er's wife (Genesis 38:6)
73 "Mordecai for _____?" (Esther 6:3)
74 Caused to go to a destination

DOWN

1 "Neither _____ they the king's laws" (Esther 3:8)
2 "_____ the Ahohite" (1 Chronicles 11:29)
3 Ear grain
4 "Righteousness and peace have _____ each other" (Psalms 85:10)
5 "O Ephraim, thou committest _____" (Hosea 5:3)
6 "Though I forbear, what am I _____?" (Job 16:6)
7 "There is but a _____ between me and death" (1 Samuel 20:3)
8 You (arch.)
9 Soup
10 Petroleum product
11 First Hebrew month (Exodus 34:18)
12 Rescue
13 Bind
22 "In the _____ which they hid is their own foot taken" (Psalm 9:15)
25 "He hath _____ his guests" (Zephaniah 1:7)
27 "Of Hena, and _____?" (2 Kings 19:13)
28 Glory
29 "Those that walk in pride he is able to _____" (Daniel 4:37)
30 "The threshingfloor of _____ the Jebusite" (1 Chronicles 21:15)
31 "_____ the office of a deacon" (1 Timothy 3:13)
33 In the midst of
34 Stories
35 Killed
36 Resounded
38 To lessen
41 "The _____ of hell and of death" (Revelation 1:18)
43 "Shall be _____ in that day" (Amos 8:3)
47 King Saul's father (Acts 13:21)
50 "For the _____ that is in the land of Assyria" (Isaiah 7:18)
52 "The _____ held their peace" (Job 29:10)
54 "Libnah, and _____" (Joshua 15:42)

by N. Teri Grottke

55 A son of Elioenai (1 Chronicles 3:24)

56 Naomi's new name (Ruth 1:20)

57 Twelve wells of water were there (Exodus 15:27)

59 "As he that lieth upon the top of a _____" (Proverb 23:34)

60 A son of Ulla (1 Chronicles 7:39)

62 Travel other than on foot

63 Baking place

64 "Their sound _____ into all the earth" (Romans 10:18)

65 A piece of baseball equipment

66 Solomon's great-grandson (1 Kings 15:8)

Answers

Puzzle 1

Puzzle 2

Puzzle 3

Puzzle 4

Puzzle 5

Puzzle 6

Puzzle 7

Puzzle 8

Puzzle 9

Puzzle 10

Puzzle 11

Puzzle 12

Puzzle 13

Puzzle 14

Puzzle 15

Puzzle 16

Puzzle 17

Puzzle 18

Puzzle 19

Puzzle 20

Puzzle 21

Puzzle 22

Puzzle 23

Puzzle 24

Puzzle 25

Puzzle 26

Puzzle 27

Puzzle 28

Puzzle 29

Puzzle 30

Puzzle 31

Puzzle 32

Puzzle 33

Puzzle 34

Puzzle 35

Puzzle 36

Puzzle 37

Puzzle 38

Puzzle 39

Puzzle 40

Puzzle 41

Puzzle 42

Puzzle 43

Puzzle 44

Puzzle 45

Puzzle 46

Puzzle 47

Puzzle 48

Puzzle 49

Puzzle 50

Puzzle 51

Puzzle 52

Puzzle 53

Puzzle 54

Puzzle 55

Puzzle 56

Puzzle 57

Puzzle 58

Puzzle 59

Puzzle 60

Puzzle 61

Puzzle 62

Puzzle 63

Puzzle 64

Puzzle 65

Puzzle 66

Puzzle 67

Puzzle 68

Puzzle 69

Puzzle 70

Puzzle 71

Puzzle 72

Puzzle 73

Puzzle 74

Puzzle 75

Puzzle 76

Puzzle 77

Puzzle 78

Puzzle 79

Puzzle 80

Puzzle 81

Puzzle 82

Puzzle 83

Puzzle 84

Puzzle 85

Puzzle 86

Puzzle 87

Puzzle 88

Puzzle 89

Puzzle 90

Puzzle 91

Puzzle 92

Puzzle 93

Puzzle 94

Puzzle 95

Puzzle 96

Puzzle 97

Puzzle 98

Puzzle 99

Looking for more fun?

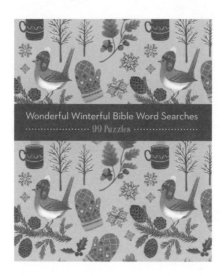

Whether it's cold and snowy where you live, or the days are just short on sunlight, wintertime can bring the blahs—here's a book to fill that time in a positive way. *Wonderful Winterful Bible Word Searches* features 99 puzzles and thousands of clues, each drawn directly from the King James Version.

Paperback / 978-1-64352-552-5 / $12.99